The Psychodynamic Approach to Drug Therapy

MORTIMER OSTOW, M.D., Med. Sc.D.
Editor

THE PSYCHOANALYTIC
RESEARCH
AND DEVELOPMENT
FUND

 VAN NOSTRAND REINHOLD COMPANY
NEW YORK   CINCINNATI   ATLANTA   DALLAS   SAN FRANCISCO
             LONDON   TORONTO   MELBOURNE

Van Nostrand Reinhold Company Regional Offices:
New York   Cincinnati   Atlanta   Dallas   San Francisco

Van Nostrand Reinhold Company International Offices:
London   Toronto   Melbourne

Library of Congress Catalog Card Number: 79-26972
ISBN: 0-442-20410-8

Manufactured in the United States of America

Published by Van Nostrand Reinhold Company
135 West 50th Street, New York, N.Y. 10020

Published simultaneously in Canada by Van Nostrand Reinhold Ltd.

15 14 13 12 11 10 9 8 7 6 5 4 3 2 1

Library of Congress Cataloging in Publication Data

Main entry under title:

The Psychodynamic approach to drug therapy.

   1. Psychopharmacology.   2. Psychopharmacology—
Case studies.   3. Psychotherapy.   4. Psychotherapy
—Case studies.   I. Ostow, Mortimer.   II. Psycho-
analytic Research and Development Fund.
RC483.P773   1980   616.8'918   79-26972
ISBN 0-442-20410-8

ACKNOWLEDGMENTS

The success of this project was achieved by virtue of the continuing earnest interest and efforts of the participants. I appreciate also the generous support, financial and moral, of the Psychoanalytic Research and Development Fund, its members, its contributors and its officers. The following pharmaceutical manufacturing companies participated in the support of this project:

Hoffmann-LaRoche, Inc.
Lederle Laboratories
Wallace Laboratories

Finally I am deeply indebted to Robin Ostow for abstracting the very large mass of transcribed material and preparing the summaries of the case presentations and the pertinent discussion. The relatively brief organized presentations of the five cases offered here, were derived from more than 60 hours of taped transcriptions. An impressive amount of industry and skill were required to achieve the compression and lucidity displayed in these abbreviated accounts.

Mortimer Ostow

Participants

Mortimer Ostow, M.D., Med. Sc. D., Editor
Edward T. Sandrow Visiting Professor of Pastoral Psychiatry,
Jewish Theological Seminary of America
Vice-President, Psychoanalytic Research & Development Fund

Bernard Bressler, M.D.
Professor of Psychiatry, Duke University Medical Center,
Durham, North Carolina

Samuel L. Feder, M.D.
Clinical Professor of Psychiatry, Cornell University
Medical College
Clinical Director, Westchester Division of The New York
Hospital - Cornell Medical Center

Sidney S. Furst, M.D.
Professional Director, Psychoanalytic Research & Development Fund
Training and Supervising Psychoanalyst, New York Psychoanalytic Institute
Associate in Clinical Psychiatry, Columbia University, College of Physicians &
  Surgeons
Associate in Pastoral Psychiatry, Jewish Theological Seminary of America

Gerald Klerman, M.D.
Professor of Psychiatry, Harvard University (on leave)
Administrator, Alcohol Drug Abuse and Mental Health Administration,
Department of Health, Education and Welfare

Louis Linn, M.D.
Clinical Professor, Department of Psychiatry, Mount Sinai
School of Medicine, City University of New York
Attending Psychiatrist, Mount Sinai Hospital
Associate in Pastoral Psychiatry, Jewish Theological Seminary of America

Earl A. Loomis, Jr., M.D.
Psychiatric Director, Blueberry Treatment Center for Emotionally Disturbed
    Children
Attending Psychiatrist, Eastern Long Island Hospital, Greenport, L.I.

Lawrence J. Roose, M.D.
Clinical Professor Emeritus, Mount Sinai School of Medicine, New York
Consultant, Psychiatry, Mount Sinai Hospital

N. William Winkelman, Jr., M.D. (deceased)
Formerly, Chairman, Department of Psychiatry and Neurology,
Sidney Hillman Medical Center

Guest Participants:

Pinhas Noy, M.D.
Professor of Psychiatry, Hadassah Hebrew Medical School, Jerusalem

Joseph Sandler, M.D.
Freud Professor of Psychoanalysis, Hebrew University, Jerusalem.
Freud Memorial Professor of Psychoanalysis,
University College London;
President, European Psycho-Analytical Federation

Gerald Sarwer-Foner, M.D.
Professor and Chairman of the Department of Psychiatry,
Faculty of Medicine, University of Ottawa

Roy Whitman, M.D.
Professor of Psychiatry, University of Cincinnati College of Medicine;
Training and Supervising Analyst, Cincinnati Psychoanalytic Institute

Contents

1. Introduction

The Psychoanalytic Research and Development Fund undertook a study of psychopharmacology in 1966 because we believed that this was an area which required intensive investigation by psychoanalysts. The efficacy of drug therapy cannot be questioned. However, the psychologic changes which these chemicals effect, and the manner in which they affect psychopathology are far from clear. Therefore a number of very important questions remain unresolved, namely, which drug to use, how much to give, when and how long to give it, and in combination with what other drugs? Phenomenologic and statistical methods, large scale, computerized and sophisticated, have been able to yield only the most general and most approximate findings.

Psychoanalysts can no longer afford to ignore organic treatment modalities, especially drug therapy.

In the first place the application of drug therapy provides abundant information about psychoanalytic psychiatry. Secondly, a number of patients who undertake psychoanalysis may break down and require supplementary drug therapy, temporary or continuing. To dismiss such patients from analysis is to deprive them of treatment which they require. Moreover, drug therapy cannot be given by another psychiatrist while the analysis continues with the original analyst. The reason is simply that the administration of medication, change of dosage, change of drug and combination of drugs, must all be determined by the psychologic state of the patient at the time, something which is available in detail only to the treating analyst. Good drug therapy cannot be administered simply by giving the patient a prescription and seeing him once a month when it must be renewed. While this can and must suffice where more intensive therapy is not available, optimal care requires a period of at least several months of experimentation with dosage and its combination while the patient is under psychotherapeutic supervision. Finally, a number of patients cannot be managed by one modality of treatment alone. Full justice to their potential requires careful combination of several varieties of treatment. In other words, the patient requires management rather than a prescription, as the cases cited in this book demonstrate.

The Psychoanalytic Research and Development Fund decided therefore to undertake a careful study of drug action, using the psychoanalytic approach to analysis of clinical phenomena, in the hope that it would provide data of both theoretical and practical value to psychoanalysts and to general psychiatrists alike. The problems of psychoanalytic research are notoriously many and difficult. It is difficult, for example, for any one analyst to study a statistically meaningful number of patients. It is difficult to collate data because of the multiplicity of variables. It is difficult to retrieve information obtained in the course of even one analysis. It is difficult to isolate truly comparable phenomena. It is difficult to eliminate the personal bias of the observer. We at the Psychoanalytic Research and Development Fund have devised a method which we think contends with, if it does not overcome, many of these difficulties. The method is described in full in a previous publication, *Sexual Deviation: Psychoanalytic Insights* (New York: Quadrangle, 1974).

Briefly, we invited between eight and twelve individuals, whom we considered experts in the field being investigated, to meet with us once a month to study a problem which we assigned to ourselves by examining the cases presented to the entire group successively by its individual members. The sessions were taped and reproduced for further study. We met an average of eight or nine times a year for a period of four years. The material which was accumulated in this way was then continually examined in order to trace out the individual themes. These themes then formed the basis of the final report.

We overcame problems of limitation of case material by assembling a number of participants. We overcame the problem of the interplay of variables by drawing upon the collective experience of the group for comparisons and contrasts of sets of unusual but truly comparable experiences. We overcame the problem of retrieving information by presenting cases for study, but only as points of departure. In the discussion of each case, the members of the group presented, as case vignettes, relevant experience from their own practice. We overcame the problem of personal bias by eliciting disagreement and consensus in discussion so that we could ascertain how generally acceptable an inference was to these select members of the profession.

What kinds of results did we obtain? Each of the groups that we organized became a coherent entity which persisted from meeting to meeting. The group became progressively more sophisticated in dealing with the subject and in formulating positions which found general acceptance. One might question the use of the word research to describe these activities. It is important to recognize that we were not merely collecting data which already existed in the records or in the minds of the participants. The presentation of the data within the group as well as the responses of the individual members created a new set of ideas. The group process created concepts, many of which did not explicitly exist previously in the mind of any of its members. For the participants, the experience was always exciting and gratifying. It was an experience of constructive group participation, together with learning, teaching and creating.

In its initial meetings, the group which was assembled to study psychopharmacology anticipated certain difficulties. If one grants that proper study of drug action requires fairly precise and accurate monitoring of drug effects, one must consider the question of just how well these effects can be monitored in patients who are seen for only one treatment session a day at most. How can one record drug effect if one doesn't know in advance what parameters to monitor and record? If one sees a change in the patient, how can one decide whether to attribute it to the change in medication or to some other concurrent influence? Our first study sessions were devoted to considering these problems. In fact, they never dropped out of consideration and were brought up again in the very last, the 34th, session. When we tried to draw up codes, protocols, and procedures, we usually found ourselves more hobbled by our design than helped by it. There were two problems. One was that if we determined to monitor only a fixed set of parameters, then we feared that we might overlook other phenomena whose importance we had not understood at the beginning of the study. Secondly, we could not arrive at a consensus to which the entire group could subscribe. Accordingly, we abandoned an attempt to achieve uniformity in record keeping. We decided to rely on the sensitivity of the group to detect regularities in the case material presented to us and available to us from our own experience. Some experiences reported by individuals found no consensual echo among the others. Other experiences did. There were some observations which at first could not be confirmed by others but subsequently were when the dissenting members of the group had time to look for such material in their own practice.

As editor, I have chosen to present the material developed in fairly systematic form, even though what we have cannot be considered a systematic psychoanalytic investigation.

Perhaps it would be more true to the spirit of the experience of the group to describe the themes which were developed without attempting to integrate these themes into any systematic whole.

A list of these themes with a descriptive sentence or two follows. The development of the themes will be described in the summaries of the discussions of the cases.

1. The latency of response to anti-depression drugs: It was not recognized by all of the members of the group at the outset that anti-depression drugs require a period of latency when taken orally before their anti-depression effect becomes manifest. The group ultimately acknowledged that they seldom saw therapeutic effects before three weeks or three and a half weeks in the case of the iminodibenzyl anti-depression agents and four weeks in the case of monoamine oxidase inhibitors (hereafter referred to as MAOI). (The fallacy of expecting response within a few days after medication was begun, which prevailed at the time, has since been corrected in the literature, though the period given now, three weeks, is still somewhat short of a more realistic three and one half or four weeks.)

2. Psychologic influences on the response to drug therapy: The fact that a patient obtained relief of his symptoms with a given dose of medication did not mean that he was protected by

the same dose from all subsequent mental stress. Relieving the patient of psychologic stress made him more responsive to drug therapy, but increasing stress could challenge the improvement which had already occurred.

3. Though drug therapy may provide the strength required to contend with psychologic problems, it does not solve these problems. Even after clinical recovery has been achieved by drug therapy, the problems in object relations or the reality frustrations continue to exert pressure upon the patient and he must find some way to deal with them other than by the clinical entity which has been alleviated.

4. Most therapeutic chemicals exert more than one effect: In fact they exert more than one pharmacologic effect. Some of these effects are therapeutic, others anti-therapeutic, some useful, and some distressing. In addition, there are psychologic consequences to being given a drug, to being given a drug in a certain way, to the experience of relief and to the experience of side effect. The conscientious therapist must try to recognize each of these effects in each case.

5. Mechanism of drug therapy: We made no effort to study the biochemistry involved though we did try to understand the psychodynamics. No consensus was achieved. There were some who thought primarily in terms of the effect of chemical agents on motivation, others who thought in terms of the effect of these agents on sensation or cognitive function, and still others who considered that both of these and other effects might be involved.

6. Psychosis as a defense: Examination of case material encouraged the group to think of schizophrenic psychosis as a method—pathologic, to be sure—for contending with a problem. Removing the option of psychotic withdrawal by drug therapy leaves the patient without this defense; and the pathology will show up in some other way, usually depression.

7. Conditions related to depression: The actual definitive depressive syndrome is merely the end state of a process. The process may be manifest before the end stage is reached in other syndromes which are not usually considered depressive in nature. Clinical examples of the anti-depression maneuvers, namely, clinging and angry repudiation, were encountered by the group.

8. What actually happens psychologically when a patient re-

covers from a depression with an anti-depression drug? Careful analytic scrutiny demonstrates that the patient attempts once again to come to terms with the object whom he had abandoned when he retreated into depression. What method he uses and how successfully he does this determines the clinical picture which will prevail after successful anti-depression drug therapy.

9. The pathogenic effect of being "trapped": It is scarcely a new discovery that individual episodes of mental illness are precipitated by specific incidents. The group learned to discern the pathogenic potential immanent in particular combinations of individual idiosyncratic weakness and external pressure.

10. Interrelation of phenothiazine treatment, agitation, depression, and schizophrenia: The group learned to expect to find a depressive component in the case of many schizophrenic patients. It also learned that the use of phenothiazine drugs for treatment of schizophrenia may result in the accentuation or creation of depressive pictures. It was interested in and puzzled by the effect of phenothiazine drugs in decreasing the agitation and sometimes other symptoms associated with depression and schizophrenia, though under other circumstances the same drugs can clearly be seen to accentuate depression.

11. Escape from anti-depression control: After a depressed patient has been satisfactorily brought to remission with the aid of an anti-depression drug, the augmentation of psychic stress may cause relapse. In such cases the patient may require an increase in the dose of anti-depression drug, the addition of another form of treatment such as electric shock treatment, or hospitalization.

12. Effectiveness of psychoanalytic understanding and technique in disturbed patients: In examining the clinical data spread before the group, the members made consistent attempts to understand the phenomena in terms of psychodynamics. They agreed, however, that even when their understanding was correct, conveying such insight to a disturbed patient could be expected to have relatively little effect on his behavior.

13. Sequence of recovery from depression: In one case report, there were two episodes of recovery from depression with the assistance of the same drug. The sequence of clinical changes occurring at varying time intervals after the drug was started was

found to be surprisingly similar in the two instances. This lends support to the idea that the progressive biochemical change brought about by the administration of the drug induced corresponding changes in the individual's psychodynamics and in his behavior. The same time schedule that controls the former will control the latter.

14. Narcissistic tranquility: A specific syndrome, namely, recurrent torpor, bulimia, weight gain, increased sexual desire, and an accumulation of possessions, was seen to occur either wholly or in part under a number of different circumstances. It was often seen especially when drug therapy alleviated gross psychopathologic symptoms while the pathogenic set of object relations and reality factors continued to oppress the patient.

15. Influence of drug therapy on psychodynamics: It was acknowledged by the group that it would be important to set down just how each of the different varieties of drugs influenced each patient's psychodynamics. It was assumed that primarily, defenses would be affected. Denial and repression were discussed in these terms but the group was not satisfied that they had achieved any significant understanding of this problem.

16. Hostility in depression: Careful study of the daily production of depressed patients permitted the group to follow the vicissitudes of aggressiveness in these patients, that is, as they were becoming depressed, when they were depressed, and as they were coming out of depression.

17. Toxicity of pharmaceutic agents: The occurrence of a toxic response to the administration of a therapeutic substance turned out to be not merely an inconvenience, but exerted significant effects upon the transference, upon the patient's self-image, upon his symptoms and his cooperativeness. Proper treatment required careful attention to manifestations of a response to toxicity.

18. Electric shock therapy and its complications: While shock treatment was not of primary interest to the group, it had to be discussed because it was employed in the management of some of the cases that were studied. The psychology of shock therapy and its influence upon psychotherapy and drug therapy were considered.

19. Implications of drug therapy for the psychoanalytic procedure: The administration of a therapeutic drug influences the way the patient looks at himself, the way the family looks at him, and the way the therapist looks at him. Therefore, the course of psychoanalytic treatment is necessarily affected. The group considered whether the ultimate effectiveness of analysis is thereby compromised and whether the use of drugs for treatment established that the patient is limited ultimately in his potential response to analysis.

20. The group was able to demonstrate the effect of four years of working together by being able to analyze together, with substantial agreement, and with more rapidity and with greater group consensus a case presented at the end of the study than cases presented at the beginning.

21. The concept of management:The idea that the patient is to be treated by the application of a coordinated group of modalities rather than a single modality was of course not novel to the members of the group at the inception of the study. However, throughout the project they worked toward achieving the ability to coordinate all variables having therapeutic potential in accordance with the prevailing psychodynamic situation. The final case report exemplified what might be considered a virtuoso performance in the management of a seriously ill patient. While the group could not take credit for the accomplishment of the individual member, they applauded it as an approach to what they considered an approximation of the ideal. Here a combination of hospitalization, nursing care, the tolerance of regression, drug therapy and psychotherapy coordinated on the basis of the therapist's clear understanding of the dynamics of the current problem, were able to restore to functioning a patient who could neither be helped nor even supported by excellent psychotherapy alone.

These are the chief themes that emerged from our study. How they were derived from the clinical data, and how one studies clinical data to understand the principal issues and to establish a treatment plan, will be presented in the individual case reports and the summaries of the discussions of them.

2. Observations on Clinical Pharmacology

While we addressed ourselves to the study of psychopharmacology, the discussions were unstructured. The individual participants responded to whichever issue in the case presentations offered them opportunity to ask a pertinent question or to make an interesting observation. Others responded to the remarks or questions offered by their colleagues. Therefore the record contains a number of observations on the clinical pharmacology of the drugs used for the treatment of mental illness. Some of these observations, or rather discussions, are worth reporting here.

One such issue is the sensitivity of a given patient to drug therapy. We have all had the experience of one patient's responding rapidly and sensitively to a small dose of a given medication while another, suffering a similar syndrome, may respond not at all to a large dose. The group had occasion to take note of this variability of response. A number of reasons were offered which are psychodynamic and these will be presented in Chapter 4. But the group also recognized that responsiveness to drug therapy might also be a matter of individual physiologic state. It was recognized that constitutional, and especially familial factors might contribute to determining sensitivity. For example, several members had observed that when one member of a family responds sensitively to a given type of medication, another member of the same family with a similar clinical syndrome is likely to respond equally sensitively. One patient (C.D.) was presented, for example, whose sister had been treated by another member of the group. The patient and his sister each responded to MAOI anti-depression medication, but only to relatively large doses. Ultimately each patient escaped from the control of anti-depression medication.

Dr. Pinhas Noy, an Israeli psychiatrist, visited with the group on one occasion when this question of family sensitivity was examined. He was asked whether biologic and cultural differences between Ashkenazi and Sephardic Jews were reflected in their differential response to psychiatric drug therapy. He replied that he had not heard of any observations of such a difference, but pointed out that those patients who were least educated and came from most primitive backgrounds were likely to fail to take their medication regularly so that treatment was less apt to be successful among them. Roose offered a confirmatory observation that immigrant Puerto Rican patients, treated at Mount Sinai Hospital, were similarly negligent about taking medication and therefore responded less well than one might expect.

Before continuing with our discussion of pharmacology, we have to take note of the fact that the administration of a pharmaceutic agent cannot be expected to produce only one single and discrete effect. A priori, since most drugs are distributed diffusely throughout the body, one must expect a number of different effects, each arising from the impact of the drug upon a particular organ system which is sensitive to that kind of chemical agent. In addition, the fact that the patient is given a drug, the fact that he takes it, the fact that his condition may be alleviated or aggravated by the drug, the fact that he may experience one or more side effects, each of these factors contributes to determining the patient's psychic response to drug therapy. Accordingly, relatively early in our transactions, a classification of drug action was offered to the group and that classification made it easier to avoid confusion in subsequent discussion. We shall use this classification to organize the material in this chapter.

A. Principal Action

Each drug is generally administered for the purpose of producing one specific effect which is arbitrarily designated as the therapeutic effect or the primary effect. In the case of most of the drugs which we considered, the primary effect was the alleviation of a state of depression, mania, or schizophrenia. Mention was made from time to time of the use of drugs whose principal action was sedation in one form or another, drugs such as Miltown (meprobamate), Librium (chlordiazepoxide), and Valium (diazepam). Our neglect of them does not imply that these drugs are not often useful, but rather that their use is less problematic than use of the others.

One of the first issues which came up for discussion was the time required for the onset of therapeutic action after the administration of the medication. With respect to the time required for the inception of the action of phenothiazine derivatives and drugs which behave similarly, it was generally agreed that the therapeutic action begins within a day or two at the latest, but continues to increase in intensity for several days even on a constant dose. There was little controversy too about the fact that the immediate quieting potency of drugs like Thorazine(chlorpromazine) is to be attributed to their sedative rather than their anti-psychosis qualities. These two actions are separate and independent and have different time courses even though they may both contribute to the desired result.

However, the problem is somewhat more complex in the case of the anti-depression drugs. Very early in the course of our discussions, a patient was reported to have shown improvement within a few days after an anti-depression drug, Elavil (amitriptyline), was started. He began to sleep; his appetite improved; he began to gain weight; and he began to read. Were these changes, all expressing an improvement of state of mind, to be attributed to the onset of anti-depression action? The group was willing to consider the proposition that the immediate response was to be attributed to the sedative effect of the medication since the anti-depression effect would require a considerably longer period. Obviously, we did not examine enough data to establish, statistically expectable norms for latency between onset of drug administration and anti-depression response. It was our impression, however, that a minimum of three to four weeks were required for a clearcut reversal of depression in the case of the iminodibenzyl derivatives and at least four weeks in the case of the MAOI. The actual latency in any given case depends upon the sensitivity of the patient, the rate at which drug dose is increased, and significant incidents affecting the patient and his object relations.

*Parenthetically, I have recently observed that for some patients,
the tricyclic anti-depression agents, before their definitive energizing effect is achieved, or in doses too low to achieve it, act like
weak phenothiazine tranquilizers. That is, in small doses, by
exerting a weak depressing influence, they may induce a defensive
energizing. This effect may set in within twelve hours after the
medication is taken. It may be this effect as well as a placebo
effect that accounts for reports of a very early onset of anti-
depression action.*

In one case (E.F.), there were data describing the patient's
recovery from depression under the influence of Niamid (nialamide)
on two separate occasions. The two episodes are not entirely comparable. At the time of the first, the patient was 56 years old; at
the time of the second, 63. In the first instance, he had had no
previous organic treatment while the second sequence followed
immediately unsuccessful treatment with Elavil and Vivactil (pro-
triptyline), and then he had three electric shock treatments which
left him feeling inert.

The first sequence of recovery can be summarized as follows:
He was started on 200 mg of Niamid per day on day 0.

Day	Status
13	Depressed, dependent, fearful, guilty, afraid of homosexual transference
14	Unchanged
15	Unchanged
19	First acknowledgment of marital difficulty
20	First acknowledgment of his wife's impatience with him; first sexual approach to his wife
21	First attempt at intercourse—no erection; concern with driving accidents; aggressive fantasies; greater interest in object relations
22	Still fearful in transference; started regular tennis game; fantasies of omniscience; sadistic fantasies
23	He felt better in the morning; complained of wife's hostility for the first time

26	Acknowledged marital difficulty and his fear to face it; depressive symptoms continue; first masturbation with voyeuristic fantasies; first morning erection
27	Felt "steadier"; forgot medication; cleaned himself up; entertained fantasies of his wife's death; diverted sexual desire to other women Niamid increased to 300 mg a day on Day 27.
28	Abdominal pains; feels discouraged
29	Felt better until session; felt threatened by the analyst
30	Insomnia; concern with threat to marriage; concern about impotence and castration anxiety
35	Homosexual anxiety; continued to complain of depression though there were fewer manifestations of it; complained about his wife; first definite improvement in mood; reduction in externally directed hostility

To summarize, the first indication of an undoing of denial of ambivalence towards his wife occurred on Days 19 and 20. Sexual desire and hostility both appeared to increase on Day 21. Motor activity was increased on Day 22 and it was associated with ideas of omniscience. Masturbation was resumed on the 26th day, at the same time that morning erection was noted for the first time, and active sexual interest in other women appeared on the 27th day, insomnia on the 30th, and a definite improvement in mood five weeks after beginning medication.

Note that the actual process of recovery, as indicated by the patient's first willingness to discuss his anger with his wife, began before the end of the third week. The fluctuations in his condition resulted from feelings and expressions of the newly activated drives and the conflicts which they created. Therefore, even at the end of the fifth week, and after an increase in dose, he was still not fully recovered.

Seven years later, he was started on 200 mg of Niamid on Day 0 and the dose was doubled to 400 on the first day.

Day	Status
1	Depressive tone and content with remarks about suicide; sleep disturbed
4	Feeling better; first time the patient did not take a daytime nap
7	Slightly depressed again
8	Sentimental feelings of attachment to the analyst
9	Sexual fantasies about his wife with a semi-erection. He felt still depressed
10	Feeling better; more active; more forceful with his wife; a frankly homosexual dream
14	Feeling slightly better; criticizes his wife for the first time
15	Continues slightly better; critical of wife
17	More active, more vigorous, more hostile toward wife
24	More confident; slight insomnia
25	Hypomanicky, overtalkative, rude and overactive

Considering the differences in circumstances, one is impressed by the similarity in the sequence of the clinical signs of recovery in the two instances.

The recovery occurred sooner in this than in the previous sequence. But the dose was twice as great, and the MAO inhibition followed close on the heels of unsuccessful treatment with tricyclic anti-depression agents and three electric shock treatments.

Ostow observed that in his experience any change in clinical state elicited by the administration of an anti-depression drug or phenothiazine or similar tranquilizer, or any change resulting from a change in dosage of these drugs, was never seen before at least one overnight sleep period.

The use of amitriptyline or imipramine administered intramuscularly was described by Bressler and Feder. Other members of the group were able to confirm that intramuscular medication for three days was in many instances sufficient to achieve true anti-depression effects.

One of the most difficult problems, and one which we failed

to resolve, is the problem of the explanation of the paradoxic effects of phenothiazines and similarly acting tranquilizing drugs. There is no doubt that these can be used effectively to subdue psychotic agitation. Perhaps the most potent drug for this purpose is Haldol (haloperidol). Stelazine (trifluoperazine) is also effective. Since some drugs which are useful in controlling agitation also possess a sedative effect, one may be led to confuse the two. However, it is quite clear that other kinds of drugs which are equally potent sedatives are not nearly as effective in controlling psychotic agitation. These anti-agitation drugs therefore possess an additional action. Many patients whose agitation has been controlled by these medications seem to be quiet but somewhat depressed. In some instances the depression is more evident, in others less. Sometimes the depression brings on an increase in agitation. Occasionally the more drug that is given, the more agitated the patient becomes, until he is almost anesthetized.

Many schizophrenic patients treated with phenothiazines and similarly acting drugs, who are not necessarily agitated, when they recover from their schizophrenic attack, seem to become depressed. While this phenomenon is occasionally observed among those who recover spontaneously, it is probably more frequently observed among those who recover with the assistance of such medications.

Feder suggested that phenothiazines might depress because they diminish self-awareness. Klerman quoted Sarwer-Foner's original suggestion that they were distressing because they impair motor control. He also suggested that the somatic side effects, autonomic and extrapyramidal, by reinforcing schizophrenic hypochondriacal concern with the body, might exert a depressing effect.

Our group also ventured a number of dynamic explanations. It was suggested that the former schizophrenic becomes depressed because after recovery, he is confronted with the loss which had precipitated the psychotic break in the first place. He may become depressed because he is confronted with challenges which he had not been able to meet before. He may become depressed because of the side effects of the drug. For example, one patient became depressed after receiving Mellaril (thioridazine) since it interfered with ejaculation. If we assume that post-schizophrenic depression is the result of the phenothiazine administration, we can formulate, then, a relatively simple hypothesis, namely, that these drugs overcome agitation, alleviate schizophrenia, and induce depression by reducing potential for activity, or by reducing physical or mental energies.

Such an explanation cannot really be the whole story. In the first place, all of these drugs exert a significant anti-schizophrenic action though they differ in their inhibition of motor activity. The ones which are most immediately effective against agitation, namely, Haldol and Thorazine, also impair motor function to the greatest degree.

Another problem is that these drugs can sometimes be used to alleviate depression itself. The group was not able to work out the mechanism accounting for these paradoxical problems.

In retrospect, as a result of clinical experience I have accumulated since then, I have learned that the action of phenothiazine and thioxanthine tranquilizers depends upon dose. At very low doses (for example, 0.5-5 mg of Navane [thiothixene], 10-50 mg of Thorazine), they may combat depression, or in susceptible patients, even induce hypomania or mania. At the same dose they might aggravate any case of schizophrenia which would be improved by a higher dose of the same agent. Above a given threshold, these same agents will depress patients susceptible to depression and undo many cases of schizophrenia. I have suggested that the mechanism for this biphasic action is that small doses exert a small depressing influence which, in many patients, elicits a counteractive anti-depression effect. Above a given threshold, this defensive mechanism is defeated and the depressing action of the drug becomes manifest.

There was some discussion about the use of Navane in the treatment of depression. I.J. was a schizophrenic young woman who seemed quite depressed or at least sad. She responded well to treatment with Navane, as well as to good psychotherapy and management. Bressler contended, however, that while he had obtained good results with the treatment of schizophrenic patients who were depressed, he had had poor results with the use of Navane for simple depression. Klerman and Feder also reported negative results with the use of Navane for the treatment of depression. Furst and Ostow, however, reported that in a few instances the depressive tendency had been arrested and in other depressed patients the depressive pain and anguish was muted so that the patient became more apathetic than agitated. Feder saw a similarity between the action of Navane and that of Stelazine in that they both tend to mobilize the patients. Taractan (chlorprothixene) seems to share with Navane the property of being minimally depressant and actually affording relief to depressed patients. Among the phenothiazines, Stelazine and Mellaril were felt to be least depressant.

Again, in retrospect, one wonders whether there is any real difference among these agents in anti-depression potency, or whether in each case the action, whether energizing or depressing, is a function primarily of dose.

It was demonstrated on more than one occasion that the administration of an anti-depression drug could at times quiet a disturbed and agitated patient. It was inferred that in these cases the agitation had been brought about by a depressive lack of energy.

It was observed several times that some psychiatrists tend to use drugs in relatively low dosage while others use drugs in relatively high dosage. For example, a psychiatrist in the former group might prescribe 25, 50, or 100 mg of Thorazine. Two hundred mg would be considered a high dose. Psychiatrists in the latter group would not hesitate to use between 1 and 4 grams of Thorazine a day. In the case of Navane, psychiatrists in the former group would use up to 6 or 10 mg a day while those in the latter group use 30 to 60. It is interesting that results obtained are similar with either large or small doses— at least so far as one can ascertain from published reports.

Having used small doses in the treatment of private patients and observed the effects of large doses in patients in the hospital, it is my impression that although psychotic or depressive distress may be eliminated by both forms of treatment, the patient on a small dose remains more like his natural self while the patient on a large dose seems limited and restricted by his medication.

B. Pharmacologic effects other than the primary effect

Many of these substances used for the treatment of mental illness exert effects other than the primary effect for which they are given. While these secondary effects may sometimes be useful, at other times they are disturbing and make the patient uncomfortable, and at worst, they may undo the therapeutic influence of the medication.

1. Sedative effect.   Of these side effects, the most common is the sedative effect exhibited by phenothiazines of the chlorpromazine series, and to a varying degree, by the iminodibenzyl derivatives among the anti-depression agents with the exception of Vivactil. The sedative effect can be used either for daytime sedation, or for facilitating sleep, or for both. In the case of A.B., who responded so promptly to the administration of Elavil, the group speculated that the prompt improvement was brought about by the sedative effect of the drug rather than by its anti-depression effect which would have required a considerably longer period to take effect. (We cannot exclude the possibility that it was the effect of marijuana which the boy took from time to time surreptitiously, or the anti-depression effect of small doses of tranquilizing agents that we mentioned above.) In contrast to the other iminodibenzyl anti-depression agents, Vivactil seems to possess a stimulating effect which is welcomed by many patients when it is taken during the day, but which might cause insomnia if it is taken toward evening. The sedative or stimulating effect of these drugs sets in within a half-hour or so after they are taken and lasts for a few hours, whereas the anti-psychosis or anti-depression influences require days or weeks to assert themselves and subside over a period of several days. Again, the individual may come to tolerate the sedative or stimulating effect, that is, the drug may lose this influence over a period of days or weeks. Yet the therapeutic effect continues as long as the drug is given.

2. Extrapyramidal disturbances.   The group had little to say about this interesting set of phenomena probably because in the case of most patients whom they treated, they avoided those side effects by using appropriate medication. It was observed that the abrupt onset of dystonic phenomena was terrifying and that these impairments of body functions could be especially disturbing to patients whose illness imposed a somatic type of cathexis.

3. Anticholinergic disturbances.   There was little occasion for comment about the usual peripheral anticholinergic disturbances such as dry mouth, constipation, urinary disturbance, or the occasional threat of precipitating glaucoma.

At one point I.J. began to experience episodes of hypotension. The dose of Navane had been raised to a higher level than previously. At the same time she had shown signs of definite clinical improvement. Ostow made the point that in the case of many patients, postural hypotension appears just when the clinical condition of the patient is beginning to improve. He reasons as follows. Most of these substances, anti-psychosis and anti-depression agents alike, have a tendency to lower blood pressure by virtue of their peripheral or central autonomic effect. While this hypotensive effect never becomes significant in some patients, in others it may become severe enough to cause disabling clinical symptoms. However, if the patient is disturbed or agitated, the accompanying increased concentration of glucocorticoids tends to counteract the hypotension. When the patient's agitation subsides, the glucocorticoid level also decreases and he loses this protection against the hypotensive effect of the medication. It often happens therefore that the onset of symptoms of hypotension announces the beginning of significant clinical improvement.

On a number of different occasions members of the group asserted that they had achieved significant clinical advantage by using a combination of MAOI with iminodibenzyl anti-depression agent. This combination, as every American psychiatrist knows, is frequently and severely interdicted in the American literature and in the package inserts provided by the manufacturers of these drugs. Accordingly, most psychiatrists refrain from using such combinations. Some believe that there is actually a significant hazard. Others believe not, but that in the case of any adverse result of whatever origin, they might be defenseless in a malpractice suit. Accordingly it is significant that on several different occasions a number of members of the group reported uniformly good experience from combining these drugs in cases in which the use of either drug singly failed to achieve the desired effect.

On a number of occasions, case studies led to a consideration of central toxicity, that is, toxic effects brought about by impairment of upper or lower brain. Slurring of speech and ataxia were encountered on at least one occasion. More commonly an acute organic syndrome appeared, manifested by confusion, inattention, memory loss and perceptual distortion. One patient reported awaking from sleep in a confused state and carrying out repetitive acts in conformity with dream thoughts. In such states he was unable to distinguish between dream and reality.

These confusional states were more common among older than younger patients, and more common among individuals who had incipient organic brain disease of any kind.

While the iminodibenzyl anti-depression agents are most apt to bring about these confusional toxic states, they may also be seen as a result of the administration of phenothiazine or similar drugs and also as a result of the administration of anti-parkinsonian drugs. All of these substances exert in common a central anticholinergic effect. When two or more drugs with this property are given at the same time, the toxicity of each reinforces that of the other. Several patients who were taking both Navane and a tricyclic anti-depression agent, reported that their driving judgment was impaired.

These confusional states, which at times approach the intensity of delirium with visual hallucinations, are sometimes misdiagnosed as a schizophrenic reaction. They must be distinguished carefully from psychotic episodes which are sometimes precipitated by the administration of an anti-depression agent to an individual with a schizophrenic tendency. The MAOI's are just as apt to produce an exacerbation of the schizophrenic psychosis as the tricyclic anti-depression drugs, and in fact some believe that they are more apt to do so. However, they do not create the acute confusional syndrome that the tricyclics do. There seem to be some individuals who are sensitive to the anticholinergic effect of tricyclics, and these do better with the MAOIs.

4. Other specific effects. For purposes of classification, we should list here toxic effects specific to only one or a small number of these agents, such as thyroid disturbances and seizures. Depersonalization has been described as a complication of the use of tricyclic anti-depression drugs, Stelazine, and Navane. It might be explained as part of the organic syndrome, or it might be given a dynamic meaning. Navane and the piperazine phenothiazines are the drugs most likely to produce dystonic side effects. Depersonalization might be regarded as a psychologic turning away from the world, while dystonia may be a motor expression of aversion. Thus both dystonia and depersonalization may be seen as automatic dissociation from the world of reality.

5. Management. There was some discussion about the management of these side effects when they occur. No one thought that it would be necessary to warn the patient of every possible side effect that he might encounter. However, most felt that when side effects did occur, they should be labeled as such and discussed with the patient. Some members of the group saw no harm in cautioning the patient that there might be some disturbing side effects without specifying their nature.

In the case of one patient an attempt was made to control the confusional state induced by tricyclic anti-depression drugs by the administration of physostigmine. However, when enough physostigmine was given to control the confusion, the patient appeared depressed as well. In other words, the physostigmine seemed to block both the anticholinergic side effect and the anti-depression effect.

C. Psychological responses to physiologic side effects

This heading is included here in the classification of drug effects. However, the subject will be discussed in Chapter 4.

D. Transference effects

These too will be discussed in Chapter 4.

E. Changes attributed erroneously to medication

Weight gain, bulimia, and night sweats are among the changes which one often sees described in the literature and on package inserts accompanying some drugs. Ostow contended, and others concurred, that they were the result of the specific psychic state induced by the drug. For example, compulsive eating and weight gain together with water retention and sleepiness were often seen in patients who had been improved by medication, but who had not resolved the pathogenic problem which had caused the illness in the first place. The state which ensues is one which he calls "narcissistic tranquility" which will be discussed below. These clinical phenomena are encountered whether the state of narcissistic tranquility accompanies spontaneous recovery, or recovery induced by electric shock treatment or any one or combination of drugs. They are not the result of the administration of a specific drug.

Sweating comes about when the patient is poised on the brink of depression. It stops when he has become completely well or when he slips into definitive depression. However, when in the course of drug therapy for depression he is able to emerge from it for a while or when he is subjected to depressing stress, night sweats may appear as he struggles to escape the downward pull of depression.

F. Toxic structural effects

Here one might include such phenomena as agranulocytosis or skin rash, or eye pigmentation.

Electric shock treatment will be mentioned in this chapter only because there was some discussion of it, though there was no discussion which focused principally around electric shock treatment. Linn contended that a brief intensive series of shock treatments is perhaps more rapidly effective in the termination of an agitated psychotic state than drug therapy.

Ostow suggested that electric shock therapy might be effective because it induces amnesia and the amnesia permits the patient to deny and therefore to be unaffected by the pathogenic stressful situation. Linn thought that this point of view was supported by the clinical observation that the patient who is confused immediately after a subarachnoid hemorrhage is euphoric rather than depressed, denying his illness. However, as the confusion clears, he tends to become more and more depressed.

E.F. became confused under the influence of a small number of electric shocks. However, the confusion was seen to have been facilitated by the anticholinergic central effect of the Vivactil which he was being given at the same time and which he tolerated poorly. Linn also pointed out that when a patient responds to electric shock treatment with confusion, he is less apt to obtain a good clinical result from the treatment.

Because of a few experiences in his practice, Ostow asked whether it had been observed by others that patients with diabetes did not respond well to anti-depression drugs. The experience of the group was not broad enough to answer this question. However, Feder did remind us that all of the drugs tend to influence the glucose tolerance curve in one way or other, as did various kinds of mental illness. The question was left open.

3. Psychoanalytic Psychiatry

In order to attempt to understand how medication might have influenced the course of the patient's illness, it became necessary to understand the psychologic changes occurring in mental illness, and the influences which elicited them. It became necessary to consider such things as the natural history of a mental illness, pathogenic influences, constitutional vulnerabilities, disease syndromes, the genesis and resolution of conflict and the circumstances under which recovery might be expected. All of these problems were approached by the group from the point of view of psychoanalysts who were dealing with mental illness, using their psychoanalytic insight to help them understand the patient's illness, and employing whatever therapeutic tools were available to psychiatrists without relying only, consistently or even primarily, on psychoanalysis as a therapeutic method. The discipline which such considerations create probably deserves the designation "psychoanalytic psychiatry." In this chapter we shall present some of these observations. The reader will see that they cover only a narrow segment of the field of psychoanalytic psychiatry.

The use of medication for the treatment of mental illness is not the primary subject of any of the observations in this chapter, though the response to medication in a number of instances helped the members of the group to understand the chain of psychologic events.

A. Pathogenic stress

Whenever a psychiatrist deals with an episode of mental illness, he tries to understand both why the patient fell ill, and why

he fell ill at that particular point in time. The question of a constitutional basis for mental illness is always raised for consideration. It was raised in these discussions in connection with the
report of a schizophrenic patient. Another member of the group
had previously treated the patient's sister and he could therefore
provide certain comparative data.

The fact that two or three siblings in a given family develop
schizophrenic illness is not a new observation nor does it surprise
the psychiatrist. Some explain it as a manifestation of a hereditary
vulnerability to schizophrenic illness. Others attribute the illness
to an unwholesome family environment. Probably most psychiatrists today see merit in both points of view. That each of the two
siblings fell ill at the same period of life, under stress which most
individuals their age are expected to handle without falling ill, tells
us only that they shared a vulnerabliity. In both cases, the stress
arose in the marriage but the circumstances were different.

Far more striking was a certain similarity in the symptoms
which prevailed during the agitated phase of the illness. In both instances the patient would perform a characteristic sequence of
movements. Someone who had witnessed the episodes of both individuals, without being asked, commented on their amazing similarity. When Ostow suggested the possibility that constitution
might have provided not only vulnerability to schizophrenic breakdown, but might also have provided patterns for symptomatic behavior, he encountered a response of intellectual outrage on the
part of the other members of the group. They preferred to believe
either that one of the patients was influenced by the other or that
both, in their expressions of illness, regressed to certain patterns of
childhood behavior which they had shared. However, the similarity went even further. Both patients responded to MAOI anti-
depression drugs, though they both required relatively high doses.
Ultimately, each escaped from the influence of these drugs and the
condition proceeded to deteriorate. In fact as the reporter
described the progressive decline despite vigorous therapeutic
efforts, Klerman speculated that what was seen was merely the
progressive unfolding of a schizophrenic life pattern. Loomis preferred to think that the parents whom both patients shared were
responsible for the behavioral similarities and for the similarity in
outcome.

This discussion resolved nothing but it did make it clear that one could not define the full extent of the contribution of constitution in general and heredity in particular to the vulnerability of a patient to illness, to the symptomatic manifestations of that illness, to its response to treatment, and to the ultimate fate of the patient.

In our discussions of the precipitating causes of breakdown, two generalizations were proposed which warrant repeating. It was clear that the patient who was presented began to break down under the stress of being expected to assume adult vocational responsibility, and being expected to marry and assume the role of a father. Breakdown on such occasions is seen not infrequently. It was an instance, Ostow suggested, of what he called the Peter Pan syndrome. A number of adolescents are unable successfully to make the transition from anaclitic dependence or narcissistic retreat to the responsibilities expected of an adult within his society. They learn in their late teens and early twenties to pretend that they have made the transition and they manage very often to give the impression of maturity. However, some time between ages 25 and 30 they ordinarily encounter inescapable challenges which they visibly either meet or fail to meet. When such a failure occurs, or when the patient fails simply by refusing to confront the challenge, he is likely to break down in one way or other, depending upon his own predisposition.

Linn noted that such Peter Pan individuals are apt to break down at either of two points in their college career. They may succumb during freshman or sophomore year as a result of separation from home and family. More malignant reactions may occur in anticipation of graduation, that is, in anticipation of leaving college to assume responsibility.

In the case of patient A.B., the episode of illness, which began with a suicide attempt, seemed to have been precipitated by the patient's having been rejected by his girl friend. During treatment, relapses occurred when the patient was moved by a resurgence of libidinal drive, or by imminent discharge from the hospital, to face reality once more. It was recognized that while the episode had been precipitated by the rejection, it was the patient's ambivalence towards his parents which made him susceptible to that rejection.

Ostow proposed the concept of a pathogenic trap. The trap might be an ambivalent relation to the principal love object; it might be personal failure, serious enough to be damaging to his narcissism; it might be a reality unacceptable for any reason. Finding oneself in a pathogenic trap, the individual must devise some way to handle the situation. As we shall discuss below, a depressive retreat and a schizophrenic break may each be considered a pathologic method of coming to terms with the trap situation.

At various points, the group saw pathogenic potential in a discrepancy between the libido supply available to the patient and external demands on the one hand, or external opportunities on the other. Inadequacy of libido supply in the face of demands could cause illness, and so could absence of opportunities when libido supply was ample.

During depressive illness, the patient may be considered to possess inadequate libido to deal with the demands made upon him. On the other hand, when libidinal energy has been restored by the administration of anti-depression medication, if the patient is still incapable of sustaining object relations, then the availability of the energy in the presence of available objects subjects the patient to stress from which he must escape. For example, patient A.B., on regaining energy, was threatened by the resurgent homosexual transference and was impelled to detach himself from the analyst in every possible way.

B. Depression

In all the case presentations, depressive tendency or depressive illness or both were important features. Our records therefore contain a good deal of discussion of the psychopathology of depression.

When a patient becomes depressed, it seems as though his whole world is collapsing. The precipitating factor is not only repressed; it is obscured by a host of other events, all of which seem to threaten the patient in one way or another. For example, in the case of patient E.F. there was good reason to believe that it was abuse by his wife upon whom he was so heavily dependent, that precipitated the episode of depression that was being reported.

However, at the same time the patient was subjected to other pressures. The family business, the income of which was supporting him, had begun to do extremely badly. Therefore, the patient in effect had very little income though, to be sure, he possessed a reassuring amount of capital. Second, the board of an eleemosynary institution, on which he served, became critical of activities which he had undertaken on behalf of the institution without authorization. Third, he was afraid that the board might discover a minor violation of trust which could, if someone wished to do so, be exaggerated so as to seem like a major abuse of trust. At the same time, too, he was scheduled to start a series of desensitizing injections for allergy. In general, the patient tends to exaggerate the importance of the secondary disappointments and frustrations, while he represses the primary ambivalence. When he recovers from the depression, however that recovery comes about, all of these hardships are ignored. Asked about them, the patient minimizes their importance.

As each symptom or manifestation of illness was presented, attempts were made to understand its dynamic significance.

As E.F. was becoming depressed, he expressed resentment for the first time that the office door was locked—from the inside—and imagined that he was being cornered in a bathroom by the nurse who looked after him in childhood. Furst interpreted this claustrophobia as a defense against a claustrophilic, anaclitic need to be protected by mother against depression.

With respect to the patient's withdrawal from contact with other individuals, Furst suggested that the function of withdrawal in depression is to control one's hostility, that is, to protect others against hostile impulses and wishes.

At one point E.F. wished to say that he felt useless. In fact, he said he felt "useful" which was a slip since he meant to say that he felt useless. Ostow commented that patients are protected against depression to the extent that someone depends upon them. The post-partum mother, for example, feels that her infant's needs prevent her from succumbing to the regression induced by depression. On the one hand the depressed patient wishes to feel that there is such a claim upon his services because it helps him to resist the depressive pull. On the other hand, he resents this claim because it interferes with his regression.

At one point the patient said that he imagined castrating himself. Bressler commented that since testicles sometimes symbolize breasts, the attack on the patient's testicles might be the expression of retroflexed anger, originally directed against mother's dry breasts. Roose observed that the patient was trying to cope with his depression by aggressivity which became an oral, sadistic rage and which in turn tightened the trap. He wished, said Bressler, for an oral, nonambivalent reunion with mother.

Roose was impressed by the degree of the patient's self-awareness and insight. Ostow pointed out that self-observation is characteristic of depression and depressed patients in general and that, as one would expect, the observations are always self-critical.

The theme of self-castration arose again a few sessions later together with thoughts about death. They appeared shortly after he complained that his wife would not stay with him. The self-destructive wishes seemed to be calculated to appease her, as though he were punishing himself for being naughty.

In reviewing all the psychologic manifestations of depression in this patient, it became possible to delineate both sides of the ambivalence to the patient's love objects, namely, mother, wife and analyst. The affectionate stream was manifested as an oral craving for food, love and protection and in clinging to the love object by demanding proximity, by confessing misbehavior, by self-humiliation, by begging, by offering physical affection, by the wish to be useful and needed, and by a recurrent religious attitude. The hostile stream of the ambivalence was expressed in the fury at being deprived, in the wish to kill, and conversely in the wish to punish himself by death, by suicide, by self-castration, and by actually striking himself.

In C.D.'s case, the initial decompensation was depressive in character. There we saw that the patient was trapped in a situation in which he was afraid of marrying, and ashamed not to marry. The trap led to depression and he attempted to combat the depression by clinging to the analyst. Since cure was not forthcoming sufficiently rapidly to meet the marriage deadline, he was disappointed and then became angry. Demands, complaints, defiance, agitation, projection of the anger and suicide threats characterized a phase of anger which seemed to succeed the phase of clinging. But even while he was angry, the patient showed a persistent dependent attitude which was confirmed by occasional weeping.

The phase of "angry repudiation" in turn gave way to definitive depression. The suicidal tendency, a sense of discouragement and a feeling of emptiness formed a transition from angry repudiation to depression.

E.F. also showed anger in his depression though he denied it. As noted above, it was expressed in suicide fantasies, in the overt hostility of dream content, in complaints about the anaclitic object, and in distrusting both analyst and wife. The hostility became overt about two or three weeks after anti-depression medication was started on each of two occasions. We shall review the actual sequence of improvement below. Linn was not sure how commonly this phenomenon was encountered. Klerman reported studies which disclosed that all depressed patients score high on inward-directed hostility, which subsides as the patient improves. He said that not all depressed patients display hostility to others. (In subsequent studies, Klerman and his associates found that hostility to others could be observed generally in depressed patients, though the hostility was focused fairly narrowly upon individuals closest to the patient and appeared in lesser degree with respect to individuals who were less important to the patient.) Ostow suggested that the hostility becomes overt when the patient, as he recovers, recathects the original disappointing object and finds the relation just as disappointing as previously. The hostility toward the original object subsides only after the energizing process has gone so far that the patient is no longer dependent upon and can ignore the original object. Feder proposed that the drug merely undoes the state of enervation so that the hostility, which existed in depressed form all along, is uncovered. Roose added that where no one is to blame, for example, in some instances of reactive depression, there should be no aggressive component. As a matter of fact, however, he acknowledged that there is always an aggressive component. The question is whether the patient would become angry as he recovers even if the external frustration is not renewed. Since in most instances the patient's expectations are unrealistic, they are almost bound to be frustrated so that crucial examples will probably be difficult to find. Relative increase in suicide potential which occasionally occurs as the patient recovers from depression may be related to this increment in hostility. This problem will be discussed below.

E.F. reported, at one point as he was becoming depressed

again, that he found himself thinking almost obsessively of previous episodes of depression. This Ostow called "the palimpsest
phenomenon." He observed that whenever a patient who had been
depressed before becomes depressed again, many of the sensations
and ideas which he had previously experienced seem to become revived. Such patients come to feel that they had never been well;
that they have been continuously or almost continuously in
depression. (In fact, this palimpsest phenomenon applies not only
to depression but to all states of mind. Whenever we fall into a
discrete state of mind, the memory of the last similar experience,
and of previous similar experiences, becomes revived. Our attention is drawn to this phenomenon when we are dealing with depressed patients because their intensified self-observation compels
them to report to us both current sensations and the past sensations which the latter revive.)

Two cases studied exhibited episodes of mania, namely, the
cases of E.F. and G.H. In each instance the manic episode could be
seen as a precursor of, and an attempt to ward off, depression. In
each case depression followed. In the first instance the occasion
for the manic-depressive sequence was an intensification of the
patient's wife's hostility toward him. She forced him to take a trip
to Europe with her, neglected him there, and on the way back
called him a homosexual. In the case of G.H., the manic attack
was precipitated by the birth of a child. It came about while he
was supposed to be taking 75 to 90 mgs a day of Nardil (phenel-
zine), though there is some reason to believe that he might have increased the dose on his own. The mania subsided when the drug
was discontinued. Subsequently it became necessary to reinstate it
for treatment of recurring depressive episodes. During the subsequent treatment, the Nardil was not always able to contain the
depression. Despite the fact that the patient had increased the
dose of Nardil, it was not the opinion of the group that this increased dose was responsible for the manic attack. Rather they believed that he increased the dose because he felt himself becoming
depressed and that the manic attack represented an attempt to
prevent the depression. Had the depression come about, it would
have been a post-partum depression in a father and the mania
could have been considered a post-partum mania.

The manifestations and dynamics of the manic episodes were not remarkable. E.F. was overactive, talked excessively, attempted to manage everybody's affairs, drank almost continuously either alcohol or coffee, or both, and felt that he was infallible. G.H. went on a buying spree and exhibited excessively affectionate behavior and obscene conversation. In the discussion of G.H., Linn pointed out that, after the baby was born, the patient returned to his mother and his behavior with her was especially inappropriate. This meant to Linn an oedipal identification with the father who was an alcoholic. Roose saw both active and passive attitudes towards both parents but he also saw identification with the new-born baby in the patient's feeling of blissful satiation.

One personally characteristic symptom of E.F. was compulsive cleaning. It is not infrequently encountered among manics. He had helped to keep the house clean after his mother died during his childhood. It was fairly evident therefore that this symptom represented an attempt to reunite with mother by identifying with her. Loomis pointed out that the identification included also a competition, that is, he was identifying with mother and wife but also supplanting them.

The vigor of the manic, for all its troublesomeness, nevertheless may quickly subside. Bressler noted in the discussion of E.F. that the manic's victory over his superego is tenuous and can be maintained only by constant activity. If he is pressed or opposed he may well break down. Furst observed that manics are defeated by any frustration. In this case it became clear that the manic syndrome included depressive components as well. Here they included hypochondria, recurrent thoughts about death, and dreams of loss. Feder observed that manics are likely to weep.

Ostow raised the question about whether there are two kinds of mania. In this instance the mania is clearly a defense against an impending depression which indeed followed immediately when the manic activity was restrained by small doses of tranquilizing drugs, for example, 50 mg of Mellaril or 100 mg of Taractan. On the other hand, one can produce a manic state artificially by giving an overdose of an anti-depression drug. Here one sees no depressive components and the mania continues so long as the drug is continued at the same dose, or so long as it is not opposed by a tranquilizing drug of the phenothiazine type. This difference has some practical significance. It would seem that the mania which occurs as a defense against depression could be effectively treated by the administration of an anti-depression drug and recurrence could be prevented by a maintenance dose of this drug, so long as the drug continues to be effective.

I have been able to do this successfully in the few cases in which I have tried it.

On the other hand the mania that is brought about by an anti-depression drug can be controlled only by an anti-psychosis tranquilizer. The anti-depression mania can also be controlled by a tranquilizing drug, but in that case there is the possibility that as the mania is conquered, the patient will slip into depression. The members of the group agreed that, in their experience, lithium, though likely to alleviate the mania, did not elicit subsequent depression. Post-manic depression, however, occurred not infrequently in the course of treatment with tranquilizing drugs of other varieties.

There was some comment about the compulsive need to eat and drink exhibited by E.F. At first he drank alcoholic beverages. When, in response to instructions, he gave these up, he replaced them with iced coffee or even cold water. He gained a great deal of weight. The excited manic usually loses weight and seems on the brink of exhaustion. By contrast, the hypomanic who is not excited but expansive is more likely to show the compulsive need to overeat and to drink excessively. Ostow related this phenomenon to what he called "the syndrome of narcissistic tranquility" which will be discussed below.

C. Schizophrenia

There was relatively little discussion of schizophrenia despite the fact that two of the cases exhibited schizophrenic components. Early in the history of the group, Bressler noted the wisdom of administering a tranquilizing drug together with an anti-depression agent to depressed, schizophrenic patients. The depression itself, he said, constitutes a kind of control over the schizophrenic process and a deterrent against further disintegration. The mutual relation between schizophrenia and depression was mentioned a number of times subsequently. The issue becomes especially important since a number of schizophrenic patients treated with phenothiazine, after initial improvement, subsequently become depressed. The group agreed that any drug which inactivates a patient's defenses may precipitate depression. Klerman acknowledged that it is a clinical fact that patients do move up and back between delusional and depressive positions. The theoretical interpretation remains uncertain. Bressler observed that when a schizophrenic loses the ability to create a restitutive delusional system after having been given a tranquilizing drug, he is then confronted with the object loss which occurred at the outset of his illness. Ostow suggested that in addition to the protective effect of schizophrenic delusion formation against the pain of object loss, there is also a more basic reciprocal opposition between detachment on the one hand and depression on the other. That is, a depressive process undoes or limits the tendency to psychic detachment, while detachment, when used as a defense, might make depression unnecessary. Feder, wondering about the mechanism of this opposition, asked whether a depressing drug undoes delusions or whether a drug that undoes delusions also produces depression. Roose asked the operational question, namely, how can one know whether, under the influence of an anti-psychosis drug, the patient will reestablish a true object relation or lapse into depression. That question was not answered.

C.D. displayed an interesting, characteristically schizophrenic phenomenon, namely, an attempt to achieve self-cure by understanding himself. The patient showed a compulsive tendency to seek "revelations" which would explain his difficulty. Linn noted that in doing so he was obviously identifying with the analyst. The patient himself conceptualized the relation between insight and recovery. He believed that the tissue covering his brain had peeled off and had fallen in front of his eyes and so obstructed his vision. Unprotected by its covering, the tissues of the brain had fallen apart. If he could now discover the truth about his illness, his brain would reconstitute. Linn observed that the mystical achievement of insight is associated with the fantasy of identifying with God, here symbolizing also identification with the analyst.

Ostow agreed that the comparison with mystical experience is appropriate because in that case, too, the image of the delusional world seems real, and the subject claims that he now sees the truth, whereas previously he had lived in a false world. This truth liberates him from the major problem of his life.

D. Narcissistic tranquility

On a number of occasions, excessive sleeping and compulsive eating were encountered as symptoms. Ostow introduced the concept of narcissistic tranquility. This is a state of affairs, he said, in which an individual attempts to cope with stress by walling himself off from the external world. It is accomplished by denial or detachment. The symptoms of narcissistic tranquility include compulsive eating, drinking or both, weight gain, afternoon or evening torpor, increased sexual desire, and a tendency to accumulate possessions. It may be considered to be the manifestation of an attempt to deal with stress without falling ill. Ostow suggested that physiologically this state might be correlated with the relative preponderance of mineralocorticoids over glucocorticoids, the converse of the situation that prevails during the general adaptation syndrome of Selye.* In a state of narcissistic tranquility, the patient may also accumulate fluid, as individuals do in the premenstrual syndrome. Linn suggested that the patient in this state seems to be attempting to escape from inner deadness by emphasizing inputs.

Referring to our discussion of compulsive eating and hypomania, we may consider the possibility that the denying, overeating, overdrinking and expansive hypomanic is indeed seeking a situation of minimal psychic stress. When he becomes agitated either in mania or in depression, he loses appetite and weight.

The compulsion to eat also suggests a kind of addiction. G.H., who was addicted to amphetamines, when he was treated with an anti-depression drug, Nardil, also showed the tendency to overeat and to gain weight. This raises the question of whether an attempt to combat stress may be considered the basis of addiction. The discussion of G.H. suggested that the following characteristics might

*Hans Selye, *The Stress of Life.* New York: McGraw-Hill, 1956.

be related to his tendency to addiction: 1) a childlike dependent character; 2) the preconsciously perceived threat of overhanging depression; 3) an anhedonic state; 4) the feeling of emptiness; 5) a psychotic core; 6) guilt for success; 7) homosexual conflict. These are features which the various members of the group thought might be operative in this case. Whether any one or group of these will be encountered more frequently among addictive personalities than among others will require investigation. In this case one may presume that they constituted threats to the patient's equilibrium. The amphetamine addiction presumably countered these threats, and when the use of amphetamines was given up, it was sufficient to throw the patient into depression. He could deal with this depression only with the aid of an anti-depression drug.

E. Notes about individual manifestations of illness

While reports of most of the discussions can be subsumed under categorical headings of nosologic entities, dynamic complexes or general principles, there were a few discussions of particular issues which deserve separate mention. These refer to questions which interest most of us from time to time. What we present here are not the results of any research in an operational sense but rather the opinions of the members of the group. The reader will wish to compare them with his own opinions and to check them out against his own experience.

1. Suicide attempts. In connection with the presentation of A.B., it was asked whether all suicidal patients are necessarily depressed. Feder believed that most suicidal patients are depressed, though others act upon psychotic impulse. Hysterics too may suicide if the hysteria is masking depression. Sarwer-Foner agreed that most suicidal patients were depressed, but in other instances the suicide attempt could be the consequence of an impulse-ridden character disorder. Winkelman agreed that the most common cause of suicide was acute depression but considered anhedonia a common cause. In Furst's opinion, most suicidal patients are depressed. The hysteria that leads to suicide may mask a psychosis. One also encounters suicide in patients with paranoid schizophrenia. Linn proposed that the danger of suicide appears when the patient feels no longer able to reach the crucial love object, no matter what the diagnostic category. Feder added that suicide may be fostered by the loss of ability to cope.

2. *"Empty" feelings.*   The meaning of "emptiness" as a sensation (as distinguished from a psychotic, hypochondriacal delusion) became a problem almost at the very beginning. Roose understood this term to be suggestive more of schizophrenia than of depression. Ostow was inclined to interpret it as depression and Linn suggested that the patient in question was both schizophrenic and depressed. Feder said that some of the patients who describe emptiness respond well to anti-depression drugs and he considers such a response, when it occurs, a practical demonstration that the condition which is being treated is depression.

Interestingly enough, the very same discussion was repeated toward the end of the project in the presentation of G.H., a very different kind of patient from A.B. He too spoke of "emptiness" and on that basis Roose suggested the existence of a "psychotic core." He acknowledged, however, that the depressed patient also feels empty but in that case the emptiness is due to lack of sustenance rather than the complete abandonment of object relations. He supported his argument by the fact that the patient did experience a definite paranoid episode. Klerman countered, however, that not everybody who reacts to amphetamine intoxication with paranoid symptoms, can be considered schizophrenic. Feder noted again that anhedonic, adolescent girls respond well to anti-depression drugs and they should not be considered schizophrenic. Ostow suggested that the schizophrenic patient usually speaks of being "numb" or "dead" rather than "empty."

3. *Wandering in the streets.*   C.D., as he became more psychotic, spent much of his time wandering through the streets. Linn and Klerman saw this as an attempt to avoid the principal love object and other individuals who are the targets of the patient's ambivalence. He avoids them for fear that he might kill them. Furst emphasized the other side of the ambivalence, namely, avoiding the love object as a defense against the patient's overwhelming need for him. Ostow observed that the psychotic's wandering must be distinguished from the prowling of the perverse patient. Both are avoiding the principal love object but the perverse

patient is seeking a substitute opportunity for gratification while the psychotic cannot accept any substitute.

4. The symbolism of space flights.   A contemporary phenomenon, the space flight, has found its way into symbolism. E.F. dreamed, as he was slipping from mania into depression, that he was in an Apollo space capsule. He was frightened when it came down. It hit the water and began to turn over. Roose interpreted the return to the water as a symbol for the lapse into depression. The presenting analyst confirmed this interpretation by noting that as he became depressed, this patient, as many other patients do, had a number of dreams of falling into the water. Ostow observed that patients threatened with hysterical or schizophrenic detachment find the idea of space flights frightening. One of his patients, a schizophrenic unable to establish any companionship, reported the fantasy that he saw himself as an astronaut on a space flight, unable to return to earth, and circling the moon forever. Furst encountered an instance in which the space flight, or at least the takeoff, was used to symbolize anal expulsion.

5. Paranoia and projection.   There was some discussion at one point about whether the term "paranoid" could properly be used of a patient with organic confusion who unrealistically blamed another individual for his difficulties. While some felt that the use of projection as a defense could be called paranoid, Furst argued that the diagnosis of paranoia requires an organized delusional system. The suspiciousness of those with organic brain disease could be called a "paranoid trend."

6. The contrast between denial and repression.   In reporting the course of his patient's recovery from an episode of depression, the reporter observed that the denial of ambivalence to his wife was undone at one point. Klerman asked whether what was undone was denial or repression. Ostow contended that it should be called denial because it was massive, and because, with the alteration of the clinical state, it was easily reversible. Feder observed that Waelder* had said that denial was an attempt to deal with a catastrophic type of situation while repression occurred when

*Robert Waelder, "The Structure of Paranoid Ideas," *International Journal of Psychoanalysis* 32 (1951), pp. 167-177.

the threat was not overwhelming. Linn contended that denial requires exclusion from apperception while repression does not require this selective inattention. It is less fragile. Roose said that repression is more restricted in content and more precise than denial. Bressler emphasized the distinction between the effect of each upon the ego. Repression, he said, frees the ego while denial splits it. Furst noted that repression gives rise to derivatives while denial doesn't.

When the discussion was reviewed at the following meeting, further discussion led to the conclusion that denial is more primitive and more likely to be associated with regression than repression is. In general, we deal with painful external reality by denial, and with unwelcome desires by repression.

Ostow asked how denial and repression each responds to medication. Klerman suggested that perhaps the phenothiazines facilitate repression by the psychotic, by reinforcing his sensory barriers. Feder agreed that some drugs cut down on sensory input. Linn asked, when alcohol alleviates the feeling of depression, do we not have to infer the existence of denial or repression or both? Perhaps, he answered, it is by creating temporary impairment of brain function, that alcohol alleviates depression. He recalled that intravenous amytal, by alleviating anxiety, may facilitate the speech of the aphasic despite the fact that its direct effect is to accentuate organic deficits.

F. Treatment and recovery

Most psychiatric literature deals with the nature of mental illness, indications for various kinds of treatment, and procedures for beginning and maintaining treatment. However, relatively less consideration has been given to a study of the process of recovery. Our group found itself dealing with the problems of recovery on a number of different occasions. Let us start, however, with a few comments about treatment.

The data presented in the description of E.F. permitted a formulation of just what it was that the patient expected of the therapist. First, he wanted protection against death. There had been a number of suicides in his family and he feared that he might be swept by his illness to suicide. However, this was merely an explicit statement of the expectation of every depressed patient that he will soon perish. Second, the patient feared that he would be castrated for sexual misbehavior and he hoped that the therapist would protect him against that danger too. There was a need, therefore, to appease the therapist and this he did by confessing his sins and by being obedient. He yearned for restitution of early protective relations, ultimately with his mother and secondarily with adults who had taken a protective interest in him subsequently. Finally he found it necessary to deny his difficulty with his wife.

Throughout the discussions, Linn emphasized the value of hospitalization for the treatment of serious mental illness. The group agreed on the importance of relieving the patient from the stress of the precipitating situation. They agreed that hospitalization is often the best way to accomplish this relief. They agreed further that until the patient is ready to resume normal activities and relations, it is useful to encourage him to regress. As Linn observed, the administration of a phenothiazine reduces drive or impairs reception of environmental messages. In either case one encourages regression so that it would be inconsistent at the same time to encourage activity. Similarly, if the patient is given an anti-depression drug, some time is required before he can emerge from his regression and isolation, and until that time has elapsed, the patient's regression must be respected, he said.

The group found itself repeatedly recurring to the following theme. If one successfully treats the presenting clinical picture, for example, schizophrenia, one is removing a defense against the stressful situation which precipitated the illness. If the patient is then exposed to the same stress without the assistance of his defenses, pathologic though they be, he will become depressed. As Furst put it, the development of symptoms represents the solution to a problem. Removing the symptoms without alleviating the pathogenic pressure brings about greater distress. Linn illustrated this principle by referring to the case of acute organic mental syndrome. In patients with acute subarachnoid hemorrhage, we usually find that the organic mental disturbance permits denial and euphoria. When mental function improves, as the hemorrhage is resorbed, the denial disappears and gives way to more appropriate unhappiness.

Ostow carried that argument further, suggesting that electric shock treatment may work on the same principle. That is, it creates an organic mental syndrome which facilitates denial. The denial spares the patient the recognition of the presenting stress and spares him the depression induced by the stress. Following electric shock treatment, the denial and the relief from depression will persist until the patient is once again overwhelmed by reality. Linn, confirming this view, noted that Fink and Kahn* demonstrated a temporal relation between the onset of slow wave activity in the electroencephalogram following electric shock therapy, and the alleviation of depression. Bressler observed that when reality is indeed intractable, insight into the mechanism of symptoms is often not sufficient to permit the patient to obtain relief. Drug therapy is also necessary.

In a sense the development of psychotic symptoms, hospitalization, and the induction of an acute organic mental syndrome which we do, for example, by giving electric shock, may all help the patient to achieve tranquility. The patient is isolated from his problem by withdrawing from object relations, by psychotic detachment, by hospitalization, and by regression. This isolation prevents object-related anxiety and undermines object-directed hostility. However, it cannot be tolerated indefinitely because in turn it induces shame, anxiety and feelings of numbness, deadness and emptiness. To a certain extent, anti-anxiety agents may permit continuing object relations by alleviating the anxiety that appears in association with them. Anti-depression drugs, on the other hand, will strengthen drives toward object relations before the patient can handle them, and thus may precipitate untoward clinical effects, for example, denial, psychotic detachment or destructive acting out.

Very early in the project the group agreed upon the following formulation: When a drug or any other therapeutic modality succeeds in removing depression, the patient is confronted once more with the pathogenic situation which provoked the depressive retreat in the first place. Unless he can bring a new approach to this situation, he will have to mobilize some other defense such as schiz-

*M. Fink and R.L. Kahn, "Relation of EEG Delta Activity to Behavioral Response in Electroshock," *Archives of Neurology and Psychiatry,* 78 (1956) pp. 516-525.

ophrenic or hysterical detachment, depersonalization, or denial. Upon the verge of recovery, the patient may be thrown back each of the first few times he attempts to resume object relations. When the depression is firmly dissipated, he will have to find another defensive position vis-a-vis the principal love object.

Specifically, in the case of the patient A.B., it was demonstrated that the resurgence of object relations as the patient was impelled toward recovery by anti-depression medication threatened him with passive homosexuality and induced a violent defense against that. It also created fears of separation and fears of fusion.

With the recovery from depression, hostility to the anacliticallyly loved object becomes more overt and the patient may provoke abandonment or punishment. In treatment, the transference is either intensified, distorted or changed from positive to negative. We discussed above (Chapter 3, page 31), the fact that the hostility which plays such a large part in depression, becomes externalized as the patient recovers. Ostow suggested that the hostility appears overtly when the patient, as a result of the energizing process, recathects the original disappointing object and finds the relation just as disappointing as previously. The hostility subsides only after the energizing process has gone so far that the patient is no longer dependent, and can ignore the original object. Feder on the other hand, said that the drug does no more than undo the state of enervation. When that happens the hostility which was there all along is uncovered.

In this connection, there was some discussion of the phenomenon of suicide occurring in patients who seemed to be recovering from depression. While some members of the group had not seen this phenomenon, others had. A number of reasons were suggested. One is that recovering patients may be discharged too soon from the hospital. The second is that, in the depths of depression, sufficient psychic energy for the suicide effort is not available. The third suggestion is that the syndrome of depression is used as a defense so that when it is removed the patient remains undefended against his libidinal and aggressive impulses. Fourth, it was suggested that the guilt attendant upon depression may act as an inhibiting factor with respect to suicide. It was Linn's impression that suicide occurring during recovery from depression is more apt to occur when the depression is one aspect of a schizophrenic psychosis.

Ostow drew attention to the fact that as a patient recovers from depression, his course usually fluctuates as he attempts again and again to deal with object relations. A day or two of relative improvement is not infrequently followed by a day or two of relapse. During the fourth and fifth week of anti-depression drug therapy, one sees relatively profound and frequent alternations between improvement and relapse. It may be that when suicide occurs during the recovery process, it does so when the patient becomes discouraged as a result of one of the relapses.

In the course of his report of patient A.B., the analyst mentioned that he was eager to have the patient obtain some regular work in order to facilitate his reintegration into the world of reality. Ostow commented that work exerts a powerful, stabilizing influence upon patients who are having difficulty establishing equilibrium by means of object relations or narcissistic investment. Linn observed that schizophrenic patients will work, but if they are paid for their work they feel that they are being challenged to function independently and such a challenge exerts a deleterious effect. Feder observed that in some "half-way houses" where patients in transitional status are maintained, it has been found helpful to reduce the rent as patients begin to earn money. The intention is to demonstrate that the patient's dependent status is not threatened by his engagement in occupational activity. The group was not entirely of one mind about whether a patient could accept the idea that his working does not threaten his dependence. Linn noted that it was important to find occupations in which potentially disturbing object relations are kept at a minimum. Loomis added that for the schizophrenic patient whose sense of time continuity has deteriorated, work can have a structuring influence.

To revert to the study of the recovery process, Ostow pointed out that when a patient has been brought out of a psychotic episode, especially when the recovery is spontaneous or occurs with the assistance of drug rather than electric shock treatment, he is eager to reconstruct what happened to him. When the recovery is based upon electric shock treatment, the amnesia and the daze discourage such an effort. The schizophrenic patient, even in the phase of acute psychosis, tries to obtain "insight." As we mentioned above, this is usually a pseudo-insight, a mystical revelation, which is meant to replace the view of reality which the patient has given up. After his recovery, the schizophrenic's search for knowledge continues, but now it is knowledge of the real world that he seeks, namely, what really happened to him and what he thought, as seen by an outside observer. By helping the patient with this reconstruction the analyst can learn a good deal about the patient's remote and recent past history and the contribution of each to his recent illness. In the case of depression, one does not wait until full recovery occurs before introducing insight.

4. Problems Involved in the Combination of Pharmaceutic Agents with Psychotherapy or Psychoanalysis

The primary purpose of our project was to try to learn how the drugs which effect mental illness do so and how they are best integrated with a total therapeutic program. In this chapter we shall deal with the use of these drugs in treatment.

In selecting a particular medication for treatment, one must first define whether one is going to try to influence the presenting symptoms or the underlying motivational state. For example, one may attempt to handle the anxiety which often appears at the beginning of depressive withdrawal, either with an anti-anxiety drug or with an anti-depression drug. The group had relatively little to say about symptomatic treatment of illness. Selecting a drug to influence the basic psychodynamic mechanism requires at least some theory of how drugs work. No consensus was achieved with respect to this central question. However, by the end of the project, most of the participants seemed ready to subscribe to the idea that it influences some aspect of motivational state.

Sandler distinguished between the subjective state of psychic pain and the depressive response to that state. The state of pain, he said, may result from a disappointment in oneself or from object loss. However, depression is not the only possible response. Other responses may be paranoid projection, acting out, and psychosomatic disorder. He said we should consider the possibility that those drugs that seem to influence depression actually act upon the state of pain which gives rise to depression.

About three weeks after patient C.D. began to take Nardil, an MAOI, he announced that he intended to commit suicide. He had attempted intercourse with his fiancée and had been unsuccessful. At this point, the group discussed what if any effect the drug was having upon the patient's condition. Loomis said that he didn't know whether the drug had become effective but if it had, it was increasing drive intensity without increasing capacity to direct and control. Bressler commented that the energy problem in depression may be either a lack of available libidinal energy, or failure on the part of the ego to handle energy properly. In the case being discussed, he said, the uncontrolled drive leads the patient to a counterphobic estimate of himself as a homosexual. The drug seemed to have brought about a state of drive intensification. It had disturbed the previously established equilibrium between heterosexual and homosexual drive. The state might result in a suicide attempt or psychotic break.

Winkelman said that the drug was impairing ego function at that point, because the degree of ego impairment seemed to exceed the degree which one would have expected from the patient's previous history. It was Feder's impression that the drug was strengthening the man's drive to a point where his ego could no longer resist, despite his fear of object relations. Though he would have preferred the passive position, the energizing medication made that position unavailable to him. Winkelman also suggested that the agitation might be attributable to a discrepancy between the patient's expectation of assistance and his failure to improve.

Ostow offered a different view. He doubted that the energizing medication had yet had a chance to become effective. In his experience a minimum of four weeks of oral therapy was required. He interpreted the increasing depression and agitation as a result of the patient's repeated failures to handle the sexual challenge with which he was presented, and to his apprehension regarding the rapidly approaching wedding. Ostow thought that the state of mind which prevailed at the moment should be considered a phase of "angry repudiation" in the course of evolving depression. This phase is characterized by demands, anger, suicide threats, and dissociative phenomena, sometimes neurotic, sometimes psychotic. It usually follows a phase of clinging and is succeeded by a phase of definitive depression. The patient's analyst supported this view with the report that the extravagant push of verbal production and the forceful attempt to achieve insight turned out in retrospect to be an attempt to overcome a threatening break with reality.

At that point, the analyst added some Thorazine to the

patient's daily medication and shortly thereafter he improved. The fact that the Thorazine was given at just about the time that the anti-depression agent might have been expected to become effective made it impossible to ascertain which of the two drugs was responsible for the patient's improvement. Ostow thought that the Thorazine had alleviated the agitation but that if it had not been given, the agitation would probably have subsided within a few days as a result of the operation of the Nardil. Bressler believed that the Thorazine had blunted the rage of the patient so that he could relate to his analyst more comfortably. With recovery, the patient attempted once more to deal with the ambivalent trap which had precipitated his illness.

I have observed only recently that when a small amount of phenothiazine or thioxanthine tranquilizer is added to a dose of anti-depression agent which is too low to reverse depression by itself, or which has not yet begun to become effective, a pronounced improvement is obtained literally overnight. The mechanism is probably the same as that which I described above in Chapter 2, page 16 but this anti-depression response is more vigorous because the system had been primed by the sub-threshold dose of the anti-depression agent.

Ostow supported the position that detachment and depression may be seen as two alternative responses to ambivalence. Energizing drugs facilitate the former and tranquilizing drugs facilitate the latter. In simple depression, therefore, merely an energizing drug is required, though if it is pressed too hard, it may precipitate a dissociated state after the patient has recovered from the depression. In that case its effect can be countered by the administration of a phenothiazine or thioxanthine, or perhaps simply by reducing the dose. In a case of psychosis, if there is merely psychotic detachment with no component of depression, the tranquilizing type of drug will handle the situation well. However, since in many cases of schizophrenia, both dissociative and depressive elements appear either together or alternating with each other, full control over the situation in those instances requires concurrent use of both energizers and tranquilizers.

Under the heading of mechanism, two additional points are worth noting. The first is that once a depressive position has been

established by exposure to psychic stress or even by the administration of a tranquilizing drug, withdrawing the stress or the drug
is not sufficient to permit the patient to recover. Some individuals
with a great deal of resilience may. Most, however, will not and an
anti-depression drug will have to be given to reverse the depression.

The second point is that the same drug given for the same
condition on different occasions is likely to elicit not only the
same effects but also precisely the same sequence of effects distributed over the same time schedule, assuming of course the absence
of serious interfering influences.

Prodded by Winkelman, the group acknowledged the importance of expectations on the outcome of drug therapy. They agreed
that the therapist's expectations and the patient's expectations
both played a role. They sought some theoretical basis for dealing
with expectation but none was forthcoming. However, Furst reminded the group of Nunberg's* distinction between the patient's
conscious and his *unconscious* expectations from treatment. Consciously the patient hopes to be relieved of his illness. Unconsciously, he hopes to be able to retain the gratification which his illness
offers but to be rid simply of the pain. However, from a practical
point of view everyone agreed on the usefulness of an optimistic
point of view on the part of the therapist. Since the anti-depression
drugs require a minimum of three to four weeks before they make
the patient feel better, Ostow has found it useful to tell the patient that recovery cannot be expected before a certain date. This
protects the patient from becoming discouraged when he does not
obtain immediate effects or when there is an immediate perceivable
effect which later disappears. If a holiday or some significant date
falls at about the time the drug effect is expected, that may be
used to pinpoint the patient's expectations for recovery.

The success of drug therapy depends not only upon proper
choice of drug and proper dose, and not only upon those features
of the patient's constitution which make him susceptible to the
drug, but also upon circumstances under which it is given. For example, the primary therapeutic effect of the drug may be rein-

---

*Herman Nunberg, "The Will to Recovery," in *Practice and Theory of Psychoanalysis,*
Vol. 1, pp. 75-88 New York: Coolidge Foundation, Publishers, 1948. [Originally published in the *International Journal of Psychoanalysis,* 7 (1926).]

forced if the pills are literally given to the patient by the doctor as an act of affectionate concern. On the other hand, the therapeutic effect may be weakened if the patient is subject to stress such as temporary abandonment by the therapist or premature discharge from the hospital to return home. If the patient experiences side effects, he may resist the drug and fail to improve as he should. To a certain extent this anti-therapeutic consequence of side effects can be overcome by warning him in advance that they may appear or by explaining them as they do appear. When the side effects are overwhelming, their anti-therapeutic influence cannot be overcome. In fact, such side effects may serve to accentuate the primary condition.

I have observed that at a dose which induces confusion (a central anticholinergic effect), the tricyclic agents lose their anti-depression effect. At a slightly lower dose, the latter may return.

Not infrequently one has the impression that the patient is resisting the effect of the drug. Reasons for such resistance may include the following. In the case of some patients, unconscious condemnation by the superego may deter recovery. We speak of negative therapeutic reaction. Other patients may become anxious as they feel instinctual drives reasserting themselves under the influence of medication. If the wrong drug or an inadequate dose is given, not only does the patient fail to improve because the treatment is inadequate but, because of his disappointment, he begins to resent and resist other attempts at drug therapy.

I have observed that despite the general rule that the administration of the same drug for the same condition on different occasions results in essentially a similar schedule of recovery, nevertheless, as relapses succeed one another, each subsequent relapse is reversed with a little more difficulty than the previous episode. While to a certain extent this progressive hardening of resistance to drug treatment may be attributed to increasing age, I have the impression also that the fact that he has experienced a relapse makes the patient more discouraged than previously and less responsive to drug therapy.

From the dynamic point of view, it was suggested that there may be an inhibition against ingesting the psychoanalyst's gift.

The patient may wish to hoard the psychoanalyst's gift. He may resist being influenced by or being dependent upon the analyst. He may resist the drug because he wishes to affirm his own self-control.

The question of the psychic effect of intra-muscular administration of medication was raised at one point. Klerman feared an interfering intensification of the homosexual* aspect of the transference. Linn, however, said that he had found no serious consequences from administering medication parenterally to psychotic patients. Furst noted that the more reality testing is disturbed, the less difference there is between oral and parenteral administration.

We commented above in Chapter 2 that a patient will sometimes be affected by his knowledge of whether someone who is important to him has been treated with a drug, or with the same drug as he is given. The discussion arose in the course of the presentation of patient C.D. The analyst selected Nardil because he wanted to give an MAOI but did not want the patient to realize that he was being treated in the same way as his psychotic sister, who had received Parnate (tranylcypromine). Linn recollected having induced a panic reaction in a male patient with homosexual problems by giving him the same anti-depression drug that he had previously given to his wife. Furst reported another patient who, upon becoming anxious, went to the physician who had treated his father for depression and insisted upon being given the same treatment.

Let us turn now to a consideration of the dynamic consequences of drug therapy. In the previous chapter we reported the discussion about the distinction between denial and repression. It was asked whether denial and repression respond differently to medication. Klerman suggested that the phenothiazines facilitate repression in the psychotic, perhaps by reinforcing sensory barriers. Feder suggested that some drugs cut down on sensory input. However, Ostow noted that if that is what was affected, then denial rather than repression would be facilitated.

As one observes patients changing under the influence of drug therapy, one finds that, as the psychic state changes, defenses change. If the patient has been dealing with a given stress by denial, and if the denial is threatened either by recovery or by a depressive confrontation with reality, the patient may have to resort to

*or heterosexual

projection or to confabulation to continue to resist the unwelcome reality. The patient may be able as a result of drug stabilization to accept direction by the analyst or to retreat from an untenable position.

Confabulation was exhibited by a patient, reported briefly by Ostow, who denied his illness after treatment with electric shock therapy and Vivactil. When phenothiazine was added, however, he began to confabulate. Ostow interpreted this phenomenon as follows. As the amnesia due to the electric shock treatment subsided and as the phenothiazine began to exert a slight depressing influence, self-observation was encouraged. Self-observation and denial conflicted with each other and confabulation was a compromise symptom. It permitted the patient to believe that he saw what was happening, while at the same time maintaining his aversion to reality.

Feder asserted that whatever the primary pharmacologic effect of the drug, if it also inactivates the defenses upon which the patient ordinarily relies before he is ready to give them up, the end result will be panic and depression. That's why we encounter paradoxical effects and inconsistent observations. He made this comment in discussing the depressing effect of phenothiazine. Klerman referred to Sarwer-Foner's early description of paradoxical excitement with rauwolfia. Sarwer-Foner had suggested that there were some individuals to whom body control was very important. When they were deprived of this body control by reserpine or by a phenothiazine like Thorazine, they became anxious. Klerman confirmed that the administration of reserpine to non-psychotic athletic individuals creates a feeling of loss and helplessness.

Klerman was not persuaded that the depression which was seen in an occasional schizophrenic patient after having been treated with phenothiazines was brought about by the drug. He preferred to believe that many schizophrenics go through a depressive phase even when they recover spontaneously. Ostow contended that the depressive tendency itself combats the schizophrenia whether the depressive tendency occurs spontaneously or is drug induced. However, some patients seem to be constitutionally disposed to depression and so slip easily from schizophrenia into frank depression. In fact, in some instances, the depression itself produces a second set of schizophrenic symptoms. These are the patients who require anti-depression support while their schizophrenic detachment is being treated with phenothiazines.

Patient C.D. demonstrated the effect of the successful use of anti-depression medication. Even though his heterosexual potency remained seriously impaired, the patient became hopeful rather than hopeless. He was able to move away from his mother toward his fiancée though he continued to feel somewhat guilty about that move. He felt less dependent upon his father and the analyst and at the same time his resistance to homosexual dependence was strengthened. He felt ashamed of taking gifts from his father. Primary process thinking and agitation both subsided. This last change, however, might possibly be attributable to the simultaneous administration of the phenothiazine. The psychosexual level at which the patient operated rose from oral to phallic.

Patient A.B. became anxious one week after he began to take Elavil and at the same time showed interest in acting out. Bressler proposed that a tranquilizer be given. Feder described a patient who improved from depression with Elavil but then became panicky and had to use Seconal(secobarbital) to overcome his anxiety. Patient C.D. was then presented in vignette form, anticipating the subsequent extensive presentation. This patient, when he came out of depression as a result of Nardil treatment, encountered a homosexual threat and then regressed to helplessness. Referring to the principle which had been discussed by the group on other occasions, Ostow proposed that when, as a result of drug administration, a patient is impelled back into the pathogenic situation, he must find some defensive maneuvers other than depression, which has now been precluded by the drug. Feder's patient resorted to barbiturate intoxication; patient C.D. to regression with a schizophrenic quality. In such situations a relatively small amount of tranquilizer will limit the extent of the pathogenic threat caused by drive intensification and the pathologic defense against that threat. However, Ostow doubted that the euphoria and restlessness of A.B. could be attributed to the Elavil because one week's treatment is insufficient to establish a true anti-depression effect. He preferred to attribute the improvement to the protection by the hospital and the opportunity for heterosexual acting out. There was also some suspicion of homosexual stimulation. The use of marijuana cannot be overlooked. A.B., C.D., and E.F., all demonstrate that, as the patient recovers from depression with the use of anti-depression medication, he finds the transference closeness which had previously been reassuring now difficult to tolerate. A.B. left. C.D. and E.F. developed additional resistance.

I.J., who was being treated for schizophrenia without a clearly visible serious depressive component, exhibited a similar effect. Each time she ventured to try to establish contact with another individual, whether the therapist or other patients, she immediately had to retreat. It wasn't until after five months of treatment with moderate doses of Navane that she was able to maintain object relations somewhat more consistently. Linn noted that at first she had been using sexual activity as a means of finding someone to rescue her from the outer space of her detachment but then proximity became too dangerous and she would run back to her private world.

One of the major purposes of this study was to ascertain the potential interrelation between drug therapy and psychoanalysis or psychotherapy. There seemed to be a tacit understanding that drugs and other organic modalities were used only when the patient required protection, or when his mental illness precluded the possibility of insight and improvement from insight. However, it was understood that these organic modalities did not replace insight therapy. They gave the patient protection and the therapist time to conduct an effective psychotherapy. As Furst put it, the medication was offered as an aid in overcoming the patient's symptomatic discomfort. It was not a substitute for the analytic work which was required to overcome C.D.'s sexual difficulties. The ability to profit from psychoanalytic therapy depends upon ego strength, Klerman said. Drug therapy permits us to work with some patients who would not otherwise be accessible to psychotherapy. However, when drug administration plays the major role in determining behavior, Ostow replied, psychodynamic understanding informs us primarily of the effect of the drug and to a lesser degree about the patient's own motivation. Even when the patient on medication is capable of taking an interpretation seriously, it may have little value in modifying his behavior. Roose added that under those circumstances, transference suffers and exerts little influence. Ostow replied that transference too comes under the influence of drugs. They may intensify, modify, or reverse transference. The result, Roose said, is that the analyst loses control of the transference. Bressler observed that a similar situation is encountered in the treatment of obese patients. Analysis alone is not sufficiently potent, and external controls must be provided at the same time. It seemed to be generally agreed that interpretative intervention is ineffectual when ego function deteriorates; when behavior is determined primarily by drug influence; in the presence of some habit or addictive state such as obesity; or in deterring the natural evolution of psychosis or depression.

When this discussion was reviewed at the subsequent meeting, Linn said that it should be made clear that when we are talking about the limitations of psychodynamic understanding, we are referring only to its usefulness in influencing behavior in the states which were enumerated. We do not question its importance for understanding what is happening to the patient and for making decisions about the case and about the treatment.

In one of the last of the sessions, Klerman said that he would still like to see whether we can demonstrate a case in which the use of drugs facilitated the analysis to the point of full resolution of the transference. Ostow observed that a priori he had hoped that, with drugs, one could analyze even psychotic patients and achieve a state in which drugs would no longer be necessary. He was able to do that in some cases. In many other cases in which drugs were required, he said that he had not been able to achieve complete independence of either the drugs or the analysis, despite some impressive improvements. Klerman asked whether it was possible to do analysis with people who are psychotic or highly narcissistic. Feder pointed out that parametric variations, other than drug therapy, are introduced in many analyses without thereby preventing full analysis. Furst replied to both questions that it isn't so much the introduction of the drug that makes the difference, as the nature of the illness. He cited a case of depression in which he used anti-depression drugs for a while, but a normal analytic process proceeded nevertheless. Klerman said that it would be important to demonstrate such an outcome in an intensive study. Some analysts believe that analytic work is possible even in schizophrenia without drugs. Linn commented that it is not realistic to assume that any analysis is free of intervention.

Even making appointments influences the patient's mental state. The problem is the same whether our interventions make the patient feel better or worse. Roose felt that to analyze the implications of varying a parameter, the variation must first be undone. Moreover the situation becomes much more complicated when several parametric variations are introduced simultaneously. At what point in the introduction of parametric variations does the procedure lose its basic analytic quality, he asked? Ostow suggested that one might consider that the analysis is interrupted for the period of crisis and resumed thereafter. Feder noted that introducing drug therapy influences the analyst's attitude toward the treatment and it influences the family's attitude toward the patient.

Klerman cited an example in which a classical analyst, presumably in the interest of classical purity, rejected a patient whom he had been treating when the patient became psychotic. It is a common observation that some psychiatrists and especially analysts become anxious when confronted with an acute psychotic relapse. Roose noted that it is anxiety in the counter-transference that induces the analyst to vary the procedure.

Continuing the discussion of the interrelation between organic therapy and analysis, Ostow commented that no matter how negative the patient may seem, in one corner of his mind he appreciates the therapist's concern and his efforts. Loomis observed that mutual trust is necessary for a therapeutic alliance.

Klerman reported that some patients in analysis view the introduction of medication as a stigma while others demand medication and reject psychotherapy. With chemically induced improvement, such patients often come to tolerate inward reflection. Roose observed that the need to introduce drugs may seem to the patient—and to the doctor—to reflect on the power of analysis. Ostow commented that to some patients the introduction of drug therapy is a kind of degradation and is taken to mean that the patient is more seriously ill than he would like to believe.

Klerman asked whether the group would attempt to treat a patient in an acute psychotic episode without drugs. Ostow replied that in a few instances the transference alone may be decisively therapeutic and Roose was able to find a case in his practice in which that was so.

The same issues were raised for review in the following session.

The chairman asked to what extent does the reality of the administration of drugs preclude the analysis of its transference manifestations? Feder replied that the fact that drug administration is real does not prevent analysis but it does make more difficult the distinction between reality and fantasy. Winkelman observed that the distinction is easier if the intervention comes after the analysis is under way rather than at the beginning. Roose repeated his earlier observation that all departures from classical technique must eventually be analyzed if they are not to become permanent contaminants. Even classical analytic abstinence exerts an influence on the patient. Linn commented that the outcome of the intervention must be taken into account in understanding its significance to the patient.

The chairman then asked whether it was possible to do a complete classical analysis with a patient who is psychotic when first seen. He said that he had not yet satisfied himself that he had been able to, though many patients improved quite satisfactorily and functioned well. Some of these have done well for years without further professional help. Roose replied that he had found that there were depths of infantile narcissism and omnipotence which could not be touched. He had learned to settle for partial insight. Linn reported that his experience with depressive and psychotic patients is that some can be analyzed well and helped to achieve fulfilling and gratifying life patterns. Proper marital choice, he said, makes an important difference. Roose commented, however, that transference is never really completely dissolved.

At this point, Feder asked to what extent does an analytic approach help us to deal with the patient who is being treated with medication? Linn replied that the large number of inputs makes it difficult to determine which are crucial in achieving the satisfactory outcome. Nor must we overlook the skill of the therapist as a determinant, Roose added.

The chairman asked how does the introduction of a drug influence the course of an analysis? Roose replied that that could be determined only after the drug is eliminated. Loomis asked how the introduction of electric shock treatment can influence the course of analysis. Ostow replied that the amnesia created by the electric shock treatment compromises the analysis. Linn added, however, that either procedure may make a patient accessible to analysis who otherwise would not be. From a practical point of view he had found that when physical intervention is required, it is usually at the outset of treatment. It seldom happens, he said, that a patient who has been in analysis for a year or two suddenly requires drug intervention. Winkelman, however, noted that sometimes a situation may escape control at least temporarily when especially traumatic material must be dealt with.

The chairman then asked whether one could compare the effect of medication as an intervention with other forms of intervention such as electric shock treatment and hospitalization. Feder replied that he had been finding recently that electric shock treatment is considerably less destructive than he used to think it was. Linn reported two cases of agitated depression which had been resolved by electric shock treatment. Each patient subsequently decided to undertake psychoanalytic therapy to resolve the precipitating problem.

Ostow mentioned one important difference between treatment of psychosis with drug therapy and with electric shock therapy. After psychotic episodes, patients try to recapture and integrate the experience of the psychosis. However, when the recovery has been brought about by electric shock treatment, the patient represses the psychotic content and excludes it from the normal conscious ego. The amnesia induced by the shock treatment encourages this repression.

Linn said that electric shock treatment can be given in a way which is minimally disruptive. Drugs on the other hand can have disruptive side effects. He felt that there was not much specificity in the significance of each of the various non-analytic forms of intervention for the transference. He considered the effectiveness of the intervention of overriding importance.

The chairman asked how much intervention vitiates the analytic quality of the treatment. Roose commented that much of the difficulty results from the influence of the intervention on the analyst. The group agreed that even the mildest intervention might stimulate fantasies in some patients.

The complexity of the relation between drug therapy and transference is illustrated by patient C.D. After he recovered from his first episode of psychotic depression with the assistance of Nardil, the transference continued to present a problem because of its passive homosexual component. He acknowledged his improved performance in social situations but insisted that he had improved because of the medication. Furst commented that the patient was afraid to acknowledge that he had become more enterprising. Klerman indicated that there was some basis for confusion about the reason for his improvement. The fact is that he had not only been given an anti-depression medication but the date for his wedding had been deferred. But Klerman acknowledged that until the anti-depression medication had taken effect, the patient was unable to accept the recommendation. Ostow observed that generally, when two or more modalities of treatment are used at the same time, the patient who feels threatened by one of them will insist that it was the other that was more efficacious. Here, Klerman observed that attributing the improvement to the pill helped the patient to resist acknowledging the homosexuality in the transference. Ostow added that the patient also preferred to overlook the possibility that his improvement could be attributed to his now being protected from the heterosexual challenge.

Ostow reported an instance in which the patient's pronounced improvement following upon the doctor's successful prescription of medication gave rise to a rescue fantasy. The patient dreamed that she obtained some pills with holes in them from her father's closet. She said that "white pills with holes in them" were "life savers." The dream also betrayed a fellatio fantasy. In other words, she interpreted the experience as having been rescued by fellatio with her father.

The question of "using the couch" came up for discussion as a minor though considerably more common "parametric variation." The group had little concern, of course, about whether the couch could or should be abandoned at times. However, they were interested in the significance and value of the departures from the standard couch situation. It was reported that when patient C.D. was agitated, he would often sit on the couch rather than lie on it. Someone asked the analyst why he let the patient sit on the couch. The analyst replied that the patient preferred to do so. When he was agitated he would stand or walk about. Someone asked whether the analyst implied that shifting from couch to desk meant regression. Linn thought that forcing a patient onto a couch promotes regression. It was his idea that vis-a-vis confrontation is helpful with psychotic patients. Ostow observed that one can encourage the patient to move to the vis-a-vis position from the couch if one wishes actively to combat regression and to encourage reality testing. On the other hand, when one wishes to encourage the patient to attempt to overcome his agitation or anxiety, at least partly by self-discipline, then one can permit him to sit on the couch.

Since many ·of the substances used for the treatment of mental illness create unwelcome and often unpleasant side effects, these often influence the patient's response to medication and also the transference. Sandler said that the side effects of the drugs should be treated like day residue. They are absorbed by the ego and brought into relation with unconscious forces. Sandler made this observation in discussing patient A.B., who expressed concern about gaining too much weight under the influence of Stelazine. Sandler interpreted this concern as a fear that the patient had been impregnated by the analyst. (Rescue fantasies often express the wish to be impregnated. Therefore, the fellatio rescue in the dream reported above by Ostow expresses the wish to be made pregnant by the analyst through the medium of the pill. Impregnation fantasies occur not infrequently in response to the beginning of medication. For some reason this did not come up for discussion.) Sandler continued his thesis. Whether the drug affects psychic structure or physiologic function, mental representations of these effects are created, which are seized upon and worked over by unconscious wishes. Ostow suggested that though the patient may not be able to make the distinction between chemical effect and unconscious wish, the analyst must try to. Bressler added that the drugs may also affect instinctual derivatives such as the functions of the gastro-intestinal tract (and the sexual organs).

Not only does obvious drug relief reinforce the positive transference, but the converse is also true. Ostow reported that on one occasion he literally gave the patient the pills he was to take. Roose offered the generalization that when you physically give the patient a pill, he may respond to it as a personal gift. Ostow said that he does that only when he feels that the patient is in trouble and requires a literal demonstration of affectionate support.

At another point in the discussion, Linn observed that the schizophrenic patient is likely to interpret side effects in the light of his feelings about the treatment. More specifically, Roose added, it is the state of the transference that determines the response to side effects. Ostow agreed that sensitivity to side effects may be overcome by positive transference.

On the other hand he illustrated the interrelation between side effects and fantasies by reporting the case of a young man who was thrown into a panic by the inhibiting effect of Mellaril on ejaculation. The patient had previously expressed fear that he was sterilized. Simply replacing the Mellaril with Thorazine alleviated both the ejaculatory inhibition and the panic.

E.F. experienced a number of side effects when he shifted from MAOI to iminodibenzyl treatment. It was generally agreed that it is advisable to discuss unpleasant side effects with patients when they occur and that it is especially important to do so in the presence of negative transference. Winkelman commented that drug toxicity may be augmented by negative transference. Feder added that a given toxic symptom may appear as a result of either psychopathogenic or pharmacogenic causes as in the case of a dystonic reaction elicited by piperazine phenothiazines.

Bressler commented that some patients interpret toxic effects as punishment for improvement. He added, too, that some patients, who do well on parenteral anti-depression agents, relapse when switched to equivalent oral doses. He felt that this was something beyond a pharmacologic effect.

He said that when he treats anorexia nervosa, he feeds the patient by tube in order to bypass the sadistic and paranoid fantasies about food. Similarly, parenteral medication may bypass the patient's resistance to receiving something physical into his mouth. Furst wondered whether one shouldn't take into account the possibility of poor gastro-intestinal absorption of the drug. Klerman added that there is a good deal of variability in blood levels. Bressler replied that blood level is not easily interpreted. A high blood level, for example, need not indicate a powerful effect. It may merely indicate that the drug metabolite is not being absorbed into the tissues so that it can exert very little clinical effect. He concurred with Linn's opinion, which we noted above, that parenteral administration of an anti-depression agent need not affect the transference adversely and in fact might reinforce it.

There was only little discussion of individual toxic symptoms though a number were mentioned. Patient E.F. reported pronounced sweating at one point. Klerman related the sweating to the Tofranil that he was being given. Ostow proposed that sweating, especially the sweating affecting the back and the posterior aspects of neck and head, occurring more often at night than during the day, are manifestations not of anti-depression drug toxicity but of the patient's struggle against depression. He compared it to the night sweats encountered in chronic, systemic illness such as tuberculosis.

5. Observations About States of Mental Illness as Illuminated by Their Response to Pharmaceutic Agents

Despite my efforts to separate the material for systematic presentation into individual chapters, a good deal of the discussion which appropriately belongs here has actually been presented previously. I shall try to avoid repetition and report in this chapter only the material which has not been reported fully or at all in previous chapters.

The complexity of drug influence upon the depressive sequence was illustrated by C.D. In that case there were situations characterized by straightforward depression with inhibition and incompetence. They seemed to have been alleviated by anti-depression medication. Second, there were attempts to recover from this depression by states characterized by psychotic anger, false independence, and self-analysis. This was the state of mind which Ostow described as the phase of angry repudiation. This state was alleviated by Thorazine. Third, there was a clinical state that was brought about when the patient was given 1200 mg of Thorazine a day and 150 mg of Stelazine. He was reported to be quiet, not agitated, but obsessed with somatic delusions, that is, about his brain, his heart and his blood pressure. He complained that his feet had changed color and complained that the other patients were calling him names, especially "homosexual." This was the state of psychotic depression associated with delusional hypochondria. Ostow inferred that it had been brought about and augmented by the large dose of phenothiazine. The group readily accepted the first two inferences but were skeptical about the third.

Our data were not sufficient to unravel the complex influence of
phenothiazines on depression, but I have mentioned above some
more recent thoughts which may be illuminating.

The concept of escape from anti-depression control was vali-
dated by group agreement. C.D. had relapsed even while taking
large doses of an anti-depression drug. Since the phenomena which
occurred at that time were similar to those which had initially
been resolved by the administration of anti-depression medication,
one could only infer that the drug which had been effective at first
subsequently failed when the patient was subjected to progressively greater stress. It was reported that the patient's sister had similarly improved in response to large doses of Parnate but after some
years she relapsed under pressure from her husband and escaped
from the influence of the anti-depression drug. In fact, by the time
she relapsed definitively, she had been getting a combination of
large doses of Parnate and of Tofranil. Bressler reported that in
three patients of his who showed a similar tendency to escape
from control of anti-depression medication, he was able to reestablish control by combining MAOI's and tricyclic anti-depression
agents. Klerman mentioned a patient who escaped from the effect
of MAO inhibition but responded when the drug was administered
again six months later. Ostow mentioned that a drug-free interval
during which electric shock treatment is administered may permit
a return of the response when the drug is resumed within a few
weeks.

Escape occurs, he said, under pressure of psychic stress. At
first one sees a relative escape and then definitive escape. That is, at
first one sees response with a small dose of medication followed
by relapse. The patient then responds to an increase in the dose of
medication and then relapses again. Ultimately the dose of medication has to be increased to a maximum and ultimately the patient relapses despite the maximum dose. In fact, patient G.H.
occasionally became depressed despite continuing treatment with
Nardil. One might interpret his manic episode as an escape from
anti-depression control because it occurred despite an increase in
the dose of Nardil. One might contend that the mania was caused
by the patient's increasing his dose of Nardil and adduce as proof

the fact that when the Nardil was discontinued, the mania subsided. However, since subsequently he could be protected against depression only relatively despite maximum doses of Nardil, one can also contend that the mania was a pre-depressive episode which signified that the medication was losing its supportive effect.

The relation between schizophrenia and depression was almost a continuing concern of the group. As reported above, they agreed that schizophrenic detachment and depression will sometimes alternate in the same patient. They agreed, too, that schizophrenic detachment and depression might be alternative responses to stress. They had seen recovery from a schizophrenic episode followed by an episode of depression, and were not sure whether to attribute the latter to the phenothiazine medication which had been given to treat the schizophrenia, or whether the depression might have occurred spontaneously. Ostow took the discussion one step further. He said that in many patients schizophrenic detachment and depressive enervation combat each other. To the schizophrenic patient we give a depressant drug, and the depressed patient, when his depression is overcome by medication, may become schizophrenic. We have difficulty with occasional patients who respond with schizophrenic withdrawal to the pain of depression. In other words, whereas depression tends to counteract schizophrenic withdrawal, when the pain of depression is itself sufficiently severe, in predisposed patients schizophrenic detachment may ensue. Therefore while in many cases of schizophrenia the depression is brought about by the phenothiazine administered to treat the primary illness, in other patients the depression is primary and itself is responsible for the schizophrenic dissociation. Then, of course, we must keep in mind the kind of suggestive depression that we see in some schizophrenic patients, which subsides as the schizophrenia subsides in response to treatment with phenothiazines only. Such was the case with patient I.J. It was this observation that made Bressler suggest that the depression in some cases of schizophrenia may be a different phenomenon from depressive illness in pure culture, or even the depressive complications in other cases of schizophrenia.

Questions were asked about such phenomena as hypochondriacal delusions and paranoid projection. Under what circumstances do they occur? Is there any drug regimen which is especially likely to resolve them? There was not enough material to warrant discussion.

Finally, there is the case (G.H.) of amphetamine addiction with chronic paranoid psychosis. When the amphetamine was withdrawn it became evident that there was an underlying depression which was fairly well handled with an anti-depression drug. Ostow offered the following reconstruction: 1) The patient was trapped in an anaclitic relation with a maternal and idealized wife. 2) He tried to alleviate his difficulty by finding manliness and sexual gratification in an extramarital affair. 3) He avoided depression by using large doses of amphetamine which exerted both an energizing and, an ego-toxic effect. 4) The schizophrenic detachment which the ego-toxicity facilitated offered him relief from the trap of his ambivalence. 5) When the amphetamine was withdrawn, the depression against which he had been defending then developed. 6) The Nardil resolved the depression but since it did not have an ego-toxic effect, it did not cause psychosis as the amphetamine had. 7) When there was additional stress, he escaped from the anti-depression effect of the Nardil. 8) The manic attack represented the incipience of just such a depressive escape. It was accompanied by a feeling of guilt toward his wife and by hypochondriacal concern about her health.

Feder objected that most chronic amphetamine users start with something more than depression, namely, a sense of emptiness and isolation. The patient's analyst contended that he saw little that was schizoid in the clinical picture after the amphetamine had been removed. Ostow replied that what amphetamine users fight is not actual depression but threatening depression. Roose felt that since there had been a definite paranoid episode, one may presume the existence of a psychotic core. Klerman objected that not everybody who exhibits a paranoid reaction to amphetamine is a schizophrenic. Ostow replied that the individual who is fully schizophrenic does not require amphetamines to make himself psychotic. G.H. had used amphetamines in the same way that A.B. had used hallucinogens: to achieve a psychotic escape from reality in preference to painful depression.

Loomis suggested that the patient was feeding himself by using amphetamines in order to supplement feeding by his wife

RESPONSES OF STATES OF MENTAL ILLNESSES: CHAPTER 5

and his employee. Subsequently, he used the therapist as a source of nourishment. He, like other addicts, wanted to have his needs anticipated and could not tolerate discomfort. Winkelman offered a somewhat different reconstruction. He said that the man had been happy in the army because he was cared for there. He married in order to secure continuing care. He had children in order to demonstrate his manliness. However, his wife chose his career. The amphetamines gave him a "sense of adequacy." The last child finally exceeded the degree of responsibility which he could take.

Postscript

Having come to the end of our presentation, we feel and we may anticipate that the reader will feel a sense of disappointment or letdown. Our contribution to psychoanalytic psychiatry and to the psychology of drug therapy has been quite limited. Yet, in retrospect, it would have been unrealistic to expect the complete solution of all outstanding problems to have been achieved in thirty-four meetings. However, the insights which we have achieved have been useful to all the participants and we believe that they will be useful to the reader.

We would like to recommend to the psychiatric community the organization of a large number of such study groups. At the very least they will constitute an educational experience, par excellence, for the participants. To the extent that the participants are teachers, as was true of this group, the group experience will improve psychiatric education. The outstanding problems of our field will be subjected to a continuing, massive, but relatively inexpensive attack by a clinician, the person who knows mental illness and the mentally ill patient best.

The Psychoanalytic Research and Development Fund is willing to share its experience in organizing and conducting these groups with our colleagues, and would welcome inquiry.

We hope that careful perusal of the case protocols and the group discussion of them which we present in the next section will repay the reader's effort with some information, some hypotheses, and most important, some inspiration to pursue this subject in clinical observations and exchanges with colleagues.

But the primary purpose of presenting these cases, as the title of the book indicates, is to demonstrate how psychodynamic

71

analysis of clinical data can contribute to the proper administration of medication, and how psychodynamic analysis of the effects of medication – both psychologic and pharmacologic effects – can help the psychiatrist to understand the changes he observes in his patient.

CASE 1

Abstract

This first presentation describes a course of treatment lasting about eighteen months. The presenting analyst prescribed, at different times, Elavil, Stelazine, Artane (trihexyphenidyl), and Mellaril to alleviate the distress of an adolescent boy who attributed his discomfort and his difficulties in maintaining object relations to an overwhelming feeling of "emptiness." This "emptiness" was interpreted by some members of the group as a depressive manifestation and by others as latent schizophrenia. The medication was prescribed for the patient in both in-patient and ambulatory settings. One of the major difficulties of the therapy was that, except during the period of his hospitalization, the patient would not take the medication regularly. Moreover, after his second acute crisis subsided, he began to see the analyst with decreasing regularity, and the treatment gradually disintegrated. At the time the treatment was terminated, the patient was functioning successfully at work and with less success in his object relations. Neither the doctor nor the patient felt that any real progress had been made toward solving the patient's basic problems.

Introduction and Background

Born in 1942, the patient, A.B., was an eighteen-year-old youth when first seen by the presenting analyst; he was about to enter college. A.B.'s mother was a manic-depressive whose illness extended back to the time of the patient's early childhood. She maintained only a distant relation with her husband, and, at the time of the patient's treatment, she was involved in an affair with another man. The boy's father, a successful businessman, was

73

passive and withdrawn in his relations with other family members. Because the mother was ineffectual, the father would often look after the children. The patient seemed fearful of his passive, homosexual wishes toward his father. The father was obese, and the patient reacted to his father's obesity with great concern about his own weight. He meticulously reported to the analyst small gains and losses. His only sibling was a sister about a year and a half older. She also had a severe emotional disturbance, and was hospitalized throughout much of the patient's course of treatment with the presenting analyst.

The patient grew up with his family in a series of suburban communities until the summer of 1955, when the family moved from the suburbs to the city. The boy performed poorly at school, frequently almost failing, and then just barely passing. His behavior was generally characterized by a great deal of impulsive acting out, which, though not particularly destructive or antisocial, put him in constant difficulties with the community, at home, and at school. A.B. had been treated, from the age of thirteen (about five years before he was seen by the presenting analyst), by a psychiatrist who did not prescribe medication. The presenting analyst had been called into the case by a colleague who was treating the patient's mother. The boy had decided to leave his previous therapist several weeks before the time that the presenting analyst was called in. The youth complained that the previous therapist was withdrawn and ungiving, and the presenting analyst, on the basis of his own contact with the latter, thought the boy's complaint was probably justified. Rorschach tests were performed in 1954 (when the patient was twelve) and in 1961. The first diagnosis was "schizophrenic process," and the second, "an individual who feels alienated from the world and shows signs of an insidious affective deterioration that has been going on for a long time."

A.B. belonged to a circle of adolescents very much like himself. His friends were either seeing psychiatrists and taking medication, or else they were taking one drug or another on their own. A.B. himself was obsessed with taking pills, and claimed that he possessed a quantity of pills large enough to kill himself twenty times over. These pills he numbered at approximately a thousand; he had hidden them somewhere in his home where no one could find them, and he planned eventually to use these pills to "finish everything." At the time he was first seen by the analyst in the group, the patient was particularly involved with a close friend Tom, who was at that time hospitalized after a serious suicide attempt. Tom remained in the hospital throughout most of the course of treatment to be described.

Initial Contact with the Patient and Beginning of Treatment

Summer 1960   The presenting analyst was asked to see the patient by a colleague in late summer 1960, when the patient, then a little over eighteen years old, was hospitalized after a suicidal gesture which consisted of swallowing an unknown (though it was suspected a small) number of pills. Relatively little evidence of toxicity was seen. At the time the analyst first saw him, the youth was a little groggy, but fairly coherent. He said he did not want to come to the hospital, and he did not come voluntarily. Moreover, he did not want to be associated with the other patients who, he felt, were very sick, and who frightened him. The patient spoke particularly about a very complicated, but as yet vague, involvement with two girls, Sylvia and Wendy.

Although at this time he spoke freely to the analyst, A.B. spoke even more freely to the night nurse about his feeling of "emptiness." Her notes described his speeches to her about the "vast, bottomless, empty void" in him and "the futility of life": "I feel empty. I have no feelings, and without any feelings I have no relationships, no contacts, no sustenance, no nothing." The monologues contained a considerable amount of exaggerated adolescent rebelliousness about "the meaning of existence" and "what good is it," but there was always the theme of an underlying emptiness.

Group Discussion

The group discussed the significance of "emptiness" as a symptom. Ostow, Furst, and Feder felt that this sense of emptiness is a symptom (Ostow considered it a primary symptom) of depressive illness. Roose contended that the feeling of emptiness signifies something different, possibly schizophrenia.

September 1960   After a period of several weeks during which the analyst saw the patient in the hospital, A.B. asked to be discharged. The analyst, seeing no further reason to prolong the hospitalization, discharged him, and began to see him in the office. The doctor discussed the patient's immediate plans with the patient and with his parents. A.B. had committed himself the previous spring to going to a college in California, and wanted to go. His mother, as a result of her understanding of her son's problems, wanted him to stay home, but the father wanted the boy out of the house because of his disruptive influence on the rest of the household. The analyst agreed to the patient's going away to school, and asked him to keep in touch, which the patient did only to the extent of coming in to see the analyst at Thanksgiving, Christmas, and during intersession.

Intersession 1961.   A.B.'s visit was preceded by a letter to the analyst in which the youth described a feeling of depression following the reading of Truman Capote's book *In Cold Blood,* the description of the apparently motiveless and very brutal murder of an entire family. The patient wrote:

My concern with it, and probably the reason I became so absorbed in it is the character of the man who committed the crime, an obviously insane thing I (hope and) feel . . . There is no need to tell you why this thing scared the hell out of me.

The point of the letter was that the book brought up many things to talk about, and A.B. looked forward to seeing the doctor shortly.

At the visit itself, A.B. reported that he had not been studying, and that he had been up at all hours of the night and staying in bed in the morning. Since Christmas, there had been several uncontrolled outbursts of destructiveness, mostly in the form of breaking his roommate's things. Most recently he had been caught shoplifting. As a result of this discussion of the patient's reported state, the patient and analyst agreed that A.B. should return to the city and start regular treatment three times a week.

Tuesday, February 21   A.B. called the analyst at 3:00 p.m.

to report that he felt "lousy" and would not come for his hour, but would call again, which he did not. The analyst, anxious, called the patient.

Wednesday, February 22   The patient came to see the analyst, and spoke of having seen Sylvia the previous evening. A.B. had originally been introduced to Sylvia by his friend Tom, the youth who had made the serious suicide attempt. Through the patient's description of his intensely ambivalent relationship with Sylvia, reviling her and at the same time clinging to her, the analyst discerned that on one level Sylvia represented the link between A.B. and Tom, with whom A.B. felt very close and very much identified. The patient reported that when he had seen Sylvia she had wanted intercourse. His first attempt was unsuccessful; at the second attempt he succeeded, but described himself as "overworked." He slept at Sylvia's home in the suburbs, and in the morning he quarreled with her. He mentioned that, for the last several days, he had been feeling tired and rundown. The next morning in the train station he felt tense and fatigued. He said: "Everything felt hostile. I was walking in circles . . . everything whirling around . . . everything sharp." This feeling subsided after the analytic hour, but the patient still felt violent and feared his violent impulses.

The Next Session   A.B. said he was in the suburbs again visiting an old friend. He told the analyst that he had begun to take Dexedrine (dextroamphetamine) on his own. He spoke again of the night with Sylvia and of attempting to build up the effectiveness of his performance in order to give her a baby; the baby would bring her closer to him. He also reported that he had had suicidal ideas the previous night. At this point the doctor suggested that the patient take an anti-depression agent, which, he said would relieve the patient's depressed feeling, but would take some time to act. The analyst felt uneasy about prescribing drugs for this patient, because A.B. was taking marijuana on and off and was preoccupied with taking LSD. However, the strength of the boy's depressive element, his suicidal threats, and his inner agitation finally convinced the analyst to prescribe Elavil for him despite his unreliability about taking it. The doctor

thought that, given A.B.'s proclivity for taking pills, he would
be better off taking pills of the analyst's choice and under medical
supervision. Thus, at the end of February the doctor prescribed
Elavil, 150 mgs daily, in three doses of 50 mgs each.

Group Discussion

Sarwer-Foner said that the strength of the therapeutic relationship between A.B. and the presenting analyst during the
month of February is evident from the following three facts. First,
that the analyst cared enough to contact the patient when he
failed to call; second, that the patient felt enough trust in the
analyst to report the extent of his homicidal and destructive
feelings; and third, that the analyst again took the initiative, this
time of prescribing a drug.

The group discussed the prescription of Elavil for this patient,
and concluded that an anti-depression drug would act as a tranquilizer to the agitated, depressed patient. Though the youth
might become subject to angry and violent impulses, as the depression was alleviated, the anger would disappear.

The First Session after the Prescription of Elavil   A.B. said
he felt tired just as he had felt tired before. He had slept much of
the day, after having had twelve hours of sleep at night. He felt he
must give up the past—Sylvia, Wendy, and Tom—but he had
nothing with which to replace them. He added that he went on
an eating binge and gained eight pounds, and that he no longer
felt depressed.

Group Discussion

Feder raised the question of whether the sleepiness was a psychologic or pharmacologic effect. Ostow responded that the effect
was pharmacologic, and that most patients sooner or later become
habituated to the medications they take, though the habituation
occurs at a different rate for each of the different effects of the
drug. Thus, habituation to the somnifacient effect of Elavil has no
relation to the response to the anti-depression effect. An individual
may become habituated to one of the effects without becoming
habituated to the others. Moreover, the sedation, which is pro-

duced within hours by Elavil or other tricyclic anti-depression drugs, sometimes alleviates the misery of the depressed patient without improving the underlying clinical state or dynamic status.

Feder suggested that drowsiness occurring with Elavil results from the fact that the depressed patient has been engaged in an intense internal conflict representing the struggle against the illness. The drowsiness reflects the exhaustion which is part of the depression and which becomes manifest under the influence of the drug.

End of February 1961 The patient and his family reported that the depression was clearing up. A.B. was "sleeping most of the time," "groggy" when he got up, "hostile to everyone," and reading a lot of sadomasochistic pornographic literature. Feder and Winkelman suggested that the fact that the patient commented that he was reading might represent an early change, that is, a response to the medication.

Within a couple of weeks the patient was no longer feeling groggy. He announced to the analyst that Sylvia was "a whore"; she had had many men. Moreover she was "bitchy and hostile." He claimed he was allowing himself to be used and he was jealous of her relations with others. A.B. said he was thinking about working, and beginning to look around for a job; he knew of one job in a library. He reported a dream:

I was a male prostitute with a big woman, kissing her thighs.

When asked by the analyst to describe the woman, he said: "The woman was about 5 feet, 10 inches tall, with big breasts, big etc." The patient spoke of how much he enjoyed "oral activity" with girls he liked (by "oral activity" he meant cunnilingus, which he regarded as demented and perverse). All during this period the youth was on an eating binge; he said that he had gained ten pounds and that he was extremely concerned about his weight. He also became progressively more silent during this hour, and complained that the analyst was not helping him.

Group Discussion

Feder commented that perhaps the medication enabled the patient for the first time to verbalize certain things. Sarwer-Foner mentioned that the analyst was becoming the giving father.

Saturday, March 4, 1961   The patient found employment
with a real estate agency, primarily through the efforts of a friend
of the family. He reported feeling "sluggish, slow, drifting, and
slightly depressed." His eating binges continued, and by this time
he had gained fifteen pounds. He told the analyst a dream of the
previous night:

> A tornado keeps coming back. I am right in the path in
> some enclosure. Finally, after several passes over me, back
> and forth, it dies down; very windy but not dangerous. I
> think I was in a train or crash. Other people got killed.

There was newspaper publicity, a day or two before the dream,
about a tornado. The analyst suggested to the patient that the
dream referred to his own inner storm, and the patient answered
that he felt suicidal, but not in a vengeful way. He added that he
had been avoiding his old crowd and that he feared getting fat.

When the patient became noticeably more anxious, the
analyst checked on the medication, and discovered that the
patient was taking it quite irregularly. The analyst and patient discussed the situation, and the medication was discontinued, though
the youth continued to take Stelazine *ad lib.* A.B. also began to
take out his thousand pills, scatter them over the floor, and play
with them.

Comments of the Presenting Analyst

The presenting analyst told the group that this dream is in-
dicative of the patient's condition at this time; he was in a state of
great turmoil, fearing a massive outburst of violence which might
occur independently or simultaneously with depressed and suicidal
thoughts.

Group Discussion

Furst raised the point that the doctor is never sure that the
patient is taking the medication as prescribed, and should check
with the patient frequently.

Linn posed the following questions: what does the discontinuation of the medication tell about the patient's illness? Does it

hint at whether the patient is suffering from depression rather than schizophrenia? Is the patient feeling threatened by a breakthrough of drives, or is he threatened by his improvement? Roose suggested that the patient could not permit himself to feel well because of his guilt. This guilt may have been derived from his extraordinary need for oral gratification, which includes a strong aggressive component. Perhaps the patient collects pills because they have a symbolic meaning for him, and the giving of the pills by the doctor is for him a significant experience. Linn noted that obese patients on total starvation tend to hoard physical objects; perhaps this hoarding is an attempt at restitution.

Ostow observed that when depression is alleviated, conscious guilt does not appear; therefore, if it is guilt that interferes with the proper medication, it must be unconscious superego condemnation. Moreover the patient's feeling of dissatisfaction with his state of improvement may have occurred after he had already reduced the dose of Elavil and added the Stelazine. The patient may have thus resisted the drug and reduced its dose. Then when he began to feel bad, he may have attributed the bad feeling to the residual drug rather than to the fact that he was taking an inadequate dose. More generally, it is quite common for people who have improved from depression with the aid of an anti-depression drug, thereupon to resist, not only taking the drug but all other kinds of treatment as well. This observation applies also to recovery from schizophrenia. What is involved is resistance to being dependent, and to being controlled. This patient in particular seems to have demonstrated by his hoarding of drugs and by his taking drugs even before he came to the presenting analyst, that he attempted to deal with his impulsiveness and lack of self-control by employing a chemical control. The idea of taking pills appeals to him, but he must retain the control.

April 1961   A.B. was still living at home, and taking Stelazine *ad lib.* He confessed that one night, after his session, he hid in the office of another doctor who shared the same suite with the analyst, and, when the analyst left, entered the analyst's office, stole a batch of pills that was on the analyst's desk, and read the notes on his case. He reported that other people felt he had improved, though he himself would not acknowledge any improvement. He was feeling relatively stable generally and relatively comfortable with the analyst. There was some feeling of closeness, and the patient appeared for his hours more or less regularly. The boy discussed with the doctor occasional suicidal feelings; he showed almost no concern for his sister, who was at that time hospitalized after a suicide attempt.

Mid-May 1961   The material in the analytic sessions dealt primarily with the patient's oral fantasies. With regard to taking the medication, the contradictory impulses remained; he both wanted and rejected external control and stimulation. He seemed to have become rather depressed again. The fear of his own violence one day would be followed the next day by increasing suicidal thoughts. He was critical of the analyst whom he accused of not giving him anything. This accusation was followed by the report of a fantasy from his fourteenth year:

> A.B.'s parents are involved in sex play with another couple of their acquaintance. The male member of the other couple is practicing cunnilingus on the boy's mother, and the female, fellatio on his father.

At this point the patient asked for "outside controls and stimulation." He spoke of his sister's hospitalization, and told the analyst the details of his friend Tom's suicide attempt; it was A.B. who discovered Tom after Tom had taken about 100 pills, and obtained assistance for him. The youth came to his next analytic session with a bag of peanuts, and offered some to the doctor.

June 1961   A.B.'s father gave him a car which he had been asking for; the boy's immediate reaction was one of guilt, that he didn't deserve it. At this time the father was away on a business trip, the sister was in the hospital, and A.B. was home alone with his mother. By the end of June he was feeling not only guilty, depressed, and anxious, but, for the first time, somewhat openly paranoid.

July 1961   A.B. took LSD for the first time. The experience was a nightmare in which he was confronted with a rapid disintegration of whatever little ego strength or boundaries he had. He took the LSD trip together with another boy. A.B. had wanted to look at his own thoughts, but his friend insisted that he look at the friend's thoughts instead. He reported seeing a telephone going up in flames, amidst a vividly colorful background. The experience threw the patient into a panic which did not stop after the effects of the LSD wore off.

July was also the month prior to the analyst's vacation, and forewarned by the patient's experiences of the previous summer, the analyst repeatedly called attention to this fact in the sessions, but without eliciting the slightest reaction from the patient. During the next to the last session, A.B. admitted that he was angry, and he skipped the final session.

August 1961   Analyst's vacation.

Thursday, September 7, 1961   The analyst returned from vacation, and the treatment resumed. The day before the scheduled first session, A.B. called the doctor to confirm his appointment. He began the first analytic hour by announcing that, during the analyst's absence, "Sylvia eloped and I had a homosexual affair," though it later turned out that the homosexual affair had preceded the news of Sylvia's marriage. A.B. then added: "I can't use Tom any more to get close to her" (at that time Tom was still in the hospital). The patient continued to deny any feeling of anger toward the analyst because of his absence, but said that he had not gone to work for four days after the analyst left.

The youth reported that he had been quite suicidal the last week of August, and drove his car at ninety miles an hour with bald tires. He had begun a relationship with a girl named Rose whom he met during August. The day before the first session he had lied needlessly to his friend Tom, whom he used to visit at the hospital. Typically during these visits the two youths would go out to smoke marijuana; Tom would return to the hospital intoxicated, and his freedom would be restricted. A.B. said he gave Tom a large sum of money (perhaps fifteen dollars), and was left broke. He then announced that he must get away from home. He was expecting a raise, and he would sell the car if necessary in order to live away from his parents.

The homosexual affair had also occurred the last week in August. Under the influence of marijuana intoxication, A.B. was propositioned in a bar by a homosexual, but went home. Later he returned to the bar where he saw the same homosexual, but left with the homosexual's boyfriend, who performed fellatio upon him. As far as the analyst knows, this was the patient's first actual homosexual experience, and it was announced in an almost indifferent tone.

On the morning of the first session, while in a stationery store, A.B. felt that two men were watching him for shoplifting. He had the same feeling in a second store, and felt very self-conscious. During this period of anxiety the patient took some Thorazine on his own. He said his next suicide attempt would be effective, but not with pills; this was to imply something more violent.

Saturday, September 9, 1961   The patient could not manage to communicate with the analyst, and spent most of the session talking about his plan of getting an apartment as soon as possible, escaping from home, and from his father. It seemed that the closer he felt to the analyst, the more he mistrusted him.

Monday, September 11, 1961   This session was two hours long because the patient's situation had become urgent. Since resuming treatment after the summer break, A.B. was increasingly uncommunicative, restless, tense, and preoccupied with suicide. He spoke of an immediate suicide attempt. He was angry at the world, and at the analyst in particular, for their indifference and lack of care. He said: "If you don't hospitalize me I will commit suicide. I want to go to a state hospital and be locked up." This threat was followed by a bargaining session between the patient and the doctor as to where the patient should go. The analyst succeeded in getting the patient to modify his demand for a state hospital, and the patient finally consented to go to the hospital where his sister was, with the understanding that he would be in a different building from his sister, and that his treatment with the analyst would continue as before. (A.B.'s friend Tom was in a different hospital.)

The analyst saw the patient at the hospital that evening, where he was quieter and more comfortable in surroundings that offered some protection. Elavil was again prescribed, 50 mgs three times a day. Within a few hours the patient felt groggy, and slept much of the day, as he had the first time he took Elavil.

Tuesday, September 12, 1961   A.B. was still groggy, but he talked some, and looked at the analyst directly. He mentioned his mistrust of the analyst, and said that he felt guilty about many things, particularly about his sister, though he could not recall what he had done to her. He suspected that he might be responsible for her illness. The analyst wondered whether there had been some incestuous play between A.B. and his sister, or whether this was mere sibling rivalry. The youth also felt guilty about spending his father's money to get the analyst's attention.

A.B. continued that he wanted to get out of bed, and was trying to ignore his sister. He did not want to see her or have anything to do with her. He said that on the morning of his admission to the hospital, prior to seeing the analyst, he had called his friend Tom, and Tom had told him not to commit suicide, but to speak to his doctor.

The patient also complained that whatever he gets from the analyst is bought with money. The analyst emphasized to the group that this theme is one of this patient's major problems. He mistrusts people and says that no one gives anything to him but, in fact, it is the patient who is incapable of giving; he is interested only in getting. Originally the non-giver was the patient's mother; that this is actually so was confirmed by her psychiatrist. Bressler added that the assumption that nothing is available externally justifies to the patient collecting narcissistic supplies, like pills, to comfort himself.

Wednesday, September 13, 1961   A.B. was still feeling sleepy. The discussion with the analyst was rather general, with no clearly expressed trend. The patient talked about his fear of insanity, and of his reluctance to speak up in the morning group therapy session. He said that his sister had baked a cake for him and had given it to him, though he was still avoiding her. There was talk about the patient's situation in the hospital generally. The boy said he felt fine, and the analyst suggested that, if he was feeling good, perhaps he should get up and get some exercise. The patient remarked that the hospital provided a safe refuge from violence and relieved him of responsibilities.

Group Discussion

Roose said that the patient seemed to show less fear of his own inner violence, though not necessarily less violence. Ostow considered the complaint about the fear of insanity to be a variant of hypochondria; there is the conviction of illness on the part of the patient though here the illness is mental and not physical.

Bressler mentioned that the hospital gives the patient both structure and nurture. He reminded the group that originally the youth had wanted not hospitalization but incarceration, and, failing that, institutionalization in a state hospital. Bressler connected this request for incarceration with the patient's strong feelings of guilt. Roose suggested that the fact of hospitalization seemed particularly important to this patient, because of his sister's hospitalization, and his fear that his sister might be getting more care than he. Ostow added that the analyst has more control over a hospitalized patient.

Linn brought up the general value of the hospital in providing a supportive structure for sanctioned regression, and Ostow too, emphasized the importance of allowing depressed patients—whether or not they are on medication—to shrug off responsibilities until they feel well enough to resume them. In a case such as this one, the disparity between the amount of libidinal energy supplies available to the patient, and the demand imposed, can be a primary determinant of anger, turning away, and illness.

Thursday, September 14, 1961   On this, the fourth day of hospitalization, the patient was out of bed; the session was conducted in one of the consultation rooms. The youth seemed much more open. He expressed a pervasive feeling that he was being pursued, similar to the feeling he had of being watched on the morning he entered the hospital, though this time he realized that he was not being pursued by real people. The patient remarked that the feeling of closeness to another person is dangerous. The closer he approaches anyone, the more he is confronted with the impulse to express his violent feelings.

In response to the analyst's inquiry about his hatred, A.B. replied that in the past everyone, and particularly his parents, had abandoned him, and, most recently, Sylvia. He added that he preferred to stay in the hospital for a while, so long as he faced such dangerous impulses. Again he referred to the fact that the analyst was being paid for his attention to the patient.

Group Discussion

Feder summarized the first few days of the patient's course since resuming the medication, by noting that anxiety, agitation, and guilt, as well as paranoid ideas increased as the boy stopped sleeping during the day, and left his bed. Ostow added that the above-mentioned phenomena might represent a reduction in the sedative effect of the Elavil. He called attention also to the definite, though as yet unfocused, paranoid coloring of the last session.

As to the patient's expressed fear of closeness, Ostow said that the fact that the patient brought it up might already mark the emergence of some sort of renewed drive toward an object relation. Ostow and Bressler both felt that the remark about his fear of closeness was the patient's way of fending off the analyst and keeping him at a distance.

Ostow suggested further that the patient's accusation that the analyst is unloving may be a projection of the patient's own unwillingness to relate to the analyst. The boy has established the expectation that everyone hates him. He must carry forward this expectation until he is ready to assume an object relation. At this point the patient is not yet ready for a real object relation, but he must have a relation of some kind.

Roose pointed out that A.B.'s relation to the analyst has the potential, at one extreme, of temptation to violence, and, at the other extreme, of passive homosexual submission in which he is fed by his father, who was actually the more mothering parent. Bressler said that submission may be even more dangerous than being fed; it could lead to being invaded completely, or, as Roose suggested, complete fusion with the mother, in which all semblance of intactness, ego boundaries, and identity are completely lost. Furst summarized the discussion by placing A.B. in a category of patients whose problems in object relations seem to center around the fact that to be close means either to devour or to be devoured, and withdrawal threatens isolation, abandonment, and loss of existence. In these patients, perhaps, the need to control really stems from an attempt to compromise between these two extremes. Hence the attempt to control a relationship represents, not necessarily the direct expression of aggressive impulses, but rather a compromise necessary for survival.

Friday, September 15, 1961   A.B. continued the theme of his mistrust of the analyst, saying that he was buying the analyst's attention with money. The analyst tried to push the patient a little further by asking A.B. what he thought the doctor would do with what he says. The youth responded that the analyst might use what he said to castrate him mentally, as a way of punishing him. He again complained that his mother left him when he was a child; he must have done something wrong, but he could not imagine what it might be. The analyst told the patient that he seemed to be acting out over and over again a need or demand for punishment. The incident of shoplifting before he left school in February 1961 would have to be seen in that light, especially as there had never been any previous history of shoplifting. Linn added briefly that the shoplifting could be considered equivalent to hoarding narcissistic supplies.

The analyst told the patient that though the latter had been quite successful in manipulating people to leave him, the analyst would not be driven away in this manner. He added that the patient was testing him and asking for affection. A.B. responded that he was up and about, more active on the unit, less anxious, and increasing his participation in the group, but he was not yet ready to leave the hospital. His father would visit him that night, and he did not want to face him. His father would ask him questions about how things were going, and the boy did not want to tell his father anything about himself.

Group Discussion

Ostow emphasized to the group the change in the state of the patient over the week. When A.B. first appealed for hospitalization, there was a completely negative relation to the analyst, with pessimism, suicidal tendencies, and practically no object relation; there was just enough narcissism to want to survive. During the week of September 11-15 three influences were brought to bear on the patient: first, the hospitalization, second, the analyst's work with the patient; and third, the medication. The medication has two effects: one is the anti-depression effect, which does not set in for three or four weeks, and the other is the sedative effect, of which there is evidence in the youth's sleepiness and grogginess, and which is gradually wearing off. One can now begin to see what is going on in the patient's mind, and there is the beginning of an attempt to get close to the analyst, and to work through his negative transference to the analyst. In this effort the analyst is reassuring the patient.

Ostow made a second point that, in this case, the analyst, in telling the patient, "I love you, I will take care of you, you can trust me," is doing something that is seldom done in straightforward psychoanalysis. This kind of assurance is necessary for this type of patient at this point; yet it is possible, when the patient has begun to recover, for the analyst, gradually and tactfully, to slip back into the analytic abstinence posture.

The group agreed that, as the patient changes, whether spontaneously, or in response to therapeutic efforts of one kind or another, he starts to face problems to which he must react and challenges against which he must defend himself. And, as he moves closer to normality, the original circumstances that threw him into illness are reconstructed. Unless the patient can bring something new to his efforts to solve this problem, he is not likely to recover fully. Linn added that hospitalized patients typically go through a period of symptom control which should not be confused with clinical recovery, because it works only in the setting of the hospital.

Furst added that, because the recovering patient encounters the pathogenic situation anew, it is important not to decrease the dosage of the medication too soon, and Ostow stressed the point that the feeling of wellbeing and remission of symptoms are interrupted by frequent temporary lapses which must be anticipated lest the patient and doctor become needlessly discouraged.

Monday, September 18, 1961   A.B. greeted the doctor quite cheerfully. He said he had been feeling better in the last two days and was planning to leave the hospital at the end of the week. Discussion of the patient's guilt continued, and the analyst told the

patient that he is a guilt collector. The youth confirmed this statement, and brought it up to date with details of his acting out in
the hospital over the week-end. The patient had been behaving in a
provocative way, and had drawn a considerable amount of attention
to himself from the entire hospital staff, particularly in reference
to his close association with another adolescent on the ward.
Specifically, the staff suspected that the two of them were taking
drugs together (at least marijuana, if not other things) on the ward.
A.B. then began an unproductive repetition of previous attempts
to pursue his feelings of guilt back into his childhood.

The patient reported further that he had had "heavy sex"
over the week-end, meaning that there was a considerable amount
of sex play with a married female patient on the unit. The doctor
suggested the interpretation that, as the acute episode begins to
subside, A.B. goes back to his endless search for a good mother.
For a moment he has found her; but, the youth hastened to add,
in describing his "heavy sex," that he felt guilty about it. Again
there was a quest into his childhood as to what he did to whom
and, as usual, he was concerned with his sister and, also as usual,
he came up with no more definite material than before. The youth
then asked the analyst to remind him about the discussion at the
last session; and, when the doctor answered that is was guilt-
collecting, A.B. gave some examples:

1. He caused a fire by throwing a piece of paper into an electric heater. To this he associated that his roommate at college was very sick; he was an arsonist.
2. At the age of four he was stealing candy from a shop, and
   jewelry from his mother.
3. At the age of ten he entertained florid superman fantasies.
4. At one time he was preoccupied with drawing the shape of
   the pressure cooker. (He drew a picture for the doctor who
   showed it to the group. Linn suggested, and the group
   agreed, that the picture suggested sexual organs, and that it
   probably depicted a screen memory.)

The patient ended the hour by commenting that the Elavil was responsible for his better spirits.

Group Discussion

The group considered possible reasons for the patient's elation on Monday. Roose attributed much of it to the effect of the medication. This increased activity is closer to the boy's former state. Linn suggested that the mild euphoria was a transference effect. The doctor abandoned the patient over the week-end, and the patient substituted people to act out with. Bressler said that because the doctor abandoned the patient over the week-end, the drug might have meant that much more to him.

Ostow felt that the change in the patient is to be attributed to the Elavil only insofar as the soporific effect of the drug is wearing off, and the patient is beginning to feel better. A.B. no longer feels panicked by the threat of suicide; he has found himself a congenial group in the hospital, and is dealing with the transference and its implicit homosexual threat. Over the weekend, in the absence of the doctor, the youth tries to find an object relation, not with a man, but with a woman. The heterosexual acting out is an anti-depression maneuver which he has tried unsuccessfully in the past. The last time he tried it was with Sylvia, and she abandoned him by eloping. Now he tries again with another woman, and this time the situation is self-limited because she is married, and she is in the hospital. Nevertheless, she does offer him an escape from the homosexual relationship with the doctor. In giving a purely perfunctory performance with the analyst, the patient tries to put him off, and at the same time to satisfy him so that he will let the patient continue acting out with the woman. Bressler suggested that, to the contrary, the youth's interest in men has not necessarily diminished, and he reminded the group of A.B.'s close relationship with another youth on the ward.

The reporting analyst recalled from previous experience that, when this patient feels better, he tends to become more and more anxious as he becomes active enough to indulge in acting out, which produces more turmoil. Linn established a connection between the stealing of jewelry from the mother and the hoarding of pills. He further felt that the fantasy of the pressure cooker is important, and he cited a study that he had done of patients at the Bronx Lebanon Hospital in which he had demonstrated that when adolescents and younger children were brought in, having set fires, he could achieve considerable alleviation of their distress by giving Elavil. He interpreted this observation to mean that pyromania is a depressive manifestation. Roose suggested that the patient sees himself as a pressure cooker, about to explode.

Ostow emphasized to the group the resilience of the youthful patient, and remarked that with an older patient, of fifty or fifty-five years, for example, the sequence of changes is much slower. Furst added that the intensity of the instinctual drives is also of a different order of magnitude.

Bressler raised the question whether it is appropriate at this time to give a tranquilizer to a patient who has been having so much trouble. He said that he personally would favor such a step. Feder felt that in the hospital setting he would wait and trust the staff to control the patient, though he would administer a tranquilizer to an ambulatory patient.

Monday evening, September 18, 1961   The reporting analyst held an interview with A.B.'s parents. He told them that the boy was very sick, and that the problem would be one of many years' duration.

Tuesday, September 19, 1961   A.B. was angry about the doctor's interview with his parents; but, although angry, as he had told the analyst previously, he had not wanted to participate in it because, he claimed, it would be too uncomfortable for him. The boy complained further that, after the interview, his father came and gloated over him because of what the analyst had revealed. The analyst asked what specifically the father had gloated about, but the patient would not say. The analyst told the patient that he pretended that his parents did not know him and did not make their own observations without necessarily being told anything by the analyst, and further, that A.B. seemed to feel that, because he withdraws from his parents, they should see, hear, and know nothing about him. The patient answered that, when he was a child, his father had ridiculed him, and now he was retaliating. The doctor then commented that the youth was retaliating by making himself even more ridiculous than he was claiming his father made him out to be. In this way he was tying himself to his parents instead of achieving any real independence.

The patient declared that he did not want to work. The doctor responded that this was tantamount to letting his father support him, and suggested that A.B. call his office (which the boy had not yet done) and inform his employers of his situation. The presenting analyst noted to the group that the patient was getting into a relationship with a married woman which seemed to be filled with an intolerable amount of anxiety, and, from that, was rebounding to a passive relationship with his father, in which he felt humiliated.

Wednesday, September 20, 1961   A.B. reported a dream:

He and his sister were stealing jewels. They were being chased, and, to avoid capture, they were killing people.

There were no associations to this dream, though the patient added that he had been waking up mornings in a cold sweat.

Group Discussion

Linn noted that in this dream the sister, the patient, and the stealing all suggest a passive, feminine, receptive posture. Roose suggested that the youth and his sister are both stealing what they never got from either parent, particularly the mother. Ostow stressed the implications of the dream for the transference: the patient is accusing the father and the doctor of being accomplices in cheating him. He, in turn is cheating them by running away with a married woman; thence, the resolution to leave the hospital. Bressler mentioned that, though the patient is being discussed in terms such as "passive feminine" and "passive homosexual," the real issue is that of the boy's pregenital needs.

Ostow, returning to the issue of possible incestuous relations between A.B. and his sister, suggested that the two, faced with distant parents, might have turned to each other, not only emotionally, but also physically, and perhaps this is the source of the patient's guilt. Furst said that the patient is now running away from the analyst, not because he does not need him, but, rather because of the homosexual transference. He very much needs the doctor, and is afraid of what he wants and needs him for. Bressler responded that the youth's relationship with the woman need not be seen as an attempt to escape from the analyst, but, by cooling it off, may make it possible for him to continue the homosexual relationship.

Thursday, September 21, 1961   A.B. was becoming increasingly restless and tense, apparently in anticipation of his approaching date of discharge from the hospital. He reported feeling "funny and strange." At first the boy denied any angry feelings, but accused the analyst of talking to others, particularly to his parents. He no longer wanted to talk to the doctor, and he complained that he was being "pushed around". The analyst replied that, though the patient obviously does not like to be pushed around, he was manipulating people into doing just that to him. As an illustration, the doctor brought up the patient's refusal to participate in the interview with his parents; in this situation a three-way exchange would clearly have been preferable. The patient continually asked about the date of discharge from the hospital, hoping the doctor would decide; again he was accusing the doctor of not having taken over and not having made a decision for him. Once the doctor had made a decision either way, the patient could contest it. When the boy again took up the theme of his intense feelings of guilt, the analyst took the occasion to return to the patient's need for punishment and his machinations to elicit punishment from those around him. The youth reported another dream of several days previously:

He saw his mother and sister in some kind of ugly homosexual relationship.

In reference to the dream he showed the analyst a crayon portrait of his mother, and said that his mother was crying tears of blood, blood meaning a wound. He had made a portrait of his sister which he did not show the doctor, and stated that the expression on his sister's face was "frightened." He also made a self portrait in which he described his face as "empty"; "I am nowhere." A.B. ended the session by stating that he wished to remain in the hospital. The analyst agreed to this and added Stelazine 5 mgs twice a day (until September 26, and then three times a day) to A.B.'s medication.

Group Discussion

Linn felt that, perhaps during the Monday elation, when the patient first suggested leaving the hospital, the doctor should have firmly vetoed the idea. Roose remarked that not forcing the issue of the patient's leaving the hospital made it necessary for the patient to acknowledge his anger.

Ostow described the events of September 12-22 as an early improvement and relapse. In the first few days the patient felt better and had become more active: first, because he had been removed from the pathogenic situation; second, because he felt strengthened by the doctor's care; and, third, because he felt nourished by the medication. He then proceeded to reestablish the pattern of object relations that had prevailed at the beginning of the breakdown. This pattern consists of, first, heterosexual acting out to see what had been withheld from him by his mother, and, second, homosexual ambivalence, i.e., the need to defy father in order to obtain heterosexual and incestuous gratification, the need for his father's love and protection, and the need to defend himself against his passive homosexual need for his father. Relapse sets in because the youth is no better equipped to handle the ambivalence stalemate now than before. The relapse is evident in the recurring signs of depression, i.e., early morning awakening, nightmares, feelings of emptiness, defeat, and guilt, and in a mild paranoia in which the patient projects his wish to be cared for upon the analyst and adds malicious intent to that wish.

Ostow saw no evidence at all that the pharmacologic effect of the anti-depression drug had played a part up to this point. The only observable effect is the placebo effect which often occurs (even when drugs are not given) when a patient begins any kind of treatment. This placebo effect may be responsible for what Ostow considers the incorrect inference that anti-depression medication takes effect within a few days after first being given. The treatment of this patient would be an ideal test case for the reliability of the anti-depression effect of Elavil if: first, one could now see a regression to depression; second, if no other drug were being given; and third, if, after three or four weeks, one would see a more reliable amelioration of the depression. In assessing the effect of the Elavil in this case, one must keep in mind the following facts:

1. Other drugs are being administered.
2. The patient prefers to believe that the drug, rather than the doctor, is helping him.
3. The patient's aggressiveness produces ambivalence which precipitates depression. Here the aggression is directed against the father, who is equivalent to the analyst, and whom the patient must kill (as he does in his dream of September 21) because they oppose his incestuous need. But the patient also needs both the father and the doctor; thence the ambivalence.
4. The patient seems psychotic on September 21 in a manner reminiscent of the paranoid feelings he described before his hospitalization. He accuses the analyst of pushing him around, though he is really complaining that the doctor is not taking proper care of him. The patient's readiness to accede to delaying his leaving the hospital confirms the interpretation that the delusional accusation reflects his increased homosexual clinging. The boy labels his psychotic state "funny and strange."
5. The patient thus shows psychosis with depression as manifested by the guilt, the early morning awakening, and the sense of emptiness. The dream about his mother and sister indicates a wish for sexual feeding by his mother, and the tears of blood are his own tears for his mother and for the analyst.

Feder contended that the dream and the pictures, rather than representing an incestuous phenomenon, show a problem of separation which involves mostly the mother. The mother and sister are seen as being together, in contrast to the patient who is off by himself. Perhaps a motivation for feminine identification in this patient is that, since the boy cannot get close to his mother as a boy, he feels he must become like his sister. The fear of being abandoned by the doctor may also account for why the patient is feeling so much better when he is told that he can stay in the hospital.

Feder's remarks were followed by a discussion of whether this patient's clinging can best be called "incestuous" or "pregenital," and whether the two kinds of possessiveness are, in fact, different. Sandler, who visited during that meeting, drew a sharp distinction between the two, but added that the former can develop from the latter. Sandler felt that, in the case of this youth, the sexuality is, to a large extent, spurious. The pathology is on the pregenital level, and the patient is trying to use instinct gratification to regain the pregenital state of closeness, security, and comfort. Sandler also distinguished between a subjective state of pain and the depressive response to it. The state of pain may be the result of a disappointment in oneself or the result of an object loss. Depression, however, is not the only possible response to this pain. In this case the sexual acting out can be seen as an alternative to depression. Perhaps the drugs that seem to influence depression actually act upon the state of pain which gives rise to depression.

Bressler said that when the medication is given regularly, the patient often counts on it as a constant reliable object. Therefore, when a patient is about to leave the hospital the dosage should not be lowered—indeed it might even be raised—because the stress resulting from leaving the hospital is an additional challenge.

Friday, September 22, 1961   A.B. again greeted the doctor cheerfully, and announced that he had been more active in the group therapy discussion on the ward that day. The night before, he had informed his father that he was staying in the hospital. He then reported another dream:

> His father bought a Rolls Royce, and was trying to park it in the garage of the house. This was in one of the family's previous suburban homes, but the garage was represented on the wrong side of the house. The boy was guiding his father in; the patient felt it was his responsibility and he was not doing a good job. His father was angry; the patient was doing it all wrong. The father finally got the car into the garage and measured the distance of the rear and front sides of the car to the right side of the garage. It had to be twelve inches and it was.

There were no spontaneous associations to this dream. In response to questions of the analyst, A.B. said that the house in the dream was the one in which his family had lived from the time he was nine until he was fourteen. This was the time when things began to go wrong with him (he started psychiatric treatment at age thirteen). The analyst suggested that it is not the father's but the patient's own standards of behavior that he was not living up to. The youth responded with two fantasies:

1. He was beaten in a game of ping-pong the previous day.
2. He rises from weakness and defeat to regain the heavy-weight title of the world. This is only the second time in history that this feat has been accomplished.

A.B. expressed concern about the picture that he drew of his mother, but could add no new data. He was also upset about a new patient who was admitted to the unit midway in the course of an operation to transform him from a male to a female. The analyst pointed out that the boy's concern for the "he-she" patient is an extreme representation of A.B.'s view of his own sexual identity. The youth also expressed interest in another patient on the ward who was being transferred to a state hospital; the analyst reminded A.B. that this was what he had originally wanted for himself. Further the patient was angry that the nurses read his chart.

Group Discussion

Sandler thought that the dream about parking the car is a homosexual dream, especially because the garage is on the wrong side. He noted the amount of omnipotence and controlling in the dream. Perhaps the patient is concerned about the extent to which he can control the doctor. Feder added that the patient can control only as the "he-she" patient did, i.e., by having himself castrated. The fantasy about being beaten at ping-pong may refer to the boy's having to admit that he was not ready to leave the hospital. Ostow felt that the dreams and fantasies show a basic phenomenon of depression, the feeling of weakness and incompetence in the broader sense of the term. The rebirth fantasy is typical of a depressive patient wishing for recovery. In the dream the youth cedes to his father the role of primary actor, but he participates in his father's exploit as a helper. It is important that all this happened before the new medication; the group can now look for a change.

Sandler suggested that the patient's interest in controlling can be attributed to his conflict between activity and passivity. He seems to project his own omnipotent impulses upon his superego introjects. On the one hand, he wishes to please these introjects by submitting to them sexually, but on the other hand, he wants to identify with them. This conflict must play a part in the pathogenesis of his depression. Very dependent individuals need to establish possessive control over their protective love objects for fear of losing them. Furst added that in patients with marked separation anxiety and feelings of dependence on a pregenital level, one often finds feelings of omnipotence and an attempt to control those around them, because to lose them would be to risk annihilation. Sandler agreed, and mentioned that colicky infants in particular need to control objects upon whom they depend to alleviate their distress, and need the feeling of control as a defense against overwhelming, unlocalized pain.

Monday, September 25, 1961   A.B. stated that he was increasingly more tense and restless. He said he was aware that others were watching him; and he added that over the week-end he had committed some minor infractions of rules, and that the nursing staff was keeping an eye on him because he was always in mischief. The patient then talked at length of his feelings about a fourteen-year-old girl on the ward who was very frightened, and again about the boy who was going to the state hospital. He complained of a vague pain in his chest, slight dizziness on exertion, and constipation. He said that the food was bad, and he was concerned about gaining weight.

The youth returned to the theme of his guilt: he claimed that he was becoming increasingly conscious of his guilt, especially with reference to his sister. He reported that he had spoken somewhat more openly to his parents about himself, and he felt that his father was paying attention to him because he was his father's son. The boy added that he finally did call the office, and mentioned leaving the hospital. He requested a pass for the following evening to attend a night class in art that he had signed up for, and the pass was granted.

Group Discussion

Both Bressler and Roose suggested that perhaps the constipation is a side effect of the Stelazine. Sandler said that the complaints might indicate a pregnancy fantasy on the part of the patient. Ostow mentioned that pregnancy fantasies are very common after beginning a drug; the complaint of the "lousy food" may refer to both the drug and the constipation which developed as a result of the drug. Feder remarked that all the minor complaints add up to the patient's real complaint, i.e., that he was abandoned over the week-end.

Ostow emphasized the fact that every drug has multiple effects. The physician prescribes the drug to achieve one of these effects, and both physician and patient must tolerate the others. The question is whether the constipation is a primary or secondary effect. Sandler felt that the side effects of a drug should be treated like the "day residue"; they are absorbed by the ego and brought into relation with unconscious forces. Moreover, whether the drug affects psychic structure or physiological function, mental representations of these effects are created, which are seized upon and worked over by unconscious wishes. Ostow emphasized that the patient does not distinguish between psychological changes and changes in physiological function, which he perceives in his body as a secondary effect of the drug, but the analyst must keep these effects separate. Bressler mentioned that the effect of the anti-psychotic drugs on the production of instinctual derivatives is not known. Artane can also produce constipation, anorexia, and malaise, especially when given alongside Elavil.

Bressler observed that generally not feeling good is a common primary effect of Stelazine. Furst and Ostow mentioned that, perhaps in retrospect, the Stelazine might not have been necessary. The patient's agitation at the end of the previous week seemed to be a response to the prospect of leaving the hospital, and it might have subsided without the drug through the reassurance that remaining in the hospital would give him. Moreover, since the patient was being hospitalized, there was no danger of his causing great harm or damage. If any drug was called for, it should have been an ordinary sedative such as meprobamate, rather than a phenothiazine tranquilizer. In this instance the Stelazine seems merely to have made the patient more depressed.

Furst thought that on Monday the patient was angry. Feder said that perhaps the youth felt that the drug was a poor substitute for the doctor, and the statement that he was being watched may be an accusation against the analyst, meaning that, though the analyst showed no concern for the patient, other people did. The presenting analyst showed the group a series of drawings that the patient had made over that week-end. Ostow commented that the features of the face seemed disjointed, and Furst remarked that the pictures represent considerable work for one day.

Tuesday, September 26, 1961   A.B. reported that he was restless and that he had eloped with his roommate for about half an hour on Monday to have lunch out. The boy felt that his restlessness was precipitated by a drawing which he showed the analyst, but would not give him. The picture was of a tree, which looked, to the analyst, like a hand with truncated fingers, and a trunk—the fingers represented the branches and the trunk going down several inches, representing a wrist. He also drew a picture of a bush and the sun. The tree, the branches, and the trunk are filled with dots. The bush and sun are filled with whirls, very much like fingerprint markings, minutely drawn around and around until the entire object was filled with these whirls. The tree looks quite lifeless, stark, and cut-off, with no roots. The branches are also cut off. The patient was so excited that he could barely talk, and the session was not very productive. The Stelazine was increased to 15 mgs a day.

Group Discussion

Ostow, Sandler, and Roose commented on the bizarre quality of the drawing done after the Stelazine was started. Ostow remarked that the patient's calling the office and going to school should be seen as efforts to be a good boy. These attempts to do the right thing are frequently a means of clinging to the parents; such measures are commonly employed by patients who feel themselves becoming depressed, and they represent an appeal for protection. Sandler felt that the patient's agitation may indicate anxiety about having seduced the doctor into acceding to his demands. Bressler said that, to the contrary, the patient may feel ashamed of having carried on, and may wish to placate the doctor.

Roose, Bressler, and Sandler all noted how the patient sees himself as a good boy and bad boy simultaneously.

Ostow summarized by saying that, on the basis of this report and the subsequent discussion, one can say three things about the results of giving tranquilizers to a patient who is basically depressed but agitated. First, there is an increase in the evidence of depression, manifested in this case as, a) increased feelings of restlessness and tension, b) hypochondria in which the side effects of the drug are used along with psychically determined ideas, and c) an identification with sick people.

Second, there is evidence of psychosis both in the ideas of being watched and in the bizarre self-image revealed in the drawings, and third, there is an attempt to be reconciled with parental representatives by confession of guilt, by appreciation of his father, and by a resolution to return to work and to school.

Wednesday, September 27, 1961   Despite the fact that Artane was added with the increased dose of Stelazine, the patient developed a marked dystonic reaction. He could scarcely walk or speak, and his speech was so thick that it was almost unintelligible. Before the analyst came, a resident had already given the boy intravenous Benadryl (diphenhydramine) which promptly removed the dystonia. The analyst eliminated the Stelazine, and gave the youth another pass to attend his evening course. A.B. said he was quite sleepy, and, as usual, restless. He was flighty in his thought, and jumped from one seemingly irrelevant detail to another. He was still upset about losing Sylvia. Rose was visiting him regularly, but he did not know what to do with her or what to say to her. He wanted to end the relationship, but did not know how to do it. The boy referred again to his guilt. He said that his last drawing of the tree, the bush, and the sun had the mood of a nightmare, but he added no details to this statement. The patient ended the hour by asking whether he was a psychotic. He seemed afraid to describe some of the more bizarre elements in his recent experiences, that is, the dream that led him to do the drawings.

Group Discussion

The reporting analyst pointed out to the group that the boy's description of his situation with the women in his life represents this patient's characteristic dilemma. When he becomes involved with a girl, though there is some sexual gratification, there is the increasing fear of closeness and of being devoured by the girl, and he eventually comes to the point where he has to break off. Here he feels more comfortable mourning the loss of a girl who is not around, than involving himself with one who is. Ostow suggested that the allusion to Sylvia at this point could indicate that the depressive tendency was precipitated by her abandoning him, and that Rose was no substitute. When A.B. speaks of Sylvia he speaks with longing, but there is no evidence of anger. The patient's flightiness might represent an akathisia of ideas, and the speculation about psychosis may again be a kind of mental hypochondria.

Friday, September 29, 1961   A.B. again brought up the theme of guilt. He felt guilty about everything; he was restless and tense. The youth spoke about his drawings, but, rather than give associations, he simply elaborated on the actual content of the drawings. The picture of the tree reminded him of Van Gogh's drawings of cypress trees, i.e., sinister and threatening. The doctor gave the boy another pass for the next Monday. The patient spoke of wanting to take another LSD trip, and reported a dream.

> He took a trip and everything was beautiful — "shapes, colors, and everything."

The patient remarked that he felt increasingly guilty, and referred to the group of drawings he had made around September 24, which had to do with eyes. He then came back to the bush, sun, and tree drawing, and spoke of the eye in the sun. The analyst commented to the patient about the relation of the sun to God and to being watched. A.B. responded by reporting a euphoric fantasy in which the phrase "the coming of the Messiah" referred to him.

> He knew he was the Messiah though no one else did.

He said more about eyes; that he could see both into the eye and out of it. The analyst suggested that his being on both sides was indirectly connected to his fantasy of the coming of the Messiah. Returning again to his last drawing, the patient said that the tree was a hand, and in response to questioning by the analyst, he specified the right one. The bush, he continued, was a pile of games. He felt guilty about some stealing that had been occurring on the ward. He said that he did not do the stealing, but that he knew who did.

A.B. reported further that he had gone to his class and felt tense. His father had accused him of running away to the hospital, but his father was wrong. The analyst deduced from this last statement that the boy must have visited his parents on the way to the class or on the way back, and that this was the basis of his conversation with his father. The analyst mentioned the conscious awareness of guilt to which the youth's increasing tension is associated, and simultaneously his tendency to act out his need for punishment rather than to experience guilt in the form of tension. He related this tendency to the patient's feelings that he was being watched. The patient than talked about the hand in the dream: the hand is related to sex, again responding to the analyst's questions, particularly to foreplay and masturbation. He used the left hand for the former and the right hand for the latter.

Group Discussion

Winkelman suggested that perhaps the patient heard that he was considered psychotic, and for that reason was comparing himself to Van Gogh. There was a discussion by the group on hand choice in masturbation: the consensus was that most people masturbate and make love with the dominant hand, except when a sense of guilt compels an attempt to dissociate the two.

Linn felt that this hour marked a psychotic breakthrough on the part of the patient. Bressler agreed, and wondered whether it was due to his reaction to the Stelazine and to its being taken away. Roose reminded the group that the paranoia which keeps breaking through preceded the administration of Stelazine and thus was not caused by it. Linn related the patient's psychotic behavior to his recent dystonic experience, and wondered whether the incident might have shaken the patient's confidence in the doctor and in the stability of things generally. Roose and Bressler agreed, the latter referring to a similar situation in which a schizoaffective patient said she had lost confidence in her doctor as a result of the side effects of a phenothiazine.

There was more general discussion about the use of delusions as a defense against psychic pain. Ostow suggested that detachment and depression can be seen as alternative responses to ambivalence. Energizing drugs facilitate detachment, and tranquilizing drugs facilitate depression.

Monday, October 2, 1961 The nurses' notes brought to the analyst's attention a considerable amount of acting out on the part of the patient over the week-end; the objectionable behavior consisted mainly of mischief, e.g., being where he should not be, being in the wrong place at the wrong time. A.B. again appeared restless and tense, and reported that he had slept poorly for the first time in the hospital. He again brought up his guilt and his feeling of being watched by others. On this occasion, however, he was aware that this feeling was paranoid, and he tried to distinguish between the feeling and how much actual watching was going on. The analyst reminded the patient that the nurses really were concerned about his meanderings. The patient replied that he wanted to leave the hospital, but was afraid to. He felt that he had wasted his life and that he was "nothing."

Group Discussion

Ostow said that the Monday session shows little change in the patient's situation since Friday. In reference to the youth's claim that he was "nothing," Ostow reported that, in his experience, this is a characteristic remark for depressives; depressed patients often refer to themselves as "empty," while schizophrenics tend to use the word "numb." but the distinction is not consistent.

Wednesday, October 4, 1961 The doctor, the patient, and one of the nurses discussed the patient's misbehavior. In the session, A.B. said he felt he was being watched, which was quite true. There was more talk about his attending school, and about the youth's guilt and its possible causes.

On Monday, October 2, A.B. had gone to visit his parents before going to class. His parents became concerned when he told them an impossible story about why he was at home and not at school. The analyst told the boy that he had been called by the boy's mother Monday evening, and he pointed out that A.B.'s refusal to deal directly and openly with his parents forced the doctor to deal with them. The analyst commented further that, in contrast to the patient's claims about his parents, the parents did seem concerned about what was happening to him. The youth replied that he doubted this. He wanted to leave the hospital, and, at the same time, he did not want to. He felt somewhat depressed, and thought that he had a number of problems, which he could not resolve. When asked to specify these problems, he stated that he felt he was being watched, and that he was interested in Ruth, a girl patient on the ward. The analyst reminded the group that when A.B. becomes involved sexually, his guilty feelings or his paranoid state increases, or becomes at least more overt.

The patient then told the analyst that he wanted to give up Rose. He had a dream the previous night:

He was dead; Sylvia was unconcerned; she paid no attention to him.

The boy then said he wanted someone to love him. When pressed to specify, he said he wanted someone to take care of him, to love him the way his father loved his mother. Bressler interpreted this statement as a reference to the transference, i.e., a wish for *rapprochement* with the doctor. When the analyst again pressed the patient for specifics, there was no response. The doctor then commented that the patient seemed quite upset, and speculated openly that it might have something to do with being sick, as his sister was sick, hinting that the sicker the patient was, the more attention he obtained from his parents. A.B. then said he would like to be a man. Again asked for details, he said that to be a man meant to love a woman, to give love as his father gave love, though he admitted that it all seemed quite confused; the analyst agreed. The entire session was in this manner confused and fragmented. The doctor had the impression that more was left unsaid than was being reported.

Group Discussion

The presenting analyst inferred that the patient would like to be a really strong man like his father but, failing to obtain love from his mother, he would take it from his father, even at the price of assuming a passive, feminine posture. Ostow said that the dream of being dead is characteristic of depression. The patient is trying to elicit responses from his mother and the doctor, threatening to kill himself if they do not comply; this is the Tom Sawyer fantasy. Furst added that this fantasy is classic in all children who feel they have been neglected. Linn went further, saying that the Tom Sawyer fantasy represents the strategy of accepting the passive posture to win love.

Friday, October 6, 1961   A.B. said he felt depressed the day before, and particularly so on his return from class. He was increasingly concerned about the future. Should he go back to the suburb where his family had lived before moving to the city? What he meant was, should he return to the environment from which he came, the hippies, the LSD trippers, and his chaotic, unstructured, disorganized group of friends and activities? He answered his own question, saying that to go back to that setting would be to go back to "nothing." He compared being "nothing" to being "straight"; "straight" meant no drugs and no wild acting out. It also meant being independent and answering to himself for his own behavior. The youth said he resented having been prohibited from visiting another ward. The hospital staff was becoming increasingly concerned about A.B.'s acting out with another male patient on the ward, Stanley, with whom he had left the hospital. The nurses suspected that the two were taking marijuana or LSD on the ward.

The boy then talked about an old childhood friend, Bob, from New Rochelle, where the family had lived earlier before moving to White Plains. Bob was shorter than A.B., and he obtained good grades in school. He was at that time at a large midwestern university where he was active in the civil rights movement. Bob represented a contrast to the patient's image of himself as a creative artist. The patient dreamed:

> There was something homosexual between himself and
> Bob,

though, in fact, as far as he could remember, there was never anything overtly homosexual between them. Although he considered Bob a friend, the two had quarreled frequently, and he had seemed to be more hurt by these quarrels than one would have expected.

A.B. mentioned that he had been depressed again on Thursday, had slept Thursday afternoon, and had spent part of Friday in bed too.

Monday, October 9, 1961   A.B. reported that he was again thinking of leaving the hospital at the end of the week. He had been sleeping during the day over the week-end. He claimed that he would have his fantasies with all their anxiety and guilt, or he would have "nothing." There was nothing in him with which to achieve anything in reality. His co-workers at the office where he worked had sent him a card. The boy reported further that another young male patient on the ward, also in treatment with the presenting analyst, wanted to tell him something about the analyst but that he did not want to hear it. This same young man knew something about Sylvia. A.B. told the analyst that he got rid of Rose by telling her that he could not have any visitors. He mentioned something vague about the girl he was interested in on the ward, but he did not follow it up. The analyst asked the patient how he was preparing to leave the hospital The youth answered by restating that he wanted mothering. He followed this declaration with a dream:

> He won a literary prize, $300, and then he saw it was
> actually $100, the same as everyone else who had entered
> the contest, but he cashed it for $300.

He added: "If I can't be a genius, I'll be nothing." He complained that he felt groggy, and said that earlier he had left the hospital for five minutes to get some fresh air and was not caught.

Group Discussion

Linn felt that the patient was stagnating at this point, remaining in a deep depression. He wondered if there was something in the hospital situation that was blocking the youth's recovery. Linn was particularly concerned about A.B.'s recurring week-end depressions that left him completely knocked out. A psychosis was becoming clinically more evident. The treatment had deprived the patient of his defenses. There were issues that were not being touched either by the medication or by the hospitalization. The boy was withdrawing into sleep, and seemed to be drifting downhill in spite of what was being done for him.

Ostow saw no significant change, but wanted to emphasize that in the past three or four days the youth had begun to sleep during the day, and reported being groggy, which he felt when he first entered the hospital. When A.B. entered the hospital, the sleepiness and grogginess were assigned to the sedative effect of the Elavil. Perhaps their recurrence indicates impending change. Subsiding agitation and readiness to sleep frequently indicates a decrease in the intensity or pressure of the depression. This can mark the beginning of what Ostow calls the state of "narcissistic tranquility." This is a state in which equilibrium has been established, perhaps by means of drugs, although the patient has not yet begun to repair object relations. The syndrome includes torpor, weight gain, greater food intake, greater sexual desire, and a need for other sensual pleasures.

The boy has reached the point, he continued, where, if the Elavil is going to work, the patient will begin to respond to it now. If he responds, he will become more independent, begin to relate more actively to objects, and, therefore, might be more motivated to run away from the doctor. His object relations have not improved, and he is being forced to recover before he is ready.

Bressler made the point that in the view of the psychoanalyst, who wants to help the patient repair object relations, if the drug therapy is successful, the patient may feel well enough, but so threatened that, as a result, he will run away before any real work can be done. From the point of view of the general psychiatrist, however, this is the desired result.

Furst saw in the session preparations for making some kind of forward movement, e.g., giving up Rose and going out for fresh air; but this reaching out is immediately checked by confronting him with the same difficulties which caused him to go into the depression in the first place. So far these gestures are aborted; there is not enough energy behind them. The patient can neither relate to objects nor live without them. He gets bogged down and dies in the dream. The sleep is a withdrawal, because all else has failed.

Feder saw the sleepiness as a way of withdrawing from the realities prior to having to make a basic decision either to face life in a more realistic way or to disengage from the doctor. Bressler felt that all along the patient has been reaching out in a positive transference to the therapist, but, since he cannot accept the homosexual implications of such a relationship, he is, by sleeping, retreating to a state of narcissistic self supply. The sleep represents here a fellatio fantasy. The boy's need to escape from treatment under the influence of the drug may, from the point of view of the analyst, be an undesirable side effect.

Wednesday, October 11, 1961   It was agreed that A.B. would leave the hospital on the 13th. The decision occasioned a long discussion in which the youth's doubts and anxieties were brought up, as well as his sources of stability and strength, namely, returning to school and to work. The patient resolved to avoid his former neighborhood. He said he wanted to form new relationships so that he would not be "isolated by others." After more discussion on this point though, the patient admitted that, at the time, he was really isolating himself from his own feelings and hence the resulting feeling of emptiness. There was talk of the patient's anxiety. The presenting analyst commented that, although anxiety is not a very pleasant feeling, it is one that the patient can call his own, observing that, in one sense, the feeling of emptiness is designed to avoid feeling an intolerable degree of anxiety. The boy responded by saying that he had again been thinking about Sylvia, and he had concluded that she gave him up because he gave her nothing and wanted everything. The analyst, in preparation for the patient's new step, started him on Mellaril, 50 mgs a day.

Group Discussion

Ostow speculated on what the results might have been if, instead of a phenothiazine, the patient had instead been discharged with a mild sedative such as meprobamate or Valium. A discussion followed about the prescription of a phenothiazine to ease the patient's separation anxiety. Linn and Ostow suggested that, if separation generates anxiety and depression, a phenothiazine would intensify the feeling of depression by cutting access to reservoirs of energy. Bressler contended that, compared to other phenothiazines, Mellaril has little or no anti-depression arousal effect. Feder thought that Mellaril might exert such an effect.

Thursday, October 12, 1961   The analyst saw the patient briefly. A.B. said he had gone for a walk the day before, and felt he was being watched. He was anxious about leaving.

Friday, October 13, 1961   On the day of discharge, A.B. reported feeling "tense and jumpy." He had a dream about the patient on the ward who had stolen things in his room:

> He beat up this boy, and broke both of his arms. He tried to punch him, but found his own arms were limp. The offender had three friends with him, whom the patient beat up.

The only association to the dream was that the boy he beat up was himself.

Saturday, October 14, 1961   The analyst saw the patient in his office. The boy said he was quite tense and restless. He attributed his discomfort to having done too much. He had had a good talk with Rose, a frank talk, but he feared that the relationship was not ended. After the talk, he had felt increasingly anxious for several hours, until Tom had come to see him. (Tom had been discharged from the hospital a few days previously.) The patient felt that Tom was still suicidal, but had apparently looked into his suicidal impulses somewhat more intensely. A.B., then, referring to himself, said he was looking into himself, and he saw "nothing." He then asked why he could not use his angry feeling for doing something constructive. The analyst interpreted that, in talking about Tom's suicidal proclivity, the patient was simultaneously talking about himself. The youth reported that he had smoked marijuana with Tom, and that it had been "the wrong time to do it." He had lost track of time.

A.B. then told the analyst about a fellow he knew in high school, Fred. Fred was "a pathological liar and an idiot." He made a girl pregnant and married her. He reported a dream about Fred:

> He was somewhere in New Hampshire with Fred and his wife, at a club or a school. There was a hurricane or a tornado, and they were caught in it outside. It looked like a tornado, but more of a hurricane. There was a storm shelter, but the patient did not know where it was. They stayed in a place where they felt it was calm, the calm of the hurricane. No harm came to the patient or to Fred. The patient was playing ping-pong with Fred. There were bundles on the table, left there by those seeking shelter from the storm. The patient was beating Fred four to one when the storm or something interrupted them. Fred was going to night school, and so was the patient. As a sideline, Fred was stealing radios from Cadillacs at the club, and selling them to some man. There were many Cadillacs at the club, and Fred would tear out the radios and straighten them with a pair of pliers. He had a second job which had something to do with fishing. Fred and his girlfriend were doing this job together. The fish would go into one end of a long net or bag, which was then rolled up. This net was about eighty inches long, and it resembled a long condom, i.e., it had a sort of cylindrical shape. Little fish were swimming into it.

A.B. added that he did not know Fred's girlfriend, and that there was some confusion between hurricane and tornado. The calm of the hurricane meant that he was in the eye of the hurricane, which gives a false sense of security. The analyst thought that the patient was referring to some real country club.

A.B. spoke more of his increased anxiety in the outside world, which recently looked larger to him. He expected to begin work on Monday, and he was thinking of taking an apartment with Stanley, his friend on the ward. He had seen Ruth, the girl patient on the ward, the night before, and decided to continue the relationship with her rather than with Rose. The analyst reminded the youth of his previous resolution to avoid his disorganized friends, which seemed already to be undone. He encouraged the patient to look at himself more straightforwardly, and gave him a prescription for Elavil and Mellaril.

Group Discussion

In reference to the eye of the hurricane, Ostow reminded the group of the patient's previous interest in eyes. Roose gave the following interpretation. With Fred there is the question of stealing vs. fishing. Another dichotomy is the hospital vs. the hurricane. Perhaps the hospital is the eye of the hurricane, with its false sense of security. But, if the hurricane is really a tornado, then the eye is really the point of maximum danger. There is risk involved in getting out of the eye of the hurricane, but perhaps less risk than in staying in the middle of a tornado. Feder wondered whether the hurricane might be a reaction to the Stelazine. Ostow disagreed and mentioned that, in the spring before he became ill, the patient had a dream of a storm passing over him. The choice of calm vs. storm might represent the patient's own choice in terms of his psychic position: the calm is what happens to the schizophrenic after he detaches. The storm is his great anger and fury which develops when he tries to resume object relations. Roose felt that with this patient the storm dream seems to be a constant repetitive dream. He thought specifically of the incident in the hospital when the boy took marijuana and then admitted that he was preoccupied with suicidal ideas.

To Feder the dream suggested a primal scene motif; the eye is the place where one is secure, but it is also the observer's position. The violence is merely being observed. Perhaps it is a reflection of the day's events for the patient, or a fantasy about the doctor in the primal scene. Roose said that the patient had always had his eye on his mother; he had sneaked into the doctor's office to ascertain the identity of her lover, thus, in fantasy, recreating the primal scene.

Monday, October 16, 1961   The patient did not appear for his session.

Wednesday, October 18, 1961   A.B. reported that he had been at work for two days, and had been assigned a fair amount of interesting work. On this day his interest seemed to be slackening, and he felt more depressed. He had called his sister and had lunch with her. When questioned by the analyst, he admitted that he was taking the medication irregularly; he was taking it in the morning and at night. In between he would forget, or he would take the day's Elavil all in one dose. He was slipping back. He had been seeing Ruth in the hospital. He had also seen Jo (a girl he met during his first hospitalization) twice "for sex only," that is, without any emotional contact. He had given up the idea of the apartment with Stanley. He admitted that he had taken an LSD trip in the hospital with Stanley at the beginning of his hospitalization. The drawings which he had refused to show the doctor (and finally did show him many months later, at the termination of his treatment) were really drawings made under the influence of the LSD. Stanley's trip had been a bad one. The patient did not believe he was on a trip until he saw Stanley's trip going bad. The patient had spoken to Jo, who is schizophrenic. He claimed that schizophrenics see more than normal people do; their world is more interesting because it has a sense of timelessness. He had begun to speak about timelessness to Jo, and she seemed to understand what he was trying to get at. Everything was going on at once.

The rest of the session was very confused, fragmented, and difficult to follow. Because the past is like the present, the patient said, he remained the same. He feared he could not be anything. His IQ of 120 was "not enough" (though the boy did not appear anxious saying this). Again the patient talked about the temptation to slip back. The choice was between Rose and Jo, who, in her confusion, demanded nothing of him.

Friday, October 20, 1961   The patient came to his session late, and said he did not know why he had decided to come. He was "locked up in a theory," trying to explain his behavior. Again he referred to the timelessness in which everything is happening at once. "The future is important." "Timelessness is common in schizophrenia." He was also convinced of the validity of ESP. He had discussed his theories and thoughts on timelessness with Jo.

He was no longer interested in his work: he was more interested in working out answers to these theoretical formulations of his problems.

Monday, October 23 and Wednesday, October 25, 1961 The patient did not come to his sessions.

Friday, October 27, 1961 A.B. arrived on time, and reported that he had been dreaming about Sylvia. When asked about his absences, the boy responded that he did not want to come. On Monday he was "too busy to come," and on Wednesday he felt "too shitty to come." He felt less "busy" and "shitty" today. The doctor asked about the medication; the patient said he was taking it regularly. He stated that he needed people, and then discussed the idea of taking an apartment alone. Primarily he wanted an apartment to escape living with his parents. He reported that he was getting on well with his sister, and that she would help him look for an apartment. He had no trouble sleeping. The analyst pointed out to the patient that, though taking an apartment would relieve the distresses of living with his parents, it might increase his feeling of isolation. The doctor and patient had both agreed that isolation is a defense against the patient's fear of closeness, and that, to the patient, both closeness and isolation generate anxiety. The youth added that he was trying to keep away from his old neighborhood.

In response to the doctor's questions, A.B. said that he was having sexual relations with Jo. The analyst used this statement as an opportunity to remind the patient of his perpetual search for physical closeness without emotional contact. The doctor further pointed out the patient's simultaneous desire for closeness and fear of closeness to the analyst. The patient responded by telling the doctor the following dream:

He had a fight with Syliva's husband. He did not feel the husband's blows, but he was cut up; his punches were harmless.

The association to this dream was another dream:

He had a fight with Sylvia herself.

The boy then said he had borrowed a few dollars from his sister to buy a tennis racket. When asked why, he said just because he wanted it. The analyst told the patient that he seemed to be settling down to his old behavior in which he would take what he wanted immediately and pay the piper later.

November and December 1961   Through November and December, A.B. continued to come to see the analyst irregularly. By the middle of December there were more absences than visits.

Treatment was terminated in February 1962. The patient saw another therapist briefly over the winter, and came back to the presenting analyst for a few visits in April. The analyst, though not sure, doubted that the medication was being taken regularly, if at all. In retrospect, the analyst felt that the primary difficulty was this patient's fear of closeness. On a superficial level this was a fear of the homosexual implications of a relationship with the analyst, and on a deeper level it was a fear of eating and of being eaten.

Group Discussion

Feder speculated that the course of the treatment reached a peak, or crisis, at about the time the patient took the LSD trip, and it began to go downhill after that. Perhaps the patient chose to take the trip because he was beginning to feel threatened by the course of the treatment, and that after the trip he gradually withdrew from the entire treatment situation.

Linn felt that a major difficulty may have been the unrealistic plan of discharging the patient from the hospital. A boy who had so little control of himself in an in-patient setting would have very little chance of controlling himself better on the outside. Such a patient would probably have done better in long-term care in a more controlled environment. Perhaps indeed the acting out should be interpreted as a request for long-term treatment. A stay for perhaps two years at an appropriate clinic, even without medication, might have brought about the desired changes.

The analyst said the patient clearly wanted long term care, but he requested it, not to control his threatening impulses, but to be taken care of like his sister. Because the hospital stay did very little for the patient, it is unclear whether or not the patient should have been hospitalized at all. Unfortunately many decisions in favor of hospitalization are based, to a large extent, on the therapist's anxiety for the welfare of an impulsive patient, and on pressure from the family rather than on what is optimal for the patient. The main argument for taking this youth out of the hospital was his work situation, the one fairly stable factor in his life, in which he was well regarded. Perhaps it was better to utilize and emphasize the few strengths that the patient had. The boy would probably have managed, by acting out, to have himself expelled from the hospital anyway, for the hospital stay also exacerbated his fear of passivity.

Feder wondered whether perhaps because of the use of drugs, doctors may now be feeling an unwarranted sense of security, and expecting too much from their patients. Ostow and Bressler agreed, Bressler adding that some doctors are even substituting drugs for a close relationship with the patient. Feder emphasized that the hospital staff has to be more sensitized to the effects of medication on a patient, and must learn to respond to these changes in the patient's condition. Too much may have been expected from this patient.

Ostow said that the case was disappointing because it did not afford the opportunity to see the day-by-day improvement from depression as a result of medication, though the course of the treatment could be observed up to the time of the patient's discharge from the hospital. At that point, the patient probably stopped taking the medication, and what was observed was a relapse. This case does bring up a number of interesting points that are important for understanding typical patterns of drug therapy. Before his hospitalization, the patient needed treatment, but kept the doctor at arm's length. Over the summer something happened: Sylvia left. The patient became so depressed, that the depression overcame his fear of the homosexual implications of the relationship to the doctor. He had to appeal for hospitalization and treatment. As soon as the patient began to feel better, he began to rebel against the transference relationship, and he took matters into his own hands. He treated himself to an LSD trip, and refused to obey rules and cooperate with the doctors and nurses. Then, as he began to feel well enough, probably as a result of the Elavil, he left the hospital, the medication, and the doctor completely, and reverted to the state which had existed before he became depressed. The description of the last months of treatment sounds very much like the treatment before the hospitalization. The hospital experience brought the patient back to the equilibrium he had before in which he would use other people but not get close to anyone. Ostow reported that he had had similar experiences in which, as soon as a drug relieves the acuteness of depression, the patient abandons all treatment, including the drug, leaving no opportunity to observe the optimal effects of the use of drugs in psychotherapy.

This pattern of drug treatment is beneficial from the point of view of a public health psychiatrist, whose goal is to get as many acutely disabled patients out of the hospitals and off the rolls of the clinics as soon as possible. However, from the point of view of someone committed to achieving an optimal level of functioning for the individual, it is hardly satisfactory. For the long run, the importance of the hospitalization consisted mostly of the opportunity it afforded this patient to resume object relations, now with a new group of companions. Judging from the effects of the negative transference that developed after his discharge, had the patient remained in the hospital, he might have become increasingly rebellious and difficult to handle in an in-patient setting as well.

Postcript

September 29, 1962   A.B. called the presenting analyst for the first time in several months, and asked to see him as soon as possible. A meeting was arranged at which the youth told the doctor that his friend Tom had attempted suicide. Tom had been discharged from the hospital the previous autumn, just a few days before the termination of A.B.'s own hospitalization, and had been living in a rented room downtown. He was not working at the time. A.B. had maintained frequent contact with Tom, and one night he called Tom and received no response. He then telephoned his father who informed him of Tom's death.

The analyst asked A.B. about his own circumstances, and the boy reported that he had left his job at which he was earning $90 a week and was now working at one of the city's more successful realty agencies for $8,000 a year.

October 1, 1962   A.B. again called the analyst, and reported that he was still terribly upset about Tom's suicide attempt. Moreover, the night before he had had a nightmare that he wanted to discuss with the doctor. The reporting analyst replied that he was, at that moment, unable to make a specific appointment, and he asked the boy to call again later in the day to arrange a meeting. A.B. did not call back. The analyst did not hear from him again until

August 1963   A.B. sought out the analyst at his summer home. He told the analyst that he was in treatment with a therapist that his mother had selected for him, who was not prescribing any medication. The youth was still working in realty and seemed to be doing well. He accused his former doctor of having abandoned him, and of not having done enough for him.

EDITOR'S NOTE. This is far from an ideal case for studying the psychodynamics associated with drug therapy. First, the patient took the prescribed medication irregularly. Second, he used marijuana and LSD during the time that he was being treated, including the period of this report. Third, the influence of individual medication was obscured by adding a second medication to the first before it was clear that the first had achieved its characteristic effect, and then adding a third.

Finally, in reviewing the case, one does not get the impression that this is a true melancholic depression, but rather is one of an anxious, embarrassed, and miserable response of an adolescent who was too fearful to meet conventional expectations. If this had been a case of melancholic depression, it would not have responded so readily to external influences, there would have been a greater concern with coenaesthestic (general body) sensations, and there would have been the usual vegetative signs.

I do not believe that it is possible from this case to draw any valid inferences about psychodynamics and drug therapy.

The case is valuable however primarily as a demonstration of how the psychoanalytic psychiatrist tries to solve a clinical problem: looking for cause and effect relations; looking for early antecedents of the current situation; looking for intrapsychic as well as interpersonal conflicts; administering medication only as one element in a general treatment plan; looking for the effect of the medication not only in the influence on specific "target symptoms," but in the influence on the total psychodynamic pattern.

And yet the material demonstrates how resistant this type of problem is. What the presenting analyst saw toward the end of this episode was that, in such cases, one must think in terms of several years of therapeutic care and not hope for significant changes in personality function within shorter periods. This case is probably also representative in demonstrating that drug therapy has relatively little to offer in the management of personality disorder.

CASE 2

Introduction

Born in 1939, C.D. was a youthful-looking, Jewish, college student when he was first seen by the presenting analyst in October 1958. He came to the doctor with the complaint of "nervousness," and described periods of extreme anxiety at school, particularly when he was called upon to recite or to go to the blackboard. He recalled several occasions in his childhood when he was overcome with stage fright in school plays and was unable to utter a word. In particular C.D. remembered an incident from his fourteenth year, when a classmate informed him that a certain girl in the class liked him. For a moment he was quite excited, since he had a crush on this girl, but he then found that, although previously he had been able to converse with this girl in a friendly manner, he suddenly could no longer face her or exchange even a word with her.

During the academic year 1957-1958, C.D. had studied accounting at an out-of-town college. His presenting complaints, however, became increasingly severe and limiting to the point that he had to consider leaving school. Instead of dropping out, however, he returned to the city where his family was living where he could obtain intensive psychiatric treatment, and he transferred to a local university. Despite the change in his situation, C.D's symptoms persisted unabated.

Background

C.D. was born in Montreal, Canada, and spent the first seventeen years of his life there. He was the middle of three children. He had a sister, two years his senior, who suffered a post-partum psychosis similar in its course to the youth's own illness, and a brother, four years younger, who showed no signs of psychic disorder.

C.D.'s father was a successful businessman who had emigrated in his youth from Europe to Canada. The patient spoke of him as a man completely dedicated to business and to making money. He had little time for his family, and when he was at home, the atmosphere was usually fraught with tension. In particular, the youth recalled frequent altercations between his parents, with violent outbursts of temper on the part of his father. The patient could not remember a time when he was not in mortal fear of his father.

C.D. described his mother as devoted and overprotective. She apparently turned to her children for the love and intimacy which she could not obtain from her husband. Though she was very close to and friendly with the patient's sister, Phyllis, C.D. himself was her avowed favorite. At an early age he became her confidant, to whom she turned with her various complaints and dissatisfactions with her husband. By emphasizing the father's frugality, his outbursts of temper, and lack of warmth and understanding, the youth's mother openly encouraged her son to grow up to be exactly the opposite of his father. She specifically instructed the children to be polite, cordial, refined, and friendly in a reserved manner. In this way she, in fact, encouraged C.D. to behave like his older sister. And, as though in repayment for her son's confidence, loyalty, and obedience, the mother was unable to refuse any of his demands. She gave him (and the other two children as well) many gifts which she knew her husband would not approve. Then, in order to avoid the father's anger, she, in effect, seduced the patient into a conspiracy against him, in which either the purchase would be kept secret, or its price would be reported incorrectly to the father.

The patient spent a great deal of time with his sister, especially during the first six years of his life. In fact he did not remember having any friends outside the house at that time, because his mother felt that "none of the other children were good enough." Instead, he was urged by his mother to love his sister above all others, and, when the time would come for him to get married, to marry someone as similar to his sister as possible.

In 1956, approximately two years before C.D. came into analysis, Phyllis (who had been married about a year at the time), gave birth to a child, and subsequently suffered a post-partum psychosis. Despite intensive therapy and several hospitalizations, she had, at the time of the report, achieved only a partial remission. The patient had little to say about his brother. Although he reported that they squabbled as children, during the course of C.D.'s analysis, the two were on friendly, though not particularly intimate terms. In contrast to C.D.'s timidity, the brother was outgoing, and apparently doing quite well.

Despite his mother's overprotectiveness, and the isolation which she imposed on him, the patient remembered his pre-school years spent in his home and at his maternal grandfather's, as quite happy. C.D. suffered acute separation anxiety, however, when the time came for him to begin school. He cried bitterly, and was extremely fearful. He felt that his mother was casting him out into a strange world where he would be in imminent and constant danger of an attack against which he could not defend himself. The boy could not forgive his mother for insisting that he go to school. He felt that she did not really understand or appreciate his feelings in the matter, for, if she had, she would never have insisted.

At school, C.D. was a good student, despite examination and recitation anxieties. When he was confronted with these uncomfortable feelings, he would appeal to his mother, often exaggerating his helplessness with the conscious intent of eliciting reassurance from her, and he always succeeded. His mother would respond by encouraging him to do as well as he could, and to remember that, no matter how poorly he performed, his mother would "take care of everything."

Though C.D. made friends at school, he always felt different from the other boys, who could indulge in horseplay, fighting, and active sports, while he felt weak, timid, and vulnerable to attack. He was quite self-conscious, and was occasionally teased about his feminine features. This feeling of being different from others, weak, and timid persisted until he began treatment.

The patient's manifest sexual history, as recalled during the course of the analysis, is as follows: C.D. began anal masturbation in his ninth or tenth year, occasionally inserting toothbrushes, and later, enema tips, into his rectum, with considerable enjoyment.

When he was about eleven years old, he discovered that he could obtain pleasure by manipulating his penis, but he was unable to achieve any real satisfaction because "there was no hole big enough to really stick something in there." As a result, C.D. resumed anal masturbation, which he continued to age thirteen, when schoolmates introduced him to phallic masturbation, which he has continued to date. C.D.'s masturbation invariably generated guilt. He believed that, by looking at him, people could tell whether he had masturbated recently. The patient's masturbation fantasies, undisguisedly incestuous, referred to his mother and/or sister.

When C.D. was fourteen, he was molested by a homosexual in a crowded subway. The stranger took C.D.'s hand and placed it on his own genitalia. Paralyzed with fear and shame, C.D. could not withdraw his hand. He later remembered this, his only homosexual contact, as one of the most humiliating episodes in his life. At about age fifteen, the youth began occasionally to visit houses of prostitution. His enjoyment was minimal, and the visits ceased after a prostitute remarked to him that his penis was particularly short.

At this time, C.D. dated schoolgirls occasionally, but with no sexual interest. During his last year in Canada (age 16-17), he "went around with Jean, but we were like brothers." When C.D. was seventeen, the family left Canada and moved to Europe. Half an hour before the boat was to leave, the patient impulsively telephoned Jean, and told her that he loved her. When he arrived in Europe, he received a letter from her in which she reciprocated his declaration of love. As a result of this letter, C.D. became panic-stricken and did not continue the correspondence. The family spent a year in Europe, where the youth functioned fairly well, despite his social and school-related anxieties. When C.D. was eighteen years old, the family came to the United States, and the youth began to study at an out-of-state college.

Course of Treatment: October 1958-March 1960

The treatment, which began as a classical analysis, progressed satisfactorily for the first year and a half. From the beginning, the work centered on the patient's passivity. In the second analytic session, C.D. brought the first dream:

I come here and you hypnotize me.

This passivity was seen by the analyst as highly overdetermined. On the most superficial level it represented a compliance with his mother's demands and expectations of him. Her admonitions to him to be kind and refined, like his sister, came to represent both the price she demanded of him for her love and favoritism, and the protection she offered him against his father's rages. To make this compliance more acceptable to her son, the mother tacitly promised to endow him with a phallus when he would grow up. This promise took the form of frequent suggestions that, if he would follow her advice and behave accordingly, he would grow up to be "the kind of man women really love," as opposed to his father, who was not loved.

On another level, C.D.'s passivity was seen as a result of an early seduction by his sister. This interpretation was reconstructed primarily from dreams such as the following:

1. I am standing on a street corner in Montreal, passionately kissing my friend's sister. She is the girl I always respected, but who wasn't sexy. I walk away, but she clings to me.

2. I meet a girl whom I knew years ago. This girl had a reputation for being loose, but was married at the time of the dream. I begin to pet with her, and then we make an appointment to meet at a hotel to have intercourse. At the time I appear at the hotel, but she is not there.

As hinted in the second dream, another consequence of this early seduction by Phyllis was C.D.'s fear of females as castrators. This fear was reinforced by fantasies which the boy entertained following his grandfather's death. C.D. was convinced that his mother had killed his grandfather, because the latter was her rival for the boy's love. His mother thus took away from him the one man with whom he could safely identify.

C.D.'s passivity was also understood by the analyst as a defense against his fear of castration, and, specifically, his great fear of his father's wrath. On a conscious level the patient was afraid that his father would find out about his extremely intimate relationship with his mother. The mother herself encouraged this conspiratorial intimacy by her admonitions to her son not to tell his father anything, but to be as quiet and polite as possible in his presence "so as not to get him excited." The boy's social anxiety in the presence of men and his difficulties at school, when called upon to recite, seemed to result from this fear (i.e., father will see, father will know). Moreover, the patient's guilt toward his father led him to interpret his father's rages as a standing threat to him not to dare to grow up, to become a man, and to defy him.

On a deeper level yet, passivity represented to C.D. his love for his father and the wish to submit to him. This last interpretation was worked through only partially in the analysis, and only with the greatest difficulty. The patient revealed this longing for his father primarily through expressions of his great disappointment in the latter for not befriending him and not serving as an object with whom he could identify. With great emotion, and tears, the youth recalled an incident from his childhood when his father took him swimming, and hoisted him on his shoulders, and "walked all around the pool so that everyone could see."

All of the trends described above were reflected in the transference relation. The patient sometimes saw the analyst as a mother who would take care of everything (that is, cure him, or endow him with a phallus) if only he would comply with the doctor's requirements. At other times the analyst was feared as a father who was eager to learn about the youth's oedipal transgressions, and, having discovered them, would castrate him.

Crisis I

Meprobamate Crisis

By March 1960, approximately eighteen months after beginning therapy with the presenting analyst, C.D.'s anxiety in school and in social situations had diminished considerably. With trepidation he resumed correspondence with his old girl friend Jean, and she responded very warmly. The patient's mother, to his surprise, encouraged the renewed relation, and even took it upon herself, with her son's permission, to invite Jean to visit. The invitation to Jean was reported to the analyst as a fait accompli. Although the analyst had indicated no disapproval of the youth's resumption of the correspondence, he told the group that, at that time, he felt that C.D. was not ready to approach the girl in person, and that, had he known the mother was planning to extend the invitation, he would have discouraged it.

The analyst's understanding of this incident was that the patient's mother, who was a true matriarch, and who made the important decisions for the family, must have believed that what her son really needed was a woman, and that settling him down in a marriage would solve his problems. The reporting analyst mentioned that such unilateral initiatives on the part of the boy's family interfered on several occasions with the course of C.D.'s treatment. The analyst felt that this family was generally suspicious of doctors; although on many occasions it appealed to doctors for help, it persisted in second guessing them.

Once it was clear that Jean was coming, the analyst felt he had to prepare C.D. for the visit. If overwhelming anxiety made it impossible for the boy to function well during the visit, it would be a severe setback to him, even more than for most patients.

Monday, April 4, 1960   In anticipation of Jean's visit, C.D. became extremely anxious. He told the analyst, "I will not be able to be with her in the same room with my parents." The anxiety was seen as primarily oedipal: the patient felt that his interest in Jean constituted a betrayal of his mother, who wanted him to remain her good little boy. Moreover, by openly showing interest in a woman, he would be defying his father. The patient reacted to these oedipal threats by regressing to a passive homosexual position, which eliminated the heterosexual conflict, and also offered him the possibility of gaining potency from the homosexual object. An illustration of this regressive strategy can be found in a dream reported in this session:

I go to a homosexual brothel where a male prostitute sticks his large, erect penis (which is bigger than mine) between my legs, so that it protrudes in front, and appears as though it were my penis.

This regression to a homosexual and anaclitic position reintroduced into the analytic work the problem of C.D.'s passivity, which he attempted to resolve by withdrawing from all objects—"I never loved anybody, I can't love anybody, and nobody loves me."

Monday, April 11, 1960   Because C.D.'s anxiety threatened to ruin what the analyst considered a favorable development, in anticipation of Jean's expected arrival on April 12, the doctor prescribed meprobamate, 400 mgs, three times a day. The drug served to reduce the level of the boy's anxiety to the point where he could show affection for Jean, at least when he was alone with her. By the time she left, after a visit of a little over two weeks, the two young people considered themselves unofficially engaged.

Group Discussion of the Prescription of Meprobamate

The group first compared meprobamate to other similar medications. Linn noted that meprobamate is a more dangerous medication than barbiturates, especially in the event of an overdose. In response to a question by Ostow, Winkelman said he felt that meprobamate is more effective than tybamate.

Feder remarked that Valium, especially when given intravenously, or over a long period of time, can impair coordination, and generally does not offer enough advantages over Librium to warrant its use. Ostow, on the other hand, had the impression that Valium is less toxic than Librium. He reported that one patient of his, an alcoholic, occasionally takes 60 mgs of Valium at a time and shows no toxic effects. Noy, who visited the group at this meeting, reported that Valium was being used for the first time in Israel, and seemed to be effective in reducing simple neurotic anxiety. No toxic effects were noted in a patient who was given 120 mgs of Valium a day. Feder felt that Librium acts different qualitatively when administered in larger doses than in smaller doses.

The discussion then turned to the prescription of meprobamate as it related to the patient's dynamic state. In answer to a question posed by Feder, the presenting analyst explained that for a patient who, when faced with anxiety, would become explosively angry rather than withdraw, he probably would have prescribed another drug. Feder then brought to the attention of the group Irwin's concept of "target function"* as an alternative to "target symptom." This concept implies that not only the symptom, but also the likely response of a patient to that symptom (whether he will fight or retreat), should be a consideration in the physician's choice of a drug. Meprobamate, for example, is said to inhibit the avoidance response.

Ostow remarked that the notion of "target function" raises the more general question of whether, in prescribing a drug, the doctor should aim at the particular manifestation of the patient's dynamic state, or at the basis for this state. If, for example, an individual, as a result of retreating from object relations, becomes anxious because of a separation, the physician could prescribe an anti-anxiety drug to help the patient handle his anxiety. At the same time he might also want to consider prescribing an anti-depression drug, if it is depression that precipitated the withdrawal. In this way one can work with both the symptom and the causative state.

Furst brought up the case of a patient trying to deal with tendencies to withdraw. Such an individual may reach out to a homosexual object and then panic when he realizes what he is doing, or he may retreat from all object relations. Furst stated that the analyst, in his use of medication, can influence the patient's choice.

Linn emphasized the countertransference element in the reaction of the presenting analyst to Jean's visit. The analyst seemed to be both approving and encouraging the relationship. Linn added that, had the medication not been available, the physician would have had to exploit his analytic tools maximally to prepare the patient for the visit. The possibility of relying on chemical agents has the potential effect of diluting the rigorousness of the psychoanalytic work. Roose commented that the mother's intervention in her son's relationship with his girl friend is a good illustration of how patients' families often, in their own acting out, interfere with and undermine the course of psychotherapy.

---

*Samuel Irwin, "A Rational Framework for the Development, Evaluation and Use of Psychoactive Drugs," 'American J. Psychiatry' 124:8 (February, 1968 supplement), pp. 1-19.

Crisis II

Nardil Crisis

Spring 1960   C.D.'s engagement, albeit unofficial, plunged him into a conflict in which his obligation to Jean was opposed by his loyalty to his mother and sister. Moreover, the patient still felt that to love a woman was an implicit challenge to his father, and was therefore a very dangerous enterprise. The boy recalled that in his childhood, he could not tolerate any affectionate gesture from his mother in his father's presence, and he generally took great pains to present himself to his father as someone who was not a rival.

Jean's visit also precipitated in the youth memories of his earlier seduction by his sister. Although he recalled no sex play with Phyllis in their childhood, during puberty and adolescence he remembered being invited into her room when she was scantily dressed. He recalled taking pictures of her lightly clad, and later masturbating while looking at the photographs.

The new relationship moreover revived in the boy's mind his brief adolescent affair with the family maid. This involvement was terminated when, after a few contacts, the maid told the boy that she had never before been unfaithful to her husband. As a result of this announcement, C.D. was overcome with guilt, and was unable to approach the maid again. In relating this incident to the analyst, the patient emphasized the maid's fear lest the two be discovered by the boy's mother, and the guilt and fear he experienced when the woman mentioned her husband. The doctor sensed in the youth a sincere regret that, although he had had intercourse with the maid several times, the relationship did not work out. The analyst also reminded the group that this affair occurred at about the time that the patient first began to feel that his penis was too small. This feeling was later to become for him an *idée fixe.*

Finally, C.D. became concerned because Jean and his mother seemed to like each other and were quite friendly. The youth understood the friendship to mean that he might ultimately have to deal with two mothers. He felt that would be too much.

End of June 1960   C.D. reported to the presenting analyst that he and Jean had decided to marry in March of the following year. The analyst confronted the youth with the problematic aspects of his having simply announced the decision to the doctor, without ever having discussed the possibility of marriage in the analystic sessions, or even having made clear that marriage in the near future was a real possibility. The analyst interpreted this pattern of behavior as a repetition of the youth's relationship to his mother. C.D. would commonly undertake a commitment or challenge, even if he was fairly certain that there might be aspects of it that he could not handle, because he was convinced that his mother would take care of everything he could not deal with. Indeed, when questioned by the doctor, C.D. admitted almost consciously thinking, regarding his plans to marry Jean, that he would set the wedding date and then the analyst would somehow see to it that by the time that date came around he would be in shape to marry.

End of July 1960   By the third week in July, C.D. started to become increasingly anxious, phobic, and convinced that he was utterly impotent and incapable of marrying Jean. He knew that he could not go through with the wedding, but at the same time he rejected the analyst's advice to postpone it. Instead, he attempted in every way to alienate his fiancée. Moreover, C.D.'s inability to face the dangers of heterosexuality in turn reawakened his passive wishes, and he began to speak of the easier times when he was his mother's "good little boy."

Alternating with these periods of passivity were times when C.D. would become restless and would demand that the doctor supply him with the courage and the potency to marry Jean. This homosexual regression, however, brought its own attendant dangers, and left as a solution only a total withdrawal from object relations. The youth would then claim that "I never really loved anyone." The inadequacies and dangers of the passive heterosexual, the homosexual, and the withdrawn stances, as solutions to C.D.'s problems, precipitated in him a depression with suicidal thoughts, and the next months were characterized by little or no analytic work. Rather, the patient remained irritable and angry with the analyst, for putting him in such an uncomfortable situation, and he frequently threatened to terminate the analysis if no immediate cure was forthcoming.

In his behavior at this time, C.D. literally regressed to being a little boy. He could not remember when his analytic hours were, and he came late to them. He became apologetic, bashful, and ashamed, and he claimed that he could not be expected to take responsibility for anything, and that he would be protected, and have all his needs taken care of by his parents. Moreover the youth, when he was feeling particularly depressed, would assert that, in his present state, neither the analysis nor anything else could help him.

The doctor interpreted this behavior to mean that he was demanding to have his anaclitic needs supplied. He tried to work with this interpretation analytically, but to no avail. The patient became more depressed as his demands went unfulfilled. When the analyst openly doubted that the patient would be able to face a wedding in March, C.D. insisted that he could not break his engagement. He stated that to cancel the wedding would represent a great humiliation, not so much to him as to Jean, for in Montreal, a broken engagement is a serious blot on a girl's reputation. Because, he claimed, he could not break the engagement, C.D. began to develop the fantasy of planning to go ahead with his marriage, and then committing suicide the day before the wedding.

July 24, 1960   To halt the deterioration of the patient's condition, the physician prescribed Nardil 15 mgs, three times a day.

Group Discussion of the Prescription of Nardil

The reporting analyst explained to the group that, although he had some qualms about prescribing the drug at this point because he was about to leave for a six-week vacation, and would thus have trouble with follow up and supervision of the medication, he felt that the debilitating effects of the youth's depression warranted drug intervention. The analyst had not chosen Parnate because Parnate had been prescribed for C.D.'s sister. The doctor assumed that C.D. would tell his family which drug he was taking, and that the family also knew what had been prescribed for Phyllis. The analyst felt it was important that the patient, at this time, did not consider himself to be as sick as his sister, and therefore tried to avoid any measures that might strengthen his identification with her.

Feder brought to the attention of the group Marks and Pare's book* which includes the suggestion that there can often be found inborn, genetic similarities in depressions of various patients. Specifically, depressed children and parents sometimes have similar responses to the same drugs.

Feder felt that, perhaps, more important than chemical similarities would be the identification of members of a family with each other. Linn confirmed this opinion, and gave an example of a male patient who had a severe unconscious homosexual problem. This man panicked when he was given a prescription for the same anti-depression agent that his wife was taking.

Furst remarked that fostering identification with a family member can, under certain circumstances, have a beneficial effect. He cited cases in which patients demanded the same medication that they knew was helping other members of their family. Ostow reported cases in which members of the same bloodline responded similarly to various anti-depression agents. The analyst in the group who had treated Phyllis mentioned that both she and her brother held up well for quite a while on large doses of anti-depression agents, and that both ultimately relapsed despite the large doses.

Noy, in response to a question by Ostow, remarked that in Israel no difference had been noted in responses of Sephardic and Ashkenazi Jews to drugs. He felt that a more important problem is the reluctance of patients with certain cultural backgrounds to take the drugs regularly over a long period of time.

August 1960   Analyst's vacation.

September 5, 1960   The physician returned from his vacation, and found C.D. feeling better, though the youth informed the doctor that he had not been taking the drug. He said he had taken it for a week, found that it did not help much, and stopped. The analyst remarked that, in retrospect, the patient had good reason for discontinuing the medication, for part of his conflict was

*John Marks and C.M.B. Pare, *The Scientific Basis of Drug Therapy in Psychiatry.* Oxford and New York: Pergamon, 1950.

eliminated by the absence of the analyst. When the analyst was away, C.D. no longer felt torn between his relationship to the doctor and the need to commit himself to a heterosexual object, and the opposition between the youth's ties to his family and to the analyst, likewise, became less immediate. Indeed, throughout his course of treatment with the reporting analyst, C.D., although he needed the doctor a great deal, seemed to feel more comfortable when the doctor was away.

During the month of September, however, C.D. became increasingly anxious and increasingly depressed. He experienced great anxiety, in the presence of men particularly. The analyst attributed the anxiety to his fantasy that he would eventually be killed by men, or castrated by his father for taking a woman. The analyst again expressed his doubts that the patient would be in shape to marry by March, and C.D. again responded by saying that to cancel or to postpone the marriage would be a great social disgrace. To alleviate this recurrence of depression, the analyst directed the patient to resume the medication.

Group Discussion

Winkelman made the point, and Ostow agreed, that the patient's failure to follow instructions concerning the administration of medication, should be analyzed like any other event in the transference. Linn felt that the patient might have interpreted the introduction of the drug at this point as the analyst's sanction of the marriage.

Saturday, December 10, 1960   Jean arrived from Montreal. She planned to remain in town until the wedding, and C.D. was able to meet her at the airport without too much difficulty.

Friday, December 23, 1960   Although C.D. had been taking Nardil for eighteen days, no therapeutic effect was evident; rather, his condition seemed to be deteriorating. The patient reported that on several occasions he had tried to have intercourse with his fiancée, but was unable to penetrate. At this time Jean was actively demanding that he perform sexually. The two would go to motels where they could be alone and he could study. She would lie down on the bed, and he would begin to read. Every so often, when he felt up to it, he would make an attempt, which she would welcome openly.

C.D. insisted that he could not find the vaginal orifice, and that his penis was too small. His inability to perform heterosexually, moreover, caused him shame and anxiety. He felt that if the situation continued, he would probably have to "back out of the marriage," and Jean now was beginning to make comments indicating that her enthusiasm was waning. Again he sensed that he was in a bind from which he could neither proceed nor retreat.

As his depression intensified, C.D. became increasingly demanding toward the analyst. He would state: "I want to know what I can expect," and thus demand a guarantee by the doctor that he would be cured by a certain date. He also became more hostile and less cooperative in his relationship with the analyst. For example, the patient, who was now in his last year of college, forgot several times to bring in his school schedule so that a schedule of analytic hours could be worked out. The doctor interpreted this forgetting not only as an expression of aggression toward the analyst, but also as a demonstration that he was really a little boy who could not be depended on to manage by himself.

In addition to his anaclitic demands and the hostile dependence described above, C.D. now, for the first time, refused to lie on the couch. Previously, lying on the couch was never questioned, except, occasionally, when he would become excited the patient would, with the analyst's permission, sit on the couch. At about this time, the youth also began to skip some of his analytic sessions.

Saturday, December 24, 1960   During this session C.D. again sat on the couch. The material he recounted dealt mostly with his childhood, when he loved his mother and was loved by her. The youth spoke at length of his alienation from his father, his fear of his father's rage, and his guilt about his incestuous relation with his mother. He also elaborated on how he used to flirt with his father, hide from the father his romance with his mother, and reassure himself, through behaving like a little boy, that he was not his father's rival. When his mother would encourage alienation from father by disparaging her husband to her son, and encouraging him to emulate his sister, the boy identified with her completely, never protesting her disparagement of his father. The patient felt that, in a sense, his mother would feed him to the father to placate the father's wrath, for example, by insisting that he go through with the marriage. With great bitterness, C.D. reported that his mother, to this day, frequently made the double slip of calling him "daughter" and calling Jean "son."

It was also during this hour that C.D. spoke very feelingly, and literally wept, about his warm relationship with his maternal grandfather, who died when he was eight years old. His grandfather was the only relative who loved him as he was, without putting a price on his love, or demanding a surrender of the boy's masculinity. The youth claimed that, since his grandfather's death, "I have not been myself. I have to cover myself with a shield from the world. I fool people into thinking I am like everyone else, but I am an empty shell." He then wept some more, and recalled something from years back—he did not know whether it was a dream or a fantasy:

> I am a very little boy, and I am in an envelope. This envelope is inside a bigger envelope. On top I can see my mother's face. It is a very large face looming over the envelope. She is dropping down little crumbs or bits of food to me, very little. They gave me very little, there was practically nothing; they took it away . . . they took it all away.

Although when questioned, the patient said he did not know what "they took away," when the analyst suggested to him that it was his grandfather, the boy wept more, and said "Yes, you are right."

The youth then told the analyst that, when his grandfather died, he at first refused to accept the fact of the grandfather's death, and insisted that his mother "shake him and wake him up." Moreover, he became furious when his mother arranged for the grandfather to be buried, since then he could not possibly wake up and live again. Indeed, the boy was convinced that when his mother realized how much her son was attached to his grandfather, she killed the latter, because she felt that the grandfather was her rival.

The patient ended the analytic hour in anger. He said: "I have come here long enough and talked enough. Now you must do something," and he left the doctor's office feeling very upset.

The Presenting Analyst's Interpretation of the Session

The presenting analyst felt that this sudden torrent of material was the patient's defense against an impending psychosis. The youth feared that he was becoming detached, and tried to protect himself against detachment by mastering intellectually his preoccupations and the important events in his life.

C.D.'s sitting on the couch referred to his seeing the analyst now, as the phallic mother who was demanding submission. By sitting, rather than lying on the couch, the patient was refusing to submit. The youth had expected the doctor to take care of everything for him, as his mother had done in his childhood. In effect he had submitted to both the doctor and his mother, and neither was now endowing him with the long-awaited phallus, or making it possible for him to go through with the wedding. In his anger and disappointment, he was turning violently on the objects upon whom he had depended. It became clear to the analyst that, in the patient's childhood too, if his mother would not take care of something for him, or if she was slow to do it, he would become quite difficult with her, and there were times when he was a stubborn, nasty little boy.

Group Discussion

The member of the group who had treated Phyllis added to the account that she too remembered the grandfather's death as a particularly tragic event in the family, and one that represented a personal deprivation for her. Ostow commented that it is unusual for a patient who is feeling so hostile and uncooperative to produce so much material. Patients, who feel as C.D. seemed to be feeling then, are generally impatient with analytic interest in the past, and do not give much information.

Linn suggested that, in producing this material which deals with the mother as destroyer, the patient was accusing the analyst of not rescuing him from the impending marriage, a fate worse than death. Feder felt, and Furst agreed, that the youth was appealing to the analyst for protection against his mother and his fiancée, who were both pushing him into the marriage. Although C.D. had objected to the analyst's suggestions that the marriage be postponed, his rejection of the doctor's recommendation may have been based on his greater fear of his mother. Ostow remarked further that, in talking about his grandfather, the youth may have been asking the analyst to be a good father like his grandfather, and to give him the courage to stand up to his mother.

Furst emphasized the patient's awe of his father who, he feared, would castrate him for marrying. C.D.'s analyst confirmed Furst's point, and added that this period marked the beginning of the youth's psychosis in that, while in truth his father approved of the marriage, in the patient's mind, the fantasy of his father's wrath at his son for defying him by openly taking a woman prevailed over the reality.

Furst suggested that perhaps the sudden torrent of past history represents an attempt on the part of the patient to recapitulate his life in order to be able to begin anew. The questions raised in the long monologue were always, who did what to him and who owed him what. Roose said that the youth was longing for a state of affairs in which nothing is demanded of him. Ostow suggested that in this context the envelope fantasy might represent burial in a grave. Furst and Linn thought that the little envelope inside the big one represented an intrauterine fantasy.

In prescribing medication for depression, Bressler emphasized, and Roose agreed, that there is always the danger of the patient's feeling that, in exchange for the medication, the therapist will expect to see signs of improvement which the patient cannot produce. Loomis added that, where a drug induces in the patient a feeling of improvement, the patient may interpret the recovery either as a liberation of his own potential, or as an extrinsic gift from the analyst. Roose pointed out that, if the invigoration is felt as extrinsic, then the patient may feel that it can be lost as easily as gained, and that he is therefore at the mercy of the analyst. The analyst added that when C.D. became angry, he would threaten to discontinue the medication if the cure was not forthcoming. Taking the drug was perhaps seen by the youth as a capitulation to his mother, who wanted him to remain impotent.

Ostow and Whitman felt that the approach of the marriage may have also elicited C.D.'s old separation anxiety; they likened the youth's current discomfort to the anxiety he had experienced when he first went off to school. Ostow summarized the discussion by calling attention to the theme of fear of marriage as a clinical phenomenon. Here the motivation for the marriage was the expectation of the parents, the expectations of the society in which the patient grew up, and his own self-esteem with respect to these expectations. The anxiety was created by the patient's oedipal guilt and fear of castration. The consequence of this conflict was clinging dependence with the demand for help, pessimism with the anticipation of failure, angry demands, and a drifting towards depression. Three modes of treatment of this situation were considered: first, manipulation of the situation, i.e., postponing the marriage; second, interpretation of the cause of the anxiety and/or of the angry response to it; and third, drug therapy to relieve the anxiety and/or to relieve the depressive tendency.

December 24, 1960, afternoon   One hour after his analytic session ended, C.D. returned to the doctor's office unannounced. Fortunately the doctor had a free hour then, and was able to see him. The patient stated that he had decided to kill himself. When the analyst asked why, the youth answered, "I have no place to go. I can't go ahead and marry Jean. I can't live at home. I can't live away from home." He then said that he had been thinking of suicide for the last two or three weeks, but that his determination had been considerably strengthened since his analytic session that morning. The doctor interpreted the patient's threat of suicide as, among other things, a reproach against him for not having taken better care of the boy.

The doctor recalled to the patient that his only predominantly affective production in the previous, very busy, hour was his assertion that the only person he felt really good with was his grandfather. The analyst wondered whether the sudden increase in the patient's urge to commit suicide represented a wish to rejoin the grandfather. C.D. neither accepted nor denied this interpretation. Instead, he replied: "I am empty. I have always been empty, and nothing will help."

On this day the analyst doubled the patient's dose of Nardil
to 30 mgs, three times a day, and C.D. at first refused the added
medication. But he then acquiesced, and added that he really did
not care anymore what happened. By the time this second hour
was over, C.D. was considerably calmer and not nearly as angry as
when he came, but he was still quite depressed—everything seemed
hopeless.

Group Discussion

Linn interpreted the youth's threat of suicide as a complaint
that the doctor was merely giving him pills and pushing him in the
same direction as everyone else. He felt, and Ostow agreed, that
the deterioration in the patient's condition was brought about by
the challenge of Jean's arrival. The analyst should have absolutely
prohibited the patient from committing himself to marry in March.
Winkelman and Furst considered the patient's feelings of inadequacy, hopelessness, emptiness, and lack of love as signs of classic
depression.

Loomis suggested that part of the patient's objection to lying
on the couch could be an increased sexual desire as a result of the
medication. The youth was finding that lying on the couch puts
him in a sexually vulnerable position. C.D.'s analyst confirmed
Loomis's suggestion, and added that he later learned that, in his
childhood, and even into adolescence, C.D. would creep into bed
with his mother in the early morning, and would rub up against
her, invariably from behind. She would lie on her side, and he
would lie behind her.

Ostow interpreted the patient's refusal to take any more
drugs as a disguised request for an increase in the medication. C.D.'s
analyst agreed, and added that, for this patient, the drug also represented the doctor's inadequacy, that is, the doctor was substituting the drug's therapeutic effect for his own.

Whitman suggested that, perhaps, because this was the first
time he tried to see the doctor during off hours, the patient may
have thought he had to use suicide as an excuse to see if the analyst
really cared enough about him to give him the extra hour. Linn
thought that the patient might have returned hoping to find the

doctor asleep in his bed, where he could crawl in and cling to him, as he was accustomed to doing with his mother. Furst said that, although the patient's reappearance might be overdetermined, primarily it represents a desperate attempt to force the analyst to rescue the boy from his own suicidal impulses.

Monday, December 26, 1960   C.D. recapitulated much of the material from the previous day. His stance toward the analyst was again one of demanding, and he emphasized particularly his feelings of emptiness.

Tuesday, December 27, 1960   The patient began the analytic hour by announcing: "I am a homosexual. I don't want Jean." During the first year of his analysis, C.D. had produced a great deal of very thinly disguised homosexual material, but he would not tolerate any attempt on the part of the analyst, no matter how subtle, to interpret it or to bring it into the analytic work. Recently, however, he had occasionally mentioned fears of being a homosexual, and now, for the first time, he began to identify as one.

The youth went on to describe how, when he would get on top of Jean to attempt intercourse, he would suddenly feel very heavy and lose all desire. The association to heaviness was "a big load on top," which was burial, especially his mother burying his grandfather and the fantasy that she buried him alive. He added to this other fantasies in which females smother males, "they cover them, they impose themselves on top and they bury them alive in lovemaking." The analyst understood this as a primal scene fantasy. C.D. further recalled that, though he had blamed his mother for his grandfather's death, his mother had in turn blamed the grandmother. Specifically his mother had spoken of her own mother (the grandfather's wife) as being stingy, selfish, not taking proper care of her husband, letting him work too hard, and starving him.

In this session it also came out that to C.D. the analyst's couch represented a coffin. To this idea he associated a dream of about nine months before.

I am lying on the floor, and a very large roach or bug is approaching me. The roach's back is shaped exactly like the

top of grandfather's coffin. I am terrified, and do not
know whether to stand up and try to kill the huge insect,
or to play dead and let it crawl over me.

In this state of indecision, the youth woke up in a panic, and
jumped up bolt-like in bed. This dream occurred for the first time
when C.D. resumed his correspondence with Jean, but before she
had been invited to New York.

The youth also remembered that, as a child, he used to play
sick deliberately and stay home from school, in order to get more
attention and love from his mother. He told the analyst what he
thought was a dream.

I am lying in bed and my mother is bending over me,
loving me.˙

The doctor commented to the patient that the dangers just alluded
to represent, not simply the fear that females smother males, but
also perhaps, a wish on his part to be smothered and engulfed by
his mother.

During this session the patient wept and talked a great deal;
he particularly gave the analyst the impression that he did not
want the analyst to respond. Because the doctor noticed increased
agitation in the patient and the beginning of dissociation in thinking, at the end of the hour he added, to the Nardil, Thorazine, 75
mgs a day.

Group Discussion

Whitman felt, and Furst agreed, that the material from this
session might reveal an hysterical psychosis. The hysterical elements are evident particularly in the patient's simultaneous
demanding and clinging, and in the dramatic way in which the
youth expressed his inability to perform sexually. From this point
of view C.D.'s opening declaration, "I am a homosexual," should
be seen as an hysterical remark, or a dramatic gesture, rather than
as a definitive statement. Ostow, by contrast, maintained that,
given that C.D. is a dramatic, histrionic type of individual, his fluc-
tuation between a clinging need for the doctor on the one hand,

and a rejection of any assistance on the other hand, should not be seen as very unusual, but could be considered merely manifestations of depressions as experienced by this type of person. Ostow further referred to the patient's rambling on, almost without stopping, as a kind of clinging by talking.

Group Discussion of the Effect of the Nardil to This Point

As Winkelman saw it, the patient was clearly falling apart: his ego had been shattered, he could not control his impulses, and he was begging for help. Perhaps the Nardil has been pushing him in this direction. MAOIs and other anti-depression drugs cannot help an individual master circumstances that are uncontrollable. Moreover, other distressing situations in which this patient had not taken medication, did not prove so debilitating to him. Feder observed that the capacity of a patient's ego to receive and to integrate certain impulses may be rendered inadequate under the influence of a drug. Winkelman emphasized that, for this patient, two independent forces are operating simultaneously; they are 1) the drug intervention, and 2) the impending marriage.

Ostow remarked that there were actually two relevant questions under consideration: first, is the drug having any perceptible effect on the patient at this point? and, second, how can one describe the change in the patient's condition in terms of metapsychology? Loomis felt that the drug was acting to increase drive availability and pressure. The youth was meeting the unpleasant situation and not liking it rather than withdrawing from it or denying it. He was facing more affect and anxiety than his ego could master. Loomis wondered whether, under these circumstances, reducing the Nardil or adding a phenothiazine would have been helpful.

Bressler said that he tended to prescribe tricyclic rather than MAOI drugs for patients who have schizoid or schizophrenia potential. He gave an example of a patient who was anxious and depressed, in whom MAOI drugs induced a tendency towards projection, and even a psychotic break. He has rarely observed such a tendency with tricyclic drugs. Feder mentioned that drug companies generally recommend MAOIs for neurotic depression.

Linn disagreed with Feder, and contended that tricyclic drugs can also induce a psychotic reaction in some patients; he cited two examples of psychotic reactions of patients on Elavil. Ostow agreed with Linn, and added that tricyclic drugs can also produce delirious reactions which rarely occur with MAOI and he described such a case. Bressler pointed out that an Elavil delirium resembles a belladonna delirium; it can be facilitated by the concurrent administration of anti-Parkinsonian drugs and phenothiazines, since all possess atropine-like qualities. This type of delirium tends to occur in warm weather. Linn added that aged patients are more susceptible to this reaction, and Ostow observed that this susceptibility can be found also in patients suffering from organic brain disease.

Bressler pointed out that it is important to distinguish between a biological or constitutional problem of making libidinal energy available, and a state in which, for some other reason, the ego cannot effectively utilize libido, and therefore, by repression, isolation, or distortion, alters a person's psychic condition. This patient, made desperate by the excessive drive produced by the Nardil, in stating "I am a homosexual," was pleading to the analyst for relief from his distress. Combined with all of C.D.'s other difficulties, the Nardil may have pushed him to a psychotic break. This situation should be seen as an ego deficit, rather than as a drive phenomenon. Whatever equilibrium the patient had set up for himself previously, in terms of how he would handle impulses towards men and women, was being upset to the point where it exceeded his ability to cope.

Winkelman observed that one component of ego deterioration is the regression from secondary to primary process thinking. An estimate of the relative prevalence of each would yield a measure of ego disintegration which could be correlated with drug dosage. A general discussion followed about whether agitation should be considered an indication of impairment of ego control. Winkelman believed that the drug was impairing ego function at this point, because the degree of ego deterioration seemed to exceed the amount one would expect from the youth's previous history.

Feder brought up the possibility of using MAOIs and tricyclic anti-depression agents together. Ostow remarked that, although they are used together in Europe, and he personally has found the combination helpful in the past, the official warnings against their combined use in this country leave the psychiatrist who does combine the two in a vulnerable position legally. Bressler cited two cases in which neither drug was effective separately though he was able to achieve therapeutic results with a combination of the two.

Feder contended that Nardil does not influence ego function. Roose and Feder saw the patient's agitation as a derivative of ego functioning, or rather as a sign that his ego was failing. Feder mentioned that both MAOIs and tricyclic drugs facilitate transmission. In the past, this patient, when faced with an overwhelming situation, has been able to withdraw either physically or psychologically. Suddenly, the Nardil was making it impossible for the patient to "shut down his nervous system" and withdrawing. Adding a phenothiazine to the present medication might help him to withdraw, and thus obtain a certain amount of tranquility.

Furst emphasized that, even before the introduction of the medication, the patient has had one way out of his bind, that is, postponement of the marriage, which he has rejected. Hence, the fundamental psychic movement observable in the youth is a regressive one in which he demands that other people resolve the situation for him. In other words, the refusal to withdraw clearly antedated the prescription of the drug. Feder disagreed with Furst, and argued that the patient could not consider postponing the wedding, because the Nardil prevented him from acknowledging his defeat and accepting assistance from the doctor. Drugs can often harm a patient by robbing him of his defenses.

At this point, Roose brought up for consideration the relationship of the dramatic deterioration of C.D.'s condition to the state of the transference. Perhaps one factor in the youth's psychic disintegration is his overwhelming rage toward the analyst. This rage is probably attributable to his suspicion of the analyst's chemical influence over him, that is, whether it is beneficial or malignant. Moreover, to regress to a passive relation to the doctor seems attractive to C.D., but also dangerous. Feder added that perhaps the patient was angry at the doctor because the doctor's drug prevented him from feeling peaceful and quiet.

Winkelman suggested thinking about the patient's condition in the framework of Festinger's theory of cognitive dissonance.* The boy expected help from the drug and did not obtain any: the discrepancy between the expectation of the drug and its actual yield increased his agitation.

Ostow felt that, up to this point, the drug has not in any way influenced C.D.'s condition. The patient became increasingly depressed and agitated as he met with repeated failure in his attempts to meet his fiancée's sexual challenge, and the wedding was drawing closer. The effect of the transference may have been helping the patient to some extent (Feder disagreed). Ostow considered the boy's most recent behavior as characteristic of what Ostow calls the third phase in the struggle against depression, namely, the phase of "angry repudiation." Ostow sees the struggle against depression, beginning when an individual unconsciously senses the inception of a tendency toward depression as a process with several stages.**

In the first phase of the struggle, the individual pursues sensual gratification in the form of sexual activities, gambling, or exciting, risky behavior. The second phase consists of anaclitic clinging to a parental object, and the third phase is angry repudiation. The manifestations of angry repudiation are: 1) anger and agitation, 2) defiance, 3) demands and complaints, 4) projection of the anger onto other people, 5) suicidal threats, and 6) incipient dissociative phenomena in thinking. Individuals predisposed to psychotic dissociation tend to become psychotic in the phase of angry repudiation.

This patient was caught in an ambivalent trap: he could neither marry nor renege; he could not leave home and he could not stay home. When the most recent deterioration started, C.D. was in the clinging phase. The clinging, however, produced no improvement, and the patient was disappointed. Although the major element in the patient's behavior at this time is angry repudiation (he was furious with the analyst and said in effect, "You are no good, you are not helping me and I in turn will no longer cooperate with you"), one can also see traces of the previous cling-

*Leon Festinger, *A Theory of Cognitive Dissonance.* New York: Harper & Row, 1957.

**Mortimer Ostow, *The Psychology of Melancholy.* New York: Harper & Row, 1970.

ing phase and precursors of the next stage of definitive depression. The residuals of the clinging phase are, first, that the patient continues to come to the analyst despite his anger, and second, his weeping. The manifestations of definitive depression are: 1) the suicidal tendency (which must be distinguished from suicidal threats that are mere displays of anger), 2) discouragement, and 3) the feeling of emptiness.

The discussion moved to the presenting analyst's interpretation of the abundance of material produced in the last sessions as an attempt by the patient to reconstruct intellectually, and thus reestablish his whole world, which was falling apart. Ostow commented that many psychotics, as they recover, feel an urgent need to understand what happened to them. Roose thought that this patient was reaching out to the doctor, and trying to rebuild the world with him. Furst said that the patient was proposing an answer to his problems, and wanted the doctor to reify this answer for him, so that together they could establish a new world. In this project the analyst was failing the youth in the same way his mother had failed him.

Friday, December 30, 1960   C.D. seemed less depressed, hopeless, and pessimistic about his future, and he was considerably less agitated. He even felt that, if his present condition would suffer no further setbacks, he would be able to go through with the wedding in March. The youth reported, however, that he was experiencing some facial, muscle, and hand twitching, and that he was quite sleepy much of the time. The doctor decreased the Thorazine to 50 mgs a day.

Group Discussion of the Prescription of Thorazine

Feder and Bressler thought that 75 mgs of Thorazine is probably too small a dose to account for such a dramatic amelioration of the patient's condition. Ostow proposed that, if the depression continues to recede on the same small dose of Thorazine, the improvement should be attributed to the Nardil. If, however, the improvement remains slight, it could be seen as a result of the Thorazine, which should achieve its maximum effect over the week-end.

Sunday, January 1, 1961   The analyst observed a definite drop in the patient's mood. The youth again elaborated on his feelings of emptiness and his fears of being homosexual, though this time he spoke with apathy rather than with agitation, and was clearly not as depressed and hopeless as he had felt the week before. In a rather firm tone of voice, C.D. repeated his demand that the doctor tell him when he would overcome his feeling of impotence. He then mentioned that he had "(done) well with Jean yesterday"—this statement referred, not to his sexual performance, but, rather, to the fact that, in her presence, he was not too anxious and erratic; instead, he behaved appropriately and in a friendly manner with both Jean and her brother-in-law (i.e., Jean's sister's husband).

There was a period, however, during the previous day when C.D. was alone with Phyllis's husband, and found that he could not look his brother-in-law in the eye. He suddenly felt weak and empty, and began to think that he was a homosexual. C.D. associated to this report that when he was alone with his father, he felt that he had to flirt with the father and act as though his father were his primary love object, and not his mother and sister.

The youth then spoke about sexual intercourse and how for him it seemed to imply the risk of being buried alive by the female. C.D. claimed that he could be potent only with a woman he does not love. He said:"If I love her, I don't want to do it; it will go down (i.e., the erection); I will come right away (premature ejaculation)."

Monday, January 2, 1961   C.D.'s mood was slightly better, and he was again somewhat optimistic. When the analyst made this observation openly, however, and questioned him about it, the youth responded that he did not want to talk, because if he would talk, his masculinity "will leak out." The patient remarked that he was occasionally trying to have intercourse with his fiancée, but he could do so only in a side position, for when either of them was on top, C.D. would be overwhelmed by his fears of burial. In the side to side position, however, the youth claimed he was unable to penetrate, partly because his penis was too small, and partly because he was feeling tired and sleepy much of the time.

Saturday, January 7, 1961   C.D. began his analytic hour by elaborating on his difficulty in relating to Jean, that is, by being close to her, he felt he was betraying his mother. He longed to return to his idyllic childhood with his mother, when he was her little child, neither potent nor even sexual. The reporting analyst told the group that it is to this state of being an asexual child that C.D. refers when he thinks of himself as a "homosexual."

During this same session, the youth remembered conscious childhood wishes not to grow up. He preferred to die rather than to grow a beard and a large penis, and in connection with this wish, he recounted a dream of two years previously.

> There are two coffins; one is mine and one is my mother's (I died as a little boy). My coffin is smaller: it is blue and it has a little window on top so I can see out.

When the analyst asked him about the window, it suddenly occurred to C.D. that the shape of the window on his coffin lid was exactly the shape of the windshield on his white Jaguar sports car, which his father had bought for him. C.D. added that he felt extremely self-conscious and hypocritical driving around in this car.

The analyst suggested to C.D. that perhaps the desire to die rather than grow up, had to do with the fact that, for him, growing up meant defying his father, and taking his mother, fantasies which provoked in him great feelings of guilt. The youth responded to this suggestion with a great deal of feeling; he elaborated on his guilt towards his father, whom he felt he had cuckolded all his life, by stealing his mother's love, and, on top of that, by taking his money.

In this session, for the first time, the patient spoke about how his father had let him down, by not befriending him, by not spending time with him, and by not serving as an object with whom he could identify. As a boy, C.D. used to encourage his father to spend time with him, but, in this enterprise, he was always unsuccessful. For example, on Sundays, he would ask his father to take him to the park; the father would say "Maybe," and then would disappoint him.

Group Discussion of the Patient's Improvement

The presenting analyst opened the discussion with some remarks on the current state of the youth's homosexual ambivalence. He emphasized to the group the implications for the transference of the homosexual anxiety reported by C.D. on Tuesday. When the patient cooperates in the analysis, he is actually flirting with the analyst, as he was accustomed to flirt with his father. This flirtation, however, causes the boy anxiety which can become intolerable, and can lead, in turn, to defiance in the form of refusal to lie down on the couch, or unreported discontinuation of the medication.

As to C.D.'s guilt toward his father, the analyst understood that what the boy was really taking from his father was the father's penis. For this patient to admit gratitude toward his father and the extent of his love for his father would threaten a breakthrough of homosexual wishes and impulses toward him.

Referring to the patient's accusation that his father denied him love, the analyst stated that, in fact, the father was quite temperamental, and wasted little time and attention on his family.

Furst and Ostow noticed that, with the beginning of his recovery from depression, the patient once more was attempting to deal with his sexual difficulties: specifically there was a push toward the object and an effort to deal with the fact that he still could not approach the object successfully. Furst added that, as the youth reached toward the object, he still expected the doctor to give him the required potency.

The dream of the two coffins reminded Ostow of the previously reported dream of two envelopes. Roose saw the small coffin as a little womb with a window, a male womb. He remarked further, and Furst agreed, that, with this patient, there are always two deeply contradictory facets to everything. The patient dreams of being incorporated by his father, and, at the same time talks about daring to oppose him. Indeed the strength to stand up to the father has to be gained passively from the father himself.

Roose suggested that, as the grandfather was in a coffin, the coffin dream may express a wish for rebirth in a masculine way through reunion with the grandfather. In response to Ostow's comparison of the coffin and envelope dreams, Roose felt that the important element in the dream was the archaic parental image; whether this was a mother or a father is less significant.

Furst observed that C.D. was accusing his father of giving him something, but not what he really needed. In buying his son a sports car, the father was endowing him with the *accoutrement*, but not with the real instrument with which to assert his manliness. The analyst likewise, in prescribing medication, offered the youth something, but did not supply C.D. with sufficient potency to master his sexual problems.

Feder and Ostow remarked that the patient's ego seems to have reconstituted: he was still ambivalent, but his ambivalence was more tolerable. Ostow emphasized the similarity of C.D.'s improvement to that of the first patient, A.B. Both youths, as they began to improve, were confronted once more with the same ambivalent problems. C.D. at this point could not resolve his sexual ambivalence, but he was able to acknowledge it, and see it as a problem. There was a general agreement that the patient was asking his father for sexual potency, but he was still demanding something oral from his mother. Previously he had identified with the oral position, and the oral position was ego-syntonic. At this point C.D. understood that he could not relate to women on a genital basis. He was asking the doctor to help him to rise above his oral fixation, to a genital level, in his heterosexual relations.

Discussion of the Effects of the Nardil and the Thorazine to This Point

Ostow suspected that the Thorazine had taken the edge off the patient's agitation, but one might have seen the same result without the drug. Bressler disagreed: he felt that the Thorazine not only alleviated the boy's agitation, but it also blunted his rage and hostility, and thus made him feel more comfortable with the analyst. He cited Hollister's report* that very angry, agitated, depressed patients often respond to phenothiazine tranquilizers alone without an accompanying anti-depression agent.

*L.E. Hollister, "Clinical Use of Psychotherapeutic Drugs: Current Status." *Clinical Pharmacology and Therapeutics* 10 (1969) pp. 170.

Regarding the youth's wishes not to grow up, i.e., the Peter Pan fantasy, Ostow suggested that C.D. was bringing up this material because the Nardil was forcing him to grow up and he was resisting. Roose proposed that the further evolution of the transference might indicate the role of drugs in the patient's improvement. Ostow mentioned that the transference had been deteriorating before the drug was given.

Bressler wondered about the implications of the youth's improvement for the transference. Specifically, was the patient feeling guilty about what he was receiving from the analyst? Ostow responded that this improvement is what C.D. had been expecting all along and had complained about not getting before. Ostow, Furst, and Bressler agreed, however, that, when the improvement did come, the youth became afraid, and a homosexual resistance developed.

Ostow characterized the discussion as an interchange on the influence of anti-depression drugs on the handling of ambivalence. In this patient, several changes were noted in the initial days of his recovery. First, with respect to heterosexual potency, C.D., so far, remained impotent, but became hopeful rather than hopeless. Second, the patient moved away from his mother towards his fiancée, but felt guilty as he did so. Third, the boy felt less dependent on his father and his analyst so that the homosexual threat was diminished. He also felt guilty about taking the father's, or the analyst's, gift while challenging him. Fourth, there was a reduction of primary process thinking and agitation, which might also be attributed to the phenothiazine. And, finally, the patient's psychosexual level rose from the oral to the phallic.

Linn added that, in his own experience in prescribing anti-depression agents for depressed patients with perverse symptoms, as the depression lifts, the perverse behavior or fantasy shifts in content, but the overall psychodynamic pattern remains the same, that is, the basic sexual stance of the patient in relation to the love object and the outside world does not shift. For C.D., too, as the depression lifted, his problem of gaining potency continued, but he perceived and approached the problem in a different manner.

Tuesday, January 10, 1961   C.D. was elated to the point of talking about *wanting* to go through with the wedding. Again he rejected the analyst's suggestion that the wedding be postponed.

Wednesday, January 11, 1961   The analyst observed a dramatic drop in the patient's feeling of well-being. C.D. wanted to call the wedding off; he stated that he could not love Jean, and the material he produced described his feeling that his mother really possessed him, and to betray her would be to lose his potency. The analyst, impressed by the youth's more marked tendency to withdraw, reduced his dose of Thorazine to 25 mgs a day.

Thursday, January 12, 1961   C.D.'s low mood continued; again he felt hopeless, and wished to call off the wedding. The doctor eliminated the Thorazine altogether.

Monday, January 16, 1961   C.D. reported that he was feeling better, and related his feeling of well-being to the fact that over the week-end he had successfully challenged his mother in a discussion. He said that during the previous week he had become depressed because his mother had called Jean a "vulgar girl," and, at the time, he felt powerless to contradict her or to defend his fiancée. Over the week-end, however, he confronted his mother with the matter, and demanded that she apologize both to him and to Jean, which she did.

Tuesday, January 17, 1961   C.D. described to the doctor his fear that, if he married Jean, he would be unable to work, because he would have to stay home and love her all the time. Work seemed to involve a homosexual threat which would render him impotent heterosexually. He expressed anger with the analyst for not having told him, on the previous day, whether or not he would be able to work once he was married. C.D. ended his session by stating that, because he could not both work and love, rather than break the engagement or postpone the marriage, he would kill himself shortly before the wedding. This state of hopelessness and anger with the analyst continued unchanged for four days.

Group Discussion

Furst and Ostow remarked that, as the depression lifted, the patient became remotivated, and again approached the problem of his inhibition with his fiancée, which again he could not master. This second failure pulled the youth back toward depression. Furst observed a deepening of the patient's depression and an increase in his hostile clinging and demands. He saw C.D.'s threat of suicide as an attempt to force the analyst to take care of everything for him as his mother had done in his childhood, and, more generally, as an effort to induce those around him to allow him both the advantages of manhood and the safety of remaining a child.

Monday, January 23, 1961   The analyst sensed an increase in C.D.'s anxiety and feeling of hopelessness. Although he denied that he was depressed, the boy blandly informed the doctor that he was planning to kill himself before his marriage. At this point the doctor insisted that the wedding be postponed. To relieve the onus of the shame that a confrontation with his fiancée over this matter would cause the patient, the analyst agreed to discuss the situation with C.D. and Jean together.

Tuesday, January 24, 1961   C.D. came with Jean to his analytic session, and the doctor spoke to them about the need to postpone the wedding. Although the analyst suggested that the wedding be postponed indefinitely, the couple agreed only to postpone it from March to June. Jean accepted the postponement with some reluctance.

Wednesday, January 25, 1961   C.D. told the doctor that plans were being made for the couple to fly back to Montreal to tell Jean's parents about the postponement.

During the period immediately following the decision to postpone the marriage, the patient developed a new symptom, which he called "ejaculation." Following urination, or, even more pronounced, following bearing down while defecating, a few drops of fluid would appear at the tip of his penis. At these times there would also be an irritation at the tip of his urethra: expelling fluid through it would relieve the irritation. C.D.'s associations to this symptom were that it drained him, it made him a weak, impotent, asexual child, and it relieved the feeling of "excitement at the tip of the penis." The production of this "ejaculate" after urination was most marked when the patient experienced anxiety connected with fear of castration. By diminishing his heterosexual drives, C.D. said, the "ejaculation" would relieve this castration anxiety. Most important, this symptom usually occurred when the youth was in the presence of other men; it never happened when he was alone with Jean.

C.D. often reported the following fantasy or dream:

My penis is like a hotdog roll which is split. My mother has a penis, and she approaches me and puts her penis into my penis. Her penis is the hotdog, my penis is the hotdog roll, and she puts it in.

Comments of the Presenting Analyst

The reporting analyst related this new symptom to C.D.'s anal erotic sensitivity; he reminded the group that the boy's masturbatory activity began with the introduction of various items into his anus. For this patient, the model of sexual excitement and activity is being penetrated.

Group Discussion

Klerman and Winkelman wondered whether this new symptom could be a side effect of the Nardil. Linn and Furst responded that they understood the "ejaculation" as part of a regression to a homosexual posture. Ostow asked, in reference to the patient's association of this symptom with being drained, whether C.D. found the symptom and the accompanying feeling disturbing. The presenting analyst thought that the youth was ambivalent about feeling drained, but that basically he was more comfortable in the depleted position. Loomis noted that the state of depletion is C.D.'s familiar stance. Feder suggested that the decision to postpone the wedding is consistent with the patient's depleted position, in the sense that he is now able to regress from manhood. Ostow commented that the patient's regressive state did not necessarily indicate depletion of libidinal energy.

Feder questioned the extent to which the medication was responsible for the patient's rising agitation and then calming. He thought that the Thorazine was unlikely to have played an important role, because it was not sustained for any length of time. Roose interpreted the patient's general retreat and the accompanying calming down as part of the anti-depression effect of the Nardil, which was then in its seventh week.

Klerman mentioned that evaluation of the effect of the drugs is complicated by the simultaneous decision to postpone the wedding. Furst felt that the drug and the wedding were both pushing the youth in the same direction, that is, towards objects: their combined action was too strong for the boy, and thus made him more and more uncomfortable. Ostow disagreed: he suggested that, by confronting him with the need to perform heterosexually, which the patient could not, the impending marriage was actually pushing C.D. to regress, while the drug was pushing him forward. Furst contended that the medication was also pushing the patient towards heterosexual performance, but, once relieved of the pressure of the marriage, he was able to regress, even with the continued drug dosage. Ostow noted that, whereas before the postponement of the marriage the patient was in a state of agitated depression, he was, at this point, discouraged, sad, and ashamed, but he was not agitated or clinically depressed.

Roose observed that the further the drug pushed the patient towards heterosexuality, the further he had to lean towards homosexuality. Once the pressure of the heterosexual stance was relieved, however, the patient was free to find his own way, and to settle down in an in-between position in which he was again oriented primarily toward his mother. This is probably the position in which he feels most comfortable. Ostow designated this position as presexual. He further pointed out that one can observe in this patient some of the same dynamics that were manifest in the last case where, likewise, a drug impelled a patient to confront his heterosexual problems and his transference problems before he was ready to work out a new solution. C.D. found himself in a trap situation. He was unable to marry and perform heterosexually, and ashamed to retreat. The clinical consequence of the trap was: dynamically, regression; clinically, depression; and behaviorally, a retreat to inactivity and suicide. The effect of the drug therapy was that it overcame the depression and thus forced the patient once more to confront the trap.

Furst added that, with this patient, the trap should be seen as three-sided. There is the heterosexual trap, the homosexual trap, and the pre-phallic trap. The patient would go from one to the other, and rest in the pre-phallic position, where he was drained of all phallic sensations and phallic urges. This state is symbolized by his symptom of "ejaculation."

End of January, 1961   In the weeks following the decision to postpone the marriage, C.D. gradually settled down to a state of tolerable depression on the same dosage of medication. He was at times, complaining, and, at times demanding, but, when he was not confronted with any particular social or sexual demand, he would occasionally feel quite good. At these times the transference would become particularly important, because the patient would have to deal with the fact that to acknowledge the doctor's responsibility for his improvement would imply an obligation to submit to his benefactor.

Monday, February 27, 1961   One month after the elimination of the Thorazine, C.D. reported, with considerable pride, that he was able to have intercourse with Jean for the first time.

Thursday, March 2, 1961   C.D. told the analyst that, especially during the past month, he had been feeling much better. He mentioned that once more he could talk to people, and particularly to men, without very much anxiety. Moreover, he felt he loved Jean more, and he had successfully attended a family gathering to celebrate his nephew's birthday, despite the fact that family gatherings were usually very difficult for him, because of the presence of many people to whom he felt he owed loyalty.

The youth attributed his recovery to the drug, and cited as evidence the extent of his improvement over a short period of time. The analyst challenged this statement, and the patient responded by admitting that the idea that he was changing was causing him to feel both happy and frightened. C.D. then spoke of feeling a persistent anxiety in connection with the need to perform sexually with his fiancée. He expressed a fear that he would not have a good erection, but then said he felt that this problem too would be resolved in time. As he put it: "It is as though I finally jumped into a swimming pool and started to swim and someone said 'Look, you have no life preserver on!' I get panicky."

Group Discussion

Klerman called attention to the patient's simile about swimming, and remarked on his oceanic feelings. Feder suggested that perhaps the boy at this point saw the analyst, not as a father who would attack him, but, rather, as a mother who was about to engulf him. Feder further noted the importance of the fact that the decision to postpone the wedding was seen by the patient, not as a failure on his part, but as a cooperative venture with the doctor. Furst felt that, on the contrary, the youth was glad to have the onus of postponing the marriage shifted to the doctor, but he continued to deny any failure on his part, and to expect the physician to repair the situation for him by the time of the new wedding date. Moreover, by attributing to the drug the responsibility for his recovery, the youth extricated himself from a potential conflict about his relationship to the man who postponed the marriage for him.

Ostow mentioned that, generally, the patient allows himself the option of deciding what was the effective element in a change of his condition, when more than one agent was operative. If, in the transference, he feels uncomfortable crediting the therapist with his improvement, he will ascribe it to the medication. If, on the other hand, he feels that the drug is a threat, he will attribute his improvement to the analysis, to the zodiac, or to any other convenient explanation. Ostow added that it would be humiliating for this patient to admit that he feels better for having been relieved of the sexual demand and challenge. Klerman speculated on the patient's possible reaction had he been offered a six-month moratorium on the marriage and continuation of the analysis without medication. After some discussion, the group agreed that it was only as a result of the drug that the boy agreed to the postponement.

Ostow wondered about the attitude of C.D.'s parents, and the role they might have played in his acceptance of the postponement. The reporting analyst responded that the parents continued, throughout, to insist the marriage would cure their son. Furst remarked that, by the time the analyst insisted on the postponement of the marriage, the patient had been taking the drug for seven weeks, had improved, and was relapsing once more. Feder commented, in reference to the analyst's limit-setting intervention, that there is a great difference between merely suggesting, and absolutely insisting, that the marriage be postponed; the drug action may be entirely different in these two settings. Loomis thought that, although on the drug, the patient had felt better and was already beginning to feel worse. Despite his uncomfortable feeling, the drug may have been bolstering the youth's judgment and capacity for self-criticism.

Ostow summarized the episode as a situation in which the young man was threatened by a heterosexual demand. He reacted by regressing: the primary manifestation of the regression was anxiety. The boy responded well to an anti-depression drug which permitted him, despite continuing anxiety, to go ahead with plans for his deferred marriage.

February 1961-May 1961   In these months C.D. continued to take 75 mgs of Nardil a day, and utilized his analytic hours to work through his various conflicts. During this period the presenting analyst noted particularly C.D.'s close association of passivity and passive wishes with depression. This association had several causes; first, for this patient, passive wishes involved the loss of his penis; second, he reacted to his passive longings with death wishes toward his castrating mother, which, in turn, generated considerable guilt; third, to C.D., passivity represented a very intense narcissistic mortification and loss of self-esteem; and finally, the youth defended himself against these passive wishes by withdrawing from objects, for example, "I can't love anyone, and I don't deserve to be loved."

The basically progressive course of the analysis was modified by moderately intense mood swings of one to three days' duration. These short reversals were usually provoked by environmental factors such as anxiety-laden social situations in which he did not perform well, inadequate sexual endeavors, and failures at school. Such setbacks, however, could invariably be handled without departing from classical psychoanalytic technique. and without any changes in the medication.

Beginning about three weeks before the wedding, the analyst observed a dramatic increase in the youth's anxiety. C.D. insisted that his anxiety centered exclusively on the need to go through with the wedding ceremony. Several times he repeated: "I am not afraid of *being* married; I am afraid of *getting* married." As during this period he was able to have intercourse with Jean, sexual performance was no longer a primary concern. More important was the need, during the ceremony, to demonstrate to the world that he was being a man and taking a woman. And this step involved separation anxiety regarding his mother, and castration in respect to his father. The wedding as such did not disturb the transference relationship because it was agreed that the analytic work would continue after the wedding.

During the last two weeks before the marriage, C.D. reported feeling anxiety concerning penetration. This anxiety was associated with claustrophobic fears, which were related to fantasies of being buried alive, and to *vagina dentata* fantasies. The youth associated to his current anxiety a memory from his seventh year.

> I was playing with one of my mother's tubular shaped hair curlers while defecating. The curlers had teeth on their inner surface. The neutral position of the clamp or curlers was closed, and the curlers could be held open only by depressing and holding a lever. Holding a curler open, I slipped it over my penis. My hand slipped, and the curler snapped shut, causing me anxiety, pain, and minor lacerations.

The patient was not depressed during this time, but he suffered considerable anxiety in anticipation of having to attend numerous pre-wedding functions, and, of course, the wedding itself. To help C.D. through these events, the analyst prescribed meprobamate, 400 mgs. The drug relieved the patient's discomfort considerably, partly through its pharmacologic action, and partly because it represented the doctor's approval, encouragement, and gift of a penis.

June-September 1961 The analyst attended the wedding, and reported that C.D., though nervous, actually handled the situation quite well. The marriage was followed by a prolonged honeymoon, which was a wedding present from C.D.'s father. The couple returned to New York, and the analysis was resumed in September.

Crisis III

First Psychotic Episode

January 1962 Jean missed her period, and C.D. suspected that she was pregnant. His reaction was a feeling of pride and also of moderate anxiety. The youth associated his anxiety with fear of a prospective child as a competitor, and, perhaps more important, with the fact that his wife's pregnancy would constitute undeniable evidence that he had had intercourse with her. At this point the patient's anxiety was manageable, and during that month the analysis went quite well as the young man began to feel increasingly proud of his anticipated fatherhood.

Saturday, February 3, 1962 The analyst decreased C.D.'s dose of Nardil from 90 to 60 mgs a day.

Thursday, February 8, 1962 C.D. appeared extremely upset, depressed, and hopeless. He stated, "I am a homosexual," and associated this statement with his wife's visit on the previous day to an obstetrician who confirmed her pregnancy.

Friday, February 9, 1962 In his analytic hour C.D. produced a great amount of narcissistic material. He described how, in his childhood, his mother had been quite verbal in her admiration of his physical appearance. Into his adolescence she proudly referred to the fact that he had less hair on his body than his sister, that his skin was fairer than hers, and that his hair was softer and curlier. He felt that much of the approval and admiration he received from people throughout his life was the result of his attractiveness, and he recalled several instances from his childhood when he gazed at himself in a full-length mirror, while naked, and became quite excited. On a number of these occasions he had an erection. The youth connected this memory with his wish to be a female with a penis.

Monday, February 12, 1962 C.D. seemed moderately depressed. He said that he felt tied to his mother, "She is holding me by the penis." He decided that he had never loved Jean, that he had deceived her, and he had deceived the analyst too. He wanted the doctor to cure him of his symptoms, but he wished to retain his mother's love.

Thursday, February 15, 1962 C.D.'s depression had intensified, and the regressive anaclitic clinging to his mother was more pronounced. The youth also began to withdraw from the doctor, and he commented on his inability to express any gratitude to the analyst for fear that appreciation of the doctor might necessitate love and loyalty to him.

Friday, February 16, 1962 The patient announced it was likely that he would terminate his analysis. He claimed that he knew the nature of his problems, and that it was now necessary for him to "go out and live." When the analyst doubted aloud the validity of this statement, as the cause for his leaving, C.D. described his loss of sexual desire for his wife: "I can't love Jean because I am not a man."

Saturday, February 17, 1962 C.D. telephoned the analyst in the morning, and requested an earlier analytic hour: the doctor explained that on that particular day he could not alter his schedule. When C.D. arrived, at his usual time, he appeared neither as upset nor as eager to see the analyst as he had sounded over the phone. He did not mention the call, but he began the hour by announcing that he was unworthy of his wife. He said that he now felt completely free of his mother, but that he was confused, since now he had no one to turn to. He then remarked that if he did not have faith in the analyst he would kill himself, and, at this point, he began to weep copiously. With much emotion, he related that when he was about three or four years old, he very much wished his father to befriend him, but his father did not respond, and did not respect him.

The analyst told C.D. that Jean's pregnancy made it necessary for him to give up his mother, that this need pushed him toward the doctor, and that he was caught between his wish to love and cling to the doctor, and a simultaneous need to withdraw from him. The doctor's inability to give the youth an earlier appointment that day had led him to expect disappointment from the analyst as he had experienced from his father.

Despite the boy's evident depressive relapse, the physician decided not to increase the anti-depression medication at this point, because he understood that C.D. was responding to the threat of depression with a highly ambivalent intensification of the transference, and with the production of much analytic material. He felt that both of these processes could still be handled by interpretation and by allowing the patient to cling to him.

Monday, February 19, 1962   C.D.'s clinical condition remained unchanged, and he continued to bring to the analysis new material which confirmed the doctor's interpretation of the previous day.

Thursday, February 22, 1962   C.D. was extremely anxious and depressed to the point of being unable to lie down on the couch. He spoke of feeling great despair, weakness, and inability to go on, and in connection with this feeling he related a dream of the previous night:

I am in a car with another doctor. I am behaving very strangely, as though I am about to break down and lose my mind. You (the analyst) tell the other doctor that you are surprised at this behavior. You approach the car, and I try to communicate with you once more, but you want

to give me a shot so that I will pass out. I desperately try
to avoid this.

The youth then elaborated on the similarity of his current anxiety
to that which he experienced when his mother forced him to go to
school for the first time. He tried desperately to convince his
mother of his inability to go to school—"to that strange, frightening place"—and begged her to allow him to remain at home with
her. He vaguely remembered being extremely frightened of his
father and not knowing why, and he spoke of his later disappointment in his mother when she did not fulfill her promise to him
that, if he obeyed her, he would grow up to be a better, more lov-
able man than his father.

The doctor told C.D. that he was anticipating castration by
his father (who was interchangeable with the analyst) for impreg-
nating his wife (who also represented his mother). He reconstructed
C.D.'s separation anxiety when he was sent to school, on that
basis, and the boy confirmed the interpretation. The doctor did not
interpret to the patient his identification with the unborn child
and the associated intrauterine primal scene fantasy.

February 23-March 1, 1962   During this period, C.D.'s
condition remained relatively stable, though the intensity of his
depression diminished somewhat. The material which the youth
brought up in the analytic hours explained his ambivalence toward
the analyst. It described the boy's childhood fear that his father
would learn about his "affair" with his mother and would kill
him, and his mother's urging him to "be nice" to his father,
that is, to behave affectionately and to flirt with him. His mother's
exhortations   thus   exacerbated   C.D.'s   repressed   homosexual
longing for his father, and his wish to replace his mother as his
father's love object.

March 2-April 8, 1962   These weeks were characterized
by a gradual improvement in C.D.'s mood and a marked dim-
inution of his anxiety. The analytic work involved an almost
continuous interpretation of the complex transference situation
in which the analyst assumed at different times the roles of
1) the phallic mother who demands loyalty, who loves, and

who castrates, 2) the father who castrates, 3) the father to whom he wished to submit, and 4) the father whose penis he wanted to steal.

Monday, April 9, 1962   Because the analyst had to be out of town that day, he cancelled the patient's hour.

Thursday, April 12, 1962   C.D. appeared distraught, somewhat confused, and very angry. He accused the analyst of not understanding him and of having harmed him, and he warned the analyst to arm himself, as over the week-end he had decided to kill the doctor. The youth then described episodes of dizziness and dissociation which he had experienced during the previous three days. He reported that he had felt his head was splitting in two and that he was two people, "a big, strong man, and a weak sissy." The patient attributed this frightening turn of events to the analyst's lack of foresight. Moreover he declared that he no longer trusted the analyst, and advised the doctor not to make any more interpretations.

Friday, April 13, 1962   C.D. again expressed a real wish to kill the analyst, and stated, with great fear, that he was "cracking up" and losing his mind. When the analyst attempted to elicit further material from him, the youth responded by warning the doctor not to try to "wash away" his responsibility for what had happened. The patient reported that two weeks previously he had read about "dual personality" in a textbook on abnormal psychology. He also mentioned that he was feeling extremely self-conscious and ashamed in the presence of his brother-in-law, and that he could no longer look his brother-in-law in the eye.

The analyst showed concern for the patient's welfare, but he made no interpretation, because, at this point, he could not determine specifically what had precipitated the psychotic episode. Rather, the physician increased the patient's daily dose of Nardil to 120 mgs, and attempted no other intervention. Toward the end of the hour the boy remarked:"You had better expect a few phone calls from me between today and tomorrow."

Saturday, April 14, 1962   C.D. remained extremely

disturbed, but he came for his analytic hour, and telephoned twice during the day.

Monday, April 16, 1962 Again the patient telephoned the analyst several times, before and after his hour. He still suffered some confusion, and he complained of occasional dizziness. His anger at the analyst, however, had diminished considerably, and was replaced by a demanding attitude towards the doctor accompanied by a great deal of self-pity and weeping.

Tuesday, April 17, 1962 C.D.'s condition had improved to the point where he apologized to the analyst for his recent behavior and for his accusations. He spontaneously began an attempt to account for the events of the past week, and he wondered aloud whether his recent "breakdown" would have any permanent effects. The analyst suggested that it would not.

Saturday, April 21, 1962 The patient's clinical state was, once more, as it had been before the acute episode. During this hour, C.D. produced material which dealt with his homosexual feelings for the analyst, which he associated with a wish to kill the doctor. Indeed, the youth confessed that conscious homosexual wishes toward the analyst had erupted over the week-end of his breakdown. The feelings were specifically: first, the analyst "kept me down" in the analysis, and, if the analyst would help him, C.D. would have to reciprocate with loyalty, love, and submission; and, second, that the analyst had become "too important in my life."

Saturday, April 28, 1962 The analyst reduced C.D.'s dose of Nardil to the previous level of 90 mgs per day.

Mid-May 1962 The presenting analyst discovered the precipitating factor in the psychotic episode. C.D.'s anxiety concerning his wife's pregnancy was augmented by his approaching graduation from college and the need to decide what to do after graduation. The two most obvious possibilities were for him to go into business with his father, or to seek employment as an accountant. Over the weekend, the patient and his wife had visited his wife's sister and her husband. They discussed C.D.'s future. The brother-in-law made a convincing argument for C.D. and Jean to return to Montreal, and for C.D. to practice his profession there. C.D. responded that he would not consider such a plan, but he refused to explain why. Finally, the brother-in-law wondered aloud whether C.D. was still seeing his analyst every day. The youth then became panic-stricken and immediately left and went home. At home, however, his anxiety was aggravated when his wife, who also wanted to return to Montreal, picked up where her brother-in-law had left off and harangued him about his dependence on the analyst.

June 1962   C.D. was graduated from college, and had a great deal of difficulty deciding what to do. He could have gone into his father's business, but that possibility posed problems, especially homosexual anxiety and fear that his father would dominate and suppress him. The youth was interviewed for many jobs, but found the interview situation highly uncomfortable. C.D. would tend to withdraw, to be cold, and to maintain a distance from the interviewer. If, however, the interviewer was friendly, the patient would experience anxiety connected with too much proximity. As C.D. himself described the situation, on first meeting, he was on the alert, and he experienced moderate anxiety. When he would become more familiar, somewhat at ease, and free to talk and to think, "I begin to feel weak, very passive, and I get the feeling that I am becoming part of the other person, that I am dissolving into him."

Late August 1962   The baby was born, one month premature.

November, 1962   Jean became, once again, available sexually, and C.D. began to complain of somatic symptoms: chest pains and skipped heartbeats. He also reported that, for the past two months, he had been occasionally skipping his medication, and that he was feeling more depressed. The patient attributed his somatic symptoms and his total loss of libido to the drug.

January 1963   After many interviews at a number of firms, C.D. found employment.

Group Discussion

Linn interpreted the patient's description of the dissolution of ego boundaries that he suffered in the interview situation as a passive homosexual issue; the youth actually felt that he was being penetrated by the interviewer. Furst suggested that the movement went both ways: the patient seemed to feel that he was both invading and being invaded. Roose emphasized how quickly C.D. would shift from the aggressive, masculine situation to the passive, homosexual position. Moreover the passive position may have been not merely a simple homosexual one where the good employer would take care of him, but the employer may also have been seen as a mother who was about to take him in and engulf him. Ostow commented that the discussion could be formulated as a debate over whether the breaking down of the patient's ego boundaries should be seen as a phallic or an oral phenomenon.

January-October 1963   At first, C.D. performed fairly well at his job, but he encountered the predictable problems: homosexual fears provoked by associating with co-workers, and conflicts between his feelings of loyalty to his superior on the one hand, and to his peers on the other. C.D. became preoccupied with his minor mistakes, and feared being watched. To alleviate the depression the young man was experiencing as a result of his difficulties functioning in this setting, the analyst increased his dose of Nardil from 60 mgs a day, to which it had been reduced, to 90.

The last job lasted ten months, during which time the patient suffered increasing anxiety. As his anxiety mounted, his work deteriorated. To some extent the deterioration in his performance consisted of the poor quality of his work, that is, he made mistakes but, more important, his output dwindled. In October 1963 he was dismissed.

October 1963-January 1964   After losing his job, C.D. made a series of attempts to procure a new position. He had the money to undertake an independent endeavor, but the prospect of negotiating with other people was too threatening. The patient therefore made several exploratory motions in that direction, but never pursued the idea seriously. The youth considered going into business with his brother-in-law, but that was also impossible, because the boy entertained homosexual wishes towards him too. The patient tried to work with his father, but that situation fell apart after three or four days. C.D. complained bitterly that his father was too domineering and treated him like a little boy, that is, his father shouted at him and gave him no decision-making power. The analyst understood that, underneath these complaints, what was involved was really the patient's fear of the homosexual posture, and of his passive wishes towards his father.

Crisis IV

Second Psychotic Episode

Mid-January 1964 Realizing that he could not hold a regular position, he could not work for his father, and he was afraid to start on his own, the patient was unoccupied, and the analyst began to see in him confusion concerning his identity (that is, whether he was a man or a woman) and a mild disorientation and denial of reality. This tendency increased during the last half of January.

Saturday, February 1, 1964 The patient experienced a dramatic decline in his self-esteem. The analyst later learned that this problem was aggravated by expressions of discontent with him, on the part of his wife, who began, directly and indirectly, to tell him that he was not a man. On the few occasions when the youth did attempt some kind of sexual approach, she, more often than not, rebuffed him.

Moreover, C.D. began to spend large amounts of his time and energy in ruminating; attempting to understand his problems and thus to alleviate his feeling of disorientation. Occasionally, he would feel he had suddenly realized exactly what was wrong with him and what had been wrong with him all his life. He would then begin to elaborate on this theory. Invariably, as he developed it, the explanation would either become repetitious and confused, or it would turn out to be a theme that had been talked about many times during the course of the analysis and that he understood, but would now repeat in a passionate and ritualistic way. Nevertheless, the patient persisted in his frantic pursuit and repetition of revelations which, he claimed, would "solve everything." He entertained a somatic delusion which related his ability to achieve insight to a membrane which fell off his brain and covered his eyes. This delusion was revealed only subsequently.

During this time there was a rapid intensification of the transference. C.D. seemed to feel that he must tell the analyst all his thoughts, but that he could not really do so because the thoughts were so numerous and involved, and because there was not enough time. At the same time, however, he began to come late to his analytic sessions, and occasionally to miss them. The analyst sensed in the boy the wish for a mother who would be completely devoted to him twenty-four hours a day.

Group Discussion

Linn saw the patient's alleged revelations as a premonitory psychotic symptom: the youth's superego was fusing with the analyst as ego ideal. Linn compared the boy's sudden insights to a mystical experience in which the achievement of understanding is associated with the fantasy of identification with God. Ostow agreed, and distinguished in the mystical experience two separate elements: first the mystical episode, or the abandonment of the real world in favor of a fantasy world, and, second, the shift in the sense of reality so that the false world becomes, for the subject, the real world and the pathogenic process serves as a restitutive process. Linn added that such a religious somatic delusion suggests a catatonic schizophrenic process with potential for either acute excitement or catatonic stupor. Roose mentioned a patient of his, who reported experiencing similar flashes of insight, but who also reported that these flashes literally fell over his eyes and were blinding.

Ostow did not think that somatic delusions by themselves could be considered reliable targets for medication. He stated that somatic delusions, as the basis for a delusional hypochondria (which is what occurred in this case), are usually found at the bottom of a schizophrenic depression. Sometimes, in a schizophrenic high, however, a patient will report delusions, but, at the same time, will indicate that he is not obsessed with these delusions. Such a patient is more likely to respond to a phenothiazine than to an anti-depression agent. Roose and Ostow agreed that the psychodynamic basis of the symptom, and not merely the symptom as such, should determine the treatment.

The Presenting Analyst's Interpretation
of the Delusions

The presenting analyst augmented the discussion by suggesting, on the basis of subsequent material, that the patient's insights were not premonitory, but were actually part of the psychotic process, though they could be described dynamically as attempts to hang on to reality. Months later the reporting analyst learned that behind the youth's need to intellectualize and reconstitute the world was the somatic delusion that the tissue on the top of his brain was peeling off, falling down in front of his eyes, and blinding him. When this tissue would peel off and fall from the top of his brain, it would allow the rest of his brain to disintegrate completely. C.D. imagined that his brain was fragile and the tissue held it together. When he would finally understand his problems, the tissue would return to the top of his head, and pull his brain together again.

Group Discussion

Roose and Ostow commented that the patient's delusion of a flap falling over his head suggests a return to the womb fantasy. Linn and Roose felt that the symptomatology of return to the mother's body, fusion, identification with God and the superego, is characteristic of mania, but the absence of euphoria is inconsistent with such a diagnosis. Feder said that the attempt to see through a veil may be a common fantasy based on the notion of the caul.

Ostow described the youth's condition as "paradoxical hypermotivation," which may appear as mania, but is really a defense against the onset of depression. In this state a tranquilizing drug might increase the patient's agitation at first, but if pressed hard and long enough would ultimately precipitate definitive depression. Roose noted that patients in this state of compulsive pursuit of insight often experience a disturbance in the sense of time. He felt that one could not predict whether, in this situation, a phenothiazine would influence the patient toward depression, toward detachment, or toward more intense object relations.

Monday, February 3, 1964   C.D. came for his morning
hour, but later in the evening he telephoned the analyst, and
requested to see him again immediately to explain some new
insights, lest they be lost over the week-end. The analyst could not
see the patient then, but talked with him over the phone for half
an hour. The boy spoke of his past, of his marriage, and of his difficulties with his brother-in-law, which involved both his homosexual problem and his incestuous feelings toward his sister. This
brother-in-law was the man who married his sister, Phyllis, about
whom the patient had many open and incestuous erotic fantasies.

Several years previously C.D. had gone to his brother-in-law
with the complaint that his penis was too small. The brother-in-
law took him to a doctor, and the doctor reassured him. Since
then he had thought of his brother-in-law as the man who knew
that he was castrated, and he could not look his brother-in-law in
the eye.

Friday, February 7, 1964   C.D.'s condition had not
changed. The youth informed the doctor that the analysis would
have to stop: the analyst must stop interpreting, and, instead,
must tell him immediately what his problem was and what he
could expect. In his demands, the patient was very insistent, confused, and agitated. The presenting analyst reminded the group
that C.D. had made this demand before, and that the analyst
understood the demand to mean that the patient felt intolerably
threatened by the homosexual aspects of the transference relationship. The doctor started the youth on 25 mgs of Thorazine in
addition to the 90 mgs of Nardil a day on which he was then being
maintained.

Beginning *February 8* the analyst observed a gradual diminu-
tion of C.D.'s agitation and psychotic ideation. By *February 20*
the patient's confusion, all the delusional attempts to understand
his life, and the agitation were completely gone. The analyst then
eliminated the Thorazine, but retained the patient's dose of Nardil.

Group Discussion

Linn though that the patient was being driven by the Nardil. The boy seemed to have a feeling that he was exploding from within; he was falling apart, and wanted some relief from the pressure. Furst argued that the attack may have been precipitated by the patient's job failure. Bressler suggested that C.D.'s daughter must have been about a year-and-a-half old at this time, old enough to walk and to make anxiety-provoking physical approaches to C.D. which in turn may have aroused old incestuous fantasies about his sister.

The presenting analyst confirmed that the patient at that time did mention that he was having difficulty with his daughter; he said he wanted to be close and affectionate with her, but that these urges would provoke incestuous feelings that he was seducing her. The analyst felt, however, that the patient's primary problem, at this point, was that he had failed in the job situation, and was finding himself incapable of moving in any direction except towards the analyst. He could tolerate closeness to the analyst only up to this point.

Roose cautioned restraint on the part of an analyst dealing with a patient in this condition, for any attempt at intervention by the doctor might provoke in the patient a homosexual panic. The reporting analyst acknowledged that C.D. was then in just such a state. He would frequently tell the doctor: "Don't say a word, because anything you say will always be your attempt to wash away your guilt." The analyst understood this statement to mean that, by talking to him, the analyst was, in effect, seducing the patient. This seduction was the source of the analyst's guilt.

Linn suggested that the patient was beginning to sound homicidal. The presenting analyst confirmed this observation, and told the group that at this time, the patient once appeared unannounced at the analyst's house, and insisted on seeing the doctor immediately. He then stated that he was going to get a gun to kill the analyst, and had come to warn the doctor to arm himself.

Feder and Ostow observed that this is one situation in which the only change in the therapy is the introduction of a new drug. The other variables in the boy's situation and treatment remained the same. Loomis particularly was surprised that the prescription of Thorazine did not increase C.D.'s agitation and attachment to the doctor. Bressler thought that, under these circumstances, Thorazine was preferable to Mellaril, because the sedative effect of Thorazine allows the patient to regress: specifically, it allowed this patient to receive care from the doctor without being homosexually destroyed. Feder commented on the importance for this patient, again in this crisis, of the opportunity for sanctioned regression. Linn agreed, and added that he would have preferred to allow C.D. to regress by hospitalizing him.

There was some general discussion about the value of hospitalizing a patient in such an agitated state, as opposed to treating him on an out-patient basis. Ostow mentioned that he tries to see such a patient every day, seven days a week, and to maintain frequent telephone contact. Roose remarked that the offer of frequent, round-the-clock contact is enough to bolster many such patients, and to prevent them from going into a panic. Linn and Bressler brought up the possibility of retaining an auxiliary therapist to help the doctor provide such services. Bressler said that he employs psychiatric nurses who work in the hospital, but are responsible only to him and his patients.

Ostow concluded, and the group agreed, that this crisis should be seen as a paranoid episode that was alleviated by increasing the patient's dose of anti-depression medication.

February and March 1964   C.D. remained at home, and continued to take 90 mgs of Nardil a day. He was supposedly reviewing and studying his profession. He wanted to find a job, but he felt that, as a result of his recent troubles, he had forgotten a great deal. He would now sit down and review everything "and really learn it," so that when he would go job hunting, he would make a good impression.

Crisis V

Third Psychotic Episode

April 1964   By April, C.D.'s condition had begun once more to deteriorate, as it became more and more obvious that he was staying home in order to avoid the anxiety of looking for a job. His wife was becoming increasingly intolerant of him. He reported that she rejected him sexually, and the doctor observed that his self-esteem was falling. At this time the youth was feeling moderately depressed and depleted, and, to a certain extent, denied what was happening to him. The analyst warned the patient of his accelerating deterioration, and of the need for some action, lest his marriage be irreparably damaged.

April 20-30, 1964   C.D. was becoming more depressed. The analyst noted a marked increase of tension, and much more complaining.

Friday, May 1, 1964   C.D.'s behavior suggested the beginning of another psychotic episode, similar to the one he had suffered on February 1. The analyst noticed in the patient the beginning of psychotic ideation, another compulsive attempt to intellectualize his problems, and renewed suspicion of the doctor. The analyst immediately started the patient again on Thorazine, 75 mgs a day.

Saturday-Monday, May 2-4, 1964   The presenting analyst saw a gradual build-up in the youth's confusion, pseudo-insights, and hostility toward the doctor. The patient seemed to have experienced a definite break with reality, and he was convinced that he now, for the first time, understood everything about himself and his life.

Tuesday, May 5, 1964   C.D. appeared acutely psychotic and extremely agitated. He insisted on standing up during his analytic hour, and he talked in one long stream. The young man literally lectured the analyst with very great emotion and animation, but he was quite confused, and had difficulty following his own train of thought. Toward the end of the hour, the boy broke into violent, uncontrolled sobbing. He was then standing near the radiator in the analyst's office, and, at one point, he slammed down with his hands on the radiator cover with all his might.
   Toward the end of the hour, when the patient had calmed down somewhat, the analyst asked him whether he had been taking the Thorazine as prescribed. C.D. responded that he had, but that he wanted to discuss this situation: he had decided that from then

on he would take the Thorazine only on the condition that the Nardil be discontinued. He would only take one drug from the analyst, though he did not care which. The analyst suspected that, despite his declaration to the contrary, C.D. had not been taking the Thorazine.

Friday-Monday, May 8-10, 1964   The youth did not come to his analytic hour, but, instead, he called the analyst each day, about five minutes after the hour should have begun, and tried to conduct the session over the telephone. In these telephone calls, the patient intellectualized further, and accused the analyst of having never understood him. Specifically, C.D. berated the doctor for having forced him into a passive role to keep him impotent, as his mother had done before.

Monday evening, May 11, 1964   C.D. telephoned the analyst from a drugstore, admitted that he had taken the Thorazine for only two days (i.e., on May 7 and May 8), and requested that the analyst instruct the pharmacist to dispense some Thorazine to him. The doctor told the druggist to dispense the Thorazine, and ordered the patient to take 100 mgs, three times a day.

Group Discussion

The reporting analyst emphasized to the group that, up to this point, it was never clear to him whether the patient was taking the Thorazine, and if so, how much. At this time the doctor began to maintain frequent contact with the patient's wife. He asked her whether C.D. was taking the medication, and she was also not sure, but had the impression that he took the drug erratically.

Feder commented that the youth may have been trying to combat his inner emptiness by identifying with the doctor. This identification, or introjection, in turn aggravated C.D.'s basic homosexual fear, which caused him to reject both the analyst and the medication. The patient has been following a course of alternately introjecting and expelling the doctor. Furst added that, from this perspective, the patient's interacting with the analyst over the telephone should be seen as a compromise. Loomis suggested that C.D., in addition to alternating the acts of taking and rejecting the medication, may have been alternately activating and suppressing his memory of when he took the drug.

Ostow commented that, while the patient was identifying with the analyst, it was a hostile identification, whose purpose was to dispense with the object relation. The youth was identifying with the doctor in order not to have to deal with him as another person. Roose emphasized that, although, at this point the boy could not bring himself to visit the analyst, he was maintaining contact by telephone. Linn interpreted the telephone call from the drugstore to mean that the patient was momentarily feeling positively towards the doctor, and was willing to follow his orders.

Ostow remarked that, sometimes, when a patient cannot be relied on to take his medication as prescribed, or even to report accurately whether or not he is taking it, the analyst can attempt to enlist the aid of the family in checking up on the medication. Klerman mentioned that, while medication can be administered intramuscularly to some patients who cannot be relied on to take it orally, in this case the possible transference effects of injecting a drug into a patient with such strong homosexual fears can be dangerous. Furst and Linn thought that when a patient is already quite psychotic, the difference between swallowing the medication and receiving it as an injection is less important. Ostow and Klerman responded that, perhaps, more important than the patient's immediate reaction to the administration of the medication is that subsequent dealing with the patient might be complicated by lending an air of erotization to the transference fantasy of being penetrated. Furst and Linn thought that, in terms of the patient's fantasies, the difference between injection and incorporation by swallowing are minimal, especially when reality testing is as severely compromised as it was with this patient in this episode.

Tuesday-Wednesday, May 12-13, 1964   The analyst observed a gradual decrease in C.D.'s agitation. The patient came to his analytic hour these two days, though he still complained that the doctor did not understand him and that the analysis was a mistake. Moreover, C.D. informed the doctor that his sister, Phyllis, who had previously been hospitalized for a post-partum psychosis, was becoming concerned about him, and had suggested to the family that the doctor who was then seeing her be called in for a consultation. The youth added that he had delayed reporting his sister's suggestion to the analyst for fear of offending him. The physician interpreted that, once again, C.D. was torn between his ties to his family and loyalty to the doctor.

Friday-Tuesday, May 15-19, 1964   C.D.'s agitation continued to ebb, giving way to a definite depressive trend. The psychotic ideation and the attempt to understand everything persisted, but decreased in their importance to the youth, while his complaints to the analyst (mostly that the analyst forced him to submit) increased in frequency and significance. In response to the analyst's questioning, C.D. insisted that he was continuing to take the medication at the prescribed dosage.

Group Discussion

The presenting analyst suspected that the complaints represented a projection of the patient's attempts to strengthen his own position in relation to his family's efforts to pull him away from the therapist. Feder and Roose saw the events of this episode as reflecting the boy's desperate struggle to maintain some degree of activity and autonomy, and, particularly in relation to the analyst, to ward off a passive, helpless situation.

Wednesday-Thursday, May 20-21, 1964   Although C.D. himself was reluctant to see another doctor, his family continued to press for an outside consultation. To this effect the patient's wife, Jean, went to see the consultant, and reported on her husband's condition. Arrangements were then made for the presenting analyst to speak with the consultant over the telephone on May 21.

Friday, May 22, 1964   The analyst told C.D. of his conversation with the consultant, and explained further that he understood the concern of the family for the patient's condition and their wish for a consultation. The doctor stated further that he would not oppose a consultation. When the youth asked whether the analyst thought that a consultation would be beneficial to him, the doctor responded that he could not advise the patient to have a consultation, but that he would in no way oppose it, nor would he hold it against the youth, should he cooperate in a consultation, especially if it was to comply with his family's wishes. The physician explained that he did not want to encourage the patient to have a consultation at the insistence of his family, because he felt that this would be pushing C.D. to do exactly what he was struggling against. The patient indicated that he understood the doctor's attitude toward the consultation, but he did not say what he should do. In order to calm the youth's libidinal turmoil and to alleviate the pressure of the immediate situation on the patient, the analyst reduced the dose of Nardil by half, to 15 mgs, three times a day.

During this week the analyst was in frequent contact with Jean. He suggested to her that, because it was now so difficult to control the youth's medication, and because his behavior was becoming so unconventional, hospitalization should be considered. Jean responded negatively to this suggestion, which she reported to her husband's parents, who also reacted negatively. The family insisted that they would agree to hospitalization only if the consultant would see the boy, and give his consent. The analyst also discussed the possibility of hospitalization with C.D. himself, who reacted to the idea with much anxiety.

The analyst later learned that, during this time, after leaving the doctor's office in the morning, C.D. would spend the day driving and walking around, all the while engaged in the conscious attempt to analyze himself and understand his problems.

Group Discussion of the Reduction of the Nardil and the Suggestion of Hospitalization

Feder agreed with the reduction of the medication. Ostow was opposed: he felt that the reduction could leave the youth exposed to depression, and thus could result, paradoxically, in more agitation or depression. In his view 90 mgs of Nardil was doing, not too much, but too little. It had supported the boy for two years, but then he escaped from its support. Ostow did not think that increasing the dosage of Nardil would have helped: he would have favored giving the patient a more powerful anti-depression agent, if one could be found.

Feder and Furst suggested that one way to reduce the pressure on an agitated patient is to take him out of circulation, i.e., to hospitalize him. Furst added that through hospitalizing the patient, the doctor also achieves greater control over the administration of the drug. The reporting analyst responded that, for the doctor to hospitalize this patient would be to do to him what C.D. thought his mother had done to his grandfather, that is, to put him in a coffin and bury him. Roose mentioned that, when he foresees even the possibility of hospitalizing a patient, he discusses that possibility long before it becomes a critical issue, and indicates that such a maneuver would be something to be decided on by the patient and the therapist together. Ostow added that generally the patient himself provides the opportunity for the analyst and patient to discuss hospitalization in advance.

Group Discussion of the Consultation Issue

The presenting analyst emphasized the fact that the issue grew out of the pressure exerted on C.D. by his family, and against his will, to see another doctor. His own analyst had become a significant homosexual threat to him and his family was, in effect, presenting him with another. Feder and Linn suggested that, since much of the patient's agitation arose from the conflicting pressures exerted on him by the analyst and by his family, an endorsement of the consultation by the doctor would have immediately reduced C.D.'s inner conflict and relieved his distress. Ostow, Furst, and Roose thought that, by endorsing the consultation, the analyst would be admitting that he was not strong enough to protect the patient against his family.

Feder remarked that, generally, by agreeing to a consultation, the doctor can dramatize the transference, and effect in a patient a more realistic appraisal of the analyst as a human being. Furst and Ostow responded that, while Feder's strategy might be useful in the treatment of neurotic patients, with a psychotic individual the analyst must utilize the transference to maintain some kind of control over the patient. Roose pointed out, and Furst agreed, that even with a psychotic patient, the analyst, in his reaction, must take into account the origin of the request for a consultation. A request for a consultation coming from the patient, for whatever reason, should be respected by the doctor. This consultation request, however, came from the boy's family, and should be considered another external pressure against which the analyst must protect the youth.

Monday-Tuesday, May 25-26, 1964   C.D.'s condition seemed to have improved slightly. His confusion and agitation had diminished somewhat, there was some increase in his overall emotional control, and he was slightly less suspicious of the analyst. In fact, on May 25 the youth at one point expressed gratitude to the doctor for having put up with so much difficulty from him. The boy was still preoccupied, however, with his psychotic ideation and with his efforts to master his problems intellectually. The analyst remained uncertain as to whether the medication was being taken as prescribed.

Wednesday-Thursday, May 27-28, 1964   C.D. did not come to his analytic hours during this period. He telephoned the analyst each day, and asked to be excused for the following day. He reported that he was feeling a little better, and he seemed to have somewhat more control of himself.

Friday, May 29, 1964   C.D.'s behavior was quite subdued. He spoke in a whisper, and lay down on the couch for the first time since the termination of his psychotic attack of the previous year. (For the past year, he had been sitting, rather than lying on the couch.) The youth said that he had spent the week-end "trying to understand everything," but he now felt unable to understand or to go on. Moreover the boy claimed that he had never understood what the analyst had been talking about since the beginning of the treatment. He assured the doctor that he was taking the medication as prescribed; the analyst was inclined to believe the youth on this point, but he was uncertain.

On that afternoon the patient's wife called the analyst, and informed him that her husband's behavior at home had become quite disturbed. He refused to talk to anyone; there were outbursts of crying, screaming, and rage; and once he threw furniture around and broke it. Although there had been brief minor episodes of this kind in the past, over the week-end the outbursts had become markedly more violent and disorganized.

Jean also told the analyst that she did not know how her husband was spending his days. He would leave the house early to attend his treatment session, and would not come home until the end of the day; nor would he account for how he had spent the time. The analyst responded that he was very concerned about this situation, that he would discuss the matter with her husband, and would request that, if the patient was planning not to go home, he should at least telephone his wife and let her know what he was doing.

The presenting analyst told the group that C.D. had spoken of his rage. He was angry with everyone. He was angry at his mother for having dominated him; he was angry at his father for having failed to pay attention to him, and for not having provided for him a model with which to identify; and he complained that the analyst did not understand him and had damaged him. The only object of his rage that he did not talk about was his wife, who, for a long time, had been humiliating him in many ways, although usually in response to his provocation.

At this time the analyst repeated to Jean his concern about the patient's condition and his suggestion that hospitalization be considered. The patient's wife continued to disagree. She again insisted on a consultation prior to hospitalization, and she berated the analyst for not encouraging her husband to accept the consultation. The doctor, in turn, explained his position to her.

Throughout this period, C.D.'s family was adamantly opposed to the idea of hospitalizing him. The analyst felt that they were using the issue of the outside consultant as a form of resistance. The doctor understood that the youth's illness was a great humiliation to his family, above and beyond the difficulties they experienced in relating to him. The family, and particularly the mother, was concerned lest her son follow in the footsteps of his sister, and hospitalization would have confirmed the fact that C.D.'s parents had two very disturbed offspring.

Group Discussion

Roose raised the question of the technical handling of this patient's great rage as a transference phenomenon. Ostow responded that, with all psychotic and depressed patients, he focuses on the rage rather than on the libidinal relationship. Further, he felt that the youth's recent subdued behavior might be attributable to the Thorazine.

Feder remarked that in this family both C.D. and his sister had to be hospitalized after parturition. Linn added that the presence of the baby might have been a disorganizing influence in the family setting. It is in the year since the birth of the baby that C.D.'s condition has been deteriorating dramatically. Klerman suggested that, from this perspective, the patient's berating of the analyst might be a displacement from the fact that the patient's wife, because of the presence of the infant, was less able to satisfy his dependency needs. Furst agreed with Linn and Klerman, but he also called attention to other factors contributing to the boy's worsening situation, namely, his inability to hold a job or to function adequately, either socially or sexually, at home.

Regarding C.D.'s unaccounted-for meanderings, Ostow mentioned that there are some psychotic patients in this condition who do not go home, and who indeed do not go anywhere, but only come to see the analyst and then wander around the streets. In contrast to perverse patients, who wander around and become involved in perverse episodes, and to depressed patients, who look for companionship, these psychotic individuals just walk around in an agitated way. Furst cited a case of street-wandering as a manifestation of obsessive indecision. Linn remarked that this kind of wandering represents an avoidance of objects, and is thus essentially a psychotic expression. Ostow agreed, and added that this psychotic wandering is comparable to the frenetic pacing often observed in agitated depressed patients. In each case the need to walk might be neurologically related to the akathesia that often develops as a side effect of phenothiazines.

Klerman and Roose proposed that, in the case of this patient, the wandering might have a defensive function: in the presence of his wife and child, the youth might lose control of his

rage and commit murder. Furst emphasized that, indeed, this patient's most bizarre behavior occurs at home. He further felt that,
for psychotics, wandering around, in addition to representing an
avoidance of objects, also functions as a defense against the
tremendous need for objects, which is even more dangerous than
the hostility.

   Saturday, May 30, 1964   C.D. telephoned the analyst in the
morning to say that he could not keep his appointment. He
sounded slightly better than the day before, and he informed the
doctor that he was actually feeling better. The analyst rescheduled
the analytic hour for later in the day. The patient kept this second
appointment, and, when he arrived, he requested permission to sit
at the desk; the analyst acquiesced. The youth then told the
doctor that he felt embarrassed about his behavior over the last
month. He said that his inability to work was a serious disgrace to
him, and that it was not anxiety, but rather shame, that made it
impossible for him to see anyone, and forced him to wander
around the streets, or to lock himself in his room. The youth
spoke of his mistrust of the analyst during the past weeks, and, for
the first time, he elaborated to the analyst the pressure his family
had been putting on him to see a consultant. During this discussion the analyst began to feel certain that it was, in fact, increased
pressure from the family that precipitated the current psychotic
episode.

   About an hour after C.D. left the analyst's office, he telephoned the doctor, and requested to see him again for a few minutes; he intimated that it was very important. The analyst told the
youth to come back at a specified time, a little later in the afternoon. Ten minutes after the appointed time, the patient again telephoned the analyst, and announced that he would not come, but
would call again later.

   Early in the evening, the patient's wife called the doctor, and
reported that she had not seen her husband since he had left the
house in the morning, and that she did not know where he was.
The analyst told Jean that he had made C.D. promise to call her, if
he was not going to return home. She, in turn, informed the doctor that she would go again that evening to see the consultant, and
she asked the analyst whether he had recently spoken with the

consultant. The analyst responded that he had not, and there ensued another discussion of the consultation issue. The analyst again explained that he personally had no objection, but that he doubted that a consultation would be helpful to the patient in his present state, and that he felt it would be detrimental for the analyst to put pressure on him.

Later in the evening, C.D. telephoned and reported simply that he would not keep his appointment for the next morning. The analyst asked the patient about his future plans, and the youth instructed the doctor merely to cancel the next morning's hour. He then added: "I think this is almost it."

Monday, June 1, 1964   C.D. did not appear for his scheduled hour, but he telephoned the analyst later in the day, and urgently requested another appointment. The analyst agreed to see him early in the evening. At the specified time, the youth again called to say that he would not keep this appointment, and that, in fact, he would not be coming to see the doctor any more.

Tuesday, June 2, 1964   Again C.D. did not appear for his scheduled session, but telephoned the analyst later in the day to make another appointment. The analyst's interpretation of this behavior was that the patient was torn between the wish to see the doctor, and the need to tear himself away, to prove to himself that he did not love or need the analyst, and that he could cure himself.

In another telephone conversation, which took place that evening, the youth displayed what the analyst considered a vivid, paranoid reaction. He said to the doctor: "You did it; you damaged me; you caused all of this; you did it; I am going to sue you." In response to the doctor's questioning, the boy admitted that he had not been taking any medication at all for several days.

Wednesday, June 3, 1964   Again C.D. called the analyst, urgently requested to see him, and then failed to appear at the specified time.

Later in the day Jean telephoned the doctor, and asked why he was not encouraging her husband to see the consultant. The analyst told her that, at that point, he was willing to do anything at all to help the patient. Jean complained further that C.D. refused to discuss doctors with her, and added that, once more, her husband was not at home, and she did not know where he was.

Thursday, June 4, 1964   The patient spoke with the analyst over the phone, but did not go to see him.

Friday, June 5, 1964   When the patient telephoned, the analyst told him firmly that their relationship could not continue in this way, and he encouraged the youth to please his family by going to see the consultant. The boy promised to do so on the next day. The analyst explained to the group that, at this point, he felt that C.D. had to be hospitalized, and that the only way to effect his hospitalization was to have him see the consultant. C.D. also agreed to resume the medication; the analyst instructed him, for the time being, to take 30 mgs of Nardil and 100 mgs of Thorazine, three times a day.

In the evening the youth came to see the analyst. He reported that he had seen the consultant in the morning, and the consultant had told him that he was confusing the analyst with his parents, whom he wanted to spite. In a fairly controlled manner, C.D. spoke of his recent behavior; the youth attributed his difficulties to his "feelings," which the analyst interpreted to mean the patient's homosexual attachment to him.

Saturday, June 6, 1964   C.D. neither appeared nor telephoned at the time of his analytic hour. When he called the analyst later, however, he sounded depressed and confused. The youth again accused the analyst of causing his present illness; he repeated about ten times over: "You did it!" The doctor responded to the patient's accusations by attempting to be supportive and reassuring: he felt that the patient was trying to accept the reassurance in a passive and childish way. The boy agreed to come to see the analyst the next day.

Monday, June 8, 1964   Not having seen or heard from C.D. by noon, the analyst became concerned, and telephoned him. Jean answered, and told the doctor that her husband was asleep; he had not slept much the night before. She described how, for the past two weeks, C.D. had been feeling restless, going to bed late, and sleeping for three or four hours, after which he would wake up, between 4:00 and 5:00 a.m., feeling confused and agitated. On these occasions, he would often behave in a bizarre manner. The youth would lock himself in the bathroom, talk to himself aloud, occasionally screaming: "I am going to die!" and lie flat on the floor. These agitated episodes would be interspersed with periods of calm, in which the patient would answer questions rationally, and would speak of his other thoughts as being "foolish and crazy." In response to the analyst's questions, Jean said she thought her husband was taking his medication erratically.

At 4:00 p.m., C.D. telephoned the doctor. He sounded very depressed and confused, and refused to see the analyst that day.

Tuesday, June 9, 1964   That night C.D.'s behavior deteriorated further. He locked himself in the bathroom, and, though he seemed to be thrashing around, he would not let anyone come in. At times he would run out of the bathroom naked, spin around, fall flat on the floor, and say he was going blind. Jean became quite frightened, and called C.D.'s brother, who came immediately; together they called the analyst at 4:00 a.m., and also Phyllis's husband.

The doctor stated that hospitalization could no longer be postponed, and he proceeded to make the necessary arrangements. One major hospital refused to admit the patient immediately; the chief of psychiatry told the analyst that the youth sounded too agitated. C.D. was admitted to a second hospital under the co-supervision of the analyst and the hospital's chief psychiatrist. The hospital was sufficiently distant from the analyst's office to make close supervision by the analyst alone virtually impossible.

C.D. was taken to the hospital by his wife and brother-in-law early in the morning; at the time he offered no objection. In the hospital Thorazine, 200 mgs, was administered to the patient five times a day; he was also given Stelazine, and Artane, 2 mgs each, three times a day.

Wednesday, June 10, 1964   It was reported by the patient's family that his behavior of the night before—especially his spinning and the movements of his eyes and hands—was remarkably similar to that of his sister, Phyllis, when she had become psychotic several years earlier. The chief psychiatrist reported to the analyst that he saw C.D. at 3:00 p.m., at which time the youth voiced many somatic delusions: he stated that his brain was peeling off, and that he was burning; that his insides were on fire. The patient claimed that he was experiencing heart attacks, and he spent a great deal of time trying to understand the hemodynamics of the somatic changes, which he imagined.

At 8:30 p.m., the analyst visited the patient at the hospital. C.D. then seemed very drowsy; his speech was slurred. The youth recognized the analyst, and seemed somewhat pleased to see him. He answered the analyst's questions fairly curtly and uninforma- tively, and offered no spontaneous remarks. After about twenty minutes, the patient appeared to doze, and, in response to the analyst's question, said he would rather go back to sleep.

Thursday, June 11, 1964   The chief psychiatrist informed the presenting analyst that C.D. was quiet and subdued. His somatic delusions persisted, but the accompanying agitation had subsided. The doctor again saw the patient personally in the even- ing, and confirmed this observation. He found the patient somewhat more talkative than the night before.

The Course of C.D.'s Hospitalization

June 12-26, 1964   In the hospital, C.D. became subdued on Thorazine, 1200 mgs, and Stelazine, 30 mgs, five times a day. His somatic delusions continued, but they troubled him only occasionally. The youth believed that his brain was peeling off, and he had fantasies of changes in his heart and blood pressure. He also was convinced that his feet would change color and become hot or cold, depending on which foot he would look at. When he looked at his right foot, it would become red, and his left foot, when he looked at it, would turn green. Further, he felt that the other patients were talking about him; they were saying that he was a "sissy" and a "homosexual," and were calling him "she."

End of June, 1964   After C.D. had been in the hospital for about two weeks, the presenting analyst and the hospital's chief psychiatrist agreed that his recovery was proceeding too slowly; they suggested to the patient's family the use of electric shock treatment as a catalyst. The family resisted this suggestion, and demanded that another consultant be called in before any new therapy was initiated. The second consultant saw the patient, and the family stated that they wanted the consultant to take over the case. C.D. again felt torn between the doctor and his family. The analyst explained to the youth, who was by now subdued and rational, that he felt that the patient's family had lost confidence in him and that the constant conflict between the physician and his family constituted a substantial hindrance to any therapeutic efforts.

The result of the negotiations described above was that the shock treatments were not administered, the consultant took over the case, and C.D. was transferred to a hospital with which his new therapist was connected. He remained at this hospital, and was driven from there by his wife to the new doctor's office three times a week for treatment.

May 1965   C.D. was still in the hospital. Although his wife, who contacted the presenting analyst sporadically, and the new doctor felt that he was ready to be discharged, the youth was fearful of leaving. No electric shock treatments were administered; rather, the new analyst continued to treat the patient with phenothiazines.

Presenting Analyst's Report on the Sudden Outbreak of the Last Psychotic Episode

In mid-June 1964, the reporting analyst learned of the incident which precipitated this last psychotic episode. C.D.'s parents had been spending the winter in Arizona, and they had invited their son to come visit them with his wife and child. This invitation again placed the youth in an ambivalent trap. The boy did not want to go; he preferred to remain in New York, to continue his analytic work and to maintain the semblance of being the head of his family in his own home. Although visiting his parents in Arizona threatened C.D. with being engulfed by his mother, he felt powerless to refuse.

The presenting analyst reminded the group that a previous psychotic episode, suffered by the patient two years earlier, had been similarly triggered when the youth's brother-in-law openly wondered whether C.D.'s unexplained reluctance to go back to Montreal to launch his career, might be due to his inability to tear himself away from his psychiatrist. Thus, in both instances, a psychotic attack was brought on by an externally stimulated intensification of the transference; specifically this patient became psychotic when he felt he was being pulled one way by his family and in the opposite direction by the analyst.

Report of the Psychosis of C.D.'s Sister, Phyllis

The analyst in the group who had been Phyllis's therapist reported briefly on her course of treatment with him. When he first saw Phyllis, she was in a post-partum psychotic state. She had been given electric shock treatments, to which she had initially responded and then relapsed. She had also been given large doses of Thorazine. After receiving the Thorazine, she would lie on the floor, say she was going blind, spin around naked, fall again to the floor, and claim she was going to die. The analyst found he could relieve her psychosis, and bring her back into a relatively normal state by administering large doses of Parnate and a small amount of Mellaril. The analyst felt that Parnate relieved her agitation, and thus allowed her to function normally. On this medication and daily visits to the doctor, she progressed well.

Phyllis became depressed once more in a schizophrenic manner, and with tremendous hostility. No amount or kind of medication alleviated her condition. The family then became angry, and took her to another doctor. She was ultimately hospitalized for almost a year, and, during the course of this hospitalization, she became seriously overweight.

Phyllis's analyst believed that, though the precipitating factors in the psychoses of C.D. and his sister were different, the fact of the identical family background suggests the importance of constitutionality in determining at least the symptoms, and the susceptibility to psychosis. The significant features in this case are: first, that sister and brother suffered breaks with reality, which were both depressive and psychotic; second, both required large doses of an anti-depression drug to relieve the depression and the psychosis; third, that, in response to stress, both escaped from the effect of the anti-depression drug, and, at that point, no drug could hold them; and, finally, when they were depressed and schizophrenic, they behaved in the same manner.

Group Discussion of this Case as an Argument for Constitutionality in Psychosis

The group was generally skeptical of the argument for constitutionality. The two presenting analysts, who made the argument, were impressed particularly by the brother-in-law's description of the similarity of the psychotic episodes of the brother and sister. Roose and Feder felt that this similarity might be attributable to direct or indirect communication between the siblings, perhaps even as children. Loomis wondered whether, in their childhood, the two had had similar tantrum patterns.

In connection with the psychotic spinning, Winkelman suggested that it might contain an element of exhibitionism. C.D.'s analyst responded that, as an adolescent, the youth took pictures of Phyllis spinning around. Roose related the psychotic spinning to children's games in which participants spin around until they collapse. Klerman pointed out the need to distinguish between genetic factors in predisposition to psychosis and in symptomatic behavior; he thought that the former was more likely than the latter. Ostow felt that, in examining the possibility of a genetic factor in symptomatology, the basic issue is not the content of the delusional idea, but rather, types of stereotyped behavior. If the brother and sister showed similar tantrum behavior in childhood, that behavior too could be attributed to genetic factors as well as to communication. Loomis cited findings of Lauretta Bender* that spinning around is a common symptom of schizophrenia.

Bressler, responding to the issue of patients escaping from the control of anti-depression drugs, reported that he has been able, on several occasions, to avoid such escapes by combining MAOI's and tricyclic drugs; he emphasized that he uses this combination

---

*Lauretta Bender, *Child Psychiatric Techniques.* Springfield, Ill: Charles C Thomas, 1952, p. 88.

only on hospitalized patients. Furst and Ostow felt that Bressler's experience was not generalizable; they cited counter examples from their own practices. Winkelman thought that such combinations are more likely to be successful with younger patients.

Feder mentioned that there is recent evidence that within families drugs are metabolized in a particular way. Klerman pointed out that, in this case, both siblings were examples of secondary failure; they responded initially to the drug, but the response subsequently diminished. This secondary failure is quite common with oral hypoglycemic agents, and seems to be more common with anti-depression agents than with phenothiazines. Loomis wondered whether the threshold of primary response could be the genetically determined element in this case. Klerman cited some cases from his practice of patients who, after exhibiting a good primary response to a drug and a secondary failure, responded well again after a rest period in which the drug was not administered. Ostow found that, among his patients, the pattern of drug response described by Klerman is common, but not universal.

Addressing himself to the problem of a patient's escape from the control of a drug, Ostow remarked that, often such an escape is related to a specific depressing event or influence. Bressler added that, to combat the possibility of escape, when he starts a patient on an MAOI, he always gives L-tryptophane with it, and oral pyridoxin for five to ten days; some patients require the added drug continually.

Discussion of C.D.'s Last Psychotic Episode

In the last phase of his treatment with the presenting analyst, Ostow considered C.D.'s illness as psychosis with agitation. The relevant signs and symptoms included rage and murderous impulses, avoiding home and family, accusations against the therapist, low self-esteem, and attempts to become independent of the therapist, by hostile identification and by rejecting medication. Three methods of treatment were considered. One was interpretation of the object of the rage, and of the transference. A second method was medication; it remained unresolved whether such a

patient should be given an anti-depression agent or a tranquilizer.
Treatment of this state with drugs also brought up the problem of
the need to distinguish between the initial and the ultimate effects
of the drug, as well as the problem of irregularity of dosage.

The third suggested treatment was hospitalization, which is
therapeutic in that it 1) allows the patient a sanctioned regression,
2) protects him against family pressure, 3) provides control of the
medication, and, finally, 4) protects the patient from the fear of
attacking his family.

The Peter Pan Syndrome

Ostow remarked that the two case histories presented so far,
as well as many patients he sees in his practice, illustrate the Peter
Pan Syndrome. This syndrome describes the young person who is
unable to face up to the responsibilities of family and of work or,
more simply, cannot grow up. These individuals are often able to
"pass"until they reach the age of about twenty-eight or twenty-
nine, though the precise age can vary. Then shame forces them to
retreat in one way or other. The retreat may take the form of
neurotic paralysis, depression or psychosis depending on the predisposition. While there is a homosexual threat implicit for men of
this type in their dependence on their fathers, friends, and analyst,
usually the homosexual threat cannot be seen as the effective
cause of the illness. Rather, the basic issue is that society will
allow young men to behave as adolescents for a while, but there is
a point at which the men are separated from the boys, and these
patients then collapse into psychosis, because they obviously cannot function as men.

Furst and Loomis agreed. They cited similar cases, emphasizing that the variety of strategies employed by these patients for
prolonging adolescence, and the age at which the strategies fail,
vary. Furst, referring back to the case of C.D., remarked that his
first psychotic episode came at about the time of his marriage; the
second coincided with his graduation from college and the birth of
his first child; and the ultimate breakdown occurred when it became clear that he could not assume an adult work role. Ostow added that, at the time of the patient's last breakdown, his obvious

inability to function at work was aggravated by his wife's with-drawal of her support, and his family's invitation to regress.

Linn referred to the findings of Farnsworth* on subsequent careers of students who drop out during their undergraduate careers. Students who drop out of school temporarily during their freshman and sophomore years, over the next five or ten years, follow career patterns indistinguishable from those of their peers who did not drop out. Students who break down towards the end of their college careers tend to have difficulties which are more serious and more debilitating in the long run. Ostow felt that, more generally, each period of life has its own peculiar challenges and supports which must be taken into account by the analyst in his prescription of medication.

Discussion of the Comparative Usefulness of Drugs and Other Strategies for Dealing with an Agitated Patient

Klerman noted the inability of the presenting analyst to detect the patient's psychosis until over a year after the beginning of the treatment. He felt that this too, seems to be a common pattern. In psychoanalysis, what appears to be a good beginning often deteriorates after a number of months, or even a year. The use of drugs frequently enables such patients to continue in therapy for longer than would have been possible before the use of drugs became so widespread.

Winkelman, in retrospect, thought that C.D. is a person who is very difficult to treat pharmacologically, and impossible to treat psychoanalytically. He is schizophrenic in a very basic way, and what he really needs is drugs, the support of friends, and advice. Throughout his course of treatment with the presenting analyst, he never handled interpretation well, or used it to work through his problems. Roose agreed, and emphasized that in C.D.'s situation, there was no equilibrium point from which the analyst could distinguish fluctuations, and on which he could base his therapy. A situation with so many sources of anxiety, so many elements which suggest regression, and so many external events, is very dif-ficult to control.

*Dana Farnsworth, *Psychiatry, Education and the Young Adult.* Springfield, Ill: Charles C Thomas, 1966.

Ostow pointed out that in following case histories of drug treatment, the drug is the independent variable and the psychodynamics of the patient often reflect the action of the drug. Therefore dynamic interpretations are often therapeutically useless. Roose added that, generally, to the extent to which the patient remains more influenced by external factors, he is less influenced by the transference. Ostow responded that, perhaps, rather than necessarily diminishing in significance, the transference, like all other manifestations of the illness, becomes a dependent variable. In such cases the transference influence often surpasses and outlasts the patient's responsiveness to interpretation. A patient who is too disorganized and too helpless to utilize interpretation may be sustained by a strong transference.

Bressler compared the treatment of agitated psychotic patients to that of obese individuals. In both cases analysis alone is not sufficiently potent: an external control must also be provided. Linn proposed that, when a patient is both hospitalized and given drugs, it may be difficult to distinguish the respective effects of two such powerful influences.

Comparison of the Psychotic Episodes

Furst pointed out, and the group agreed, that whereas C.D.'s psychotic episode of April 1962 began with depressive symptoms, his ultimate breakdown in May 1964 seems more directly a psychotic response to his homosexual longing. Moreover, by late Winter 1964 the patient was already taking a significant dose of medication (e.g., 90 mgs of Nardil), which was, perhaps, providing him with an excessive amount of libidinal energy. Although in the final episode there was no antecedent depressive trend, both cases involved a breakthrough of paranoid ideation.

Linn suggested that paranoid trends emerging in a depressive setting may represent part of a depression. Ostow responded that paranoid ideation can develop as a manifestation of the struggle against depression, in the depths of a depression, or as a result of libidinal plethora; each case calls for a different approach on the part of the therapist. The mere existence of ideas of reference is therefore not a clear indication of which drugs should be given.

Furst added that, when he sees strong ideas of reference and intense paranoid ideation, even when he feels that these are manifestations of a depressive trend, and uses an anti-depression drug as the basic medication, he always adds some phenothiazine. Ostow cited a case, from his practice, of a psychotic patient who could function normally only when maintained on the proper combination of anti-depression agent and phenothiazine. A deviation in either direction would produce paranoid ideation, though, errors in different directions resulted in paranoid ideas with different themes. The ideation of the paranoia arising from a depressive trend was quite different from that associated with excess psychic energy. In prescribing medication for paranoid patients, the therapist must take into account both the patient's paranoia, and his affective condition.

Discussion of the Reporting Analyst's Use of the Couch

The presenting analyst reminded the group that, during most of C.D.'s sessions, the patient sat up on the couch, and looked at the analyst, who retained his accustomed seat behind the couch. This position seemed to be the most comfortable one for the patient. When he became agitated, however, the youth would often stand up or walk around. The analyst saw nothing that suggested to him that the patient might want to move over to the desk.

Linn suggested that face-to-face contact maximizes the opportunity for a psychotic patient to relate to the therapist as a real person, and is therefore important for the efficacy of the treatment. Klerman proposed that the patient's wish to remain on the couch should be seen as a regressive wish. Ostow observed that many agitated psychotic patients sit up because they are anxious. Moreover, the therapist can encourage the use of either the chair or the couch to underscore or to de-emphasize the patient's state of regression. The physician can suggest that the patient move to a face-to-face position if he wishes to combat regression actively and to encourage reality testing. On the other hand, when the doctor wishes to urge the patient to attempt to overcome his agitation or anxiety, at least partly, by self-discipline, then one can permit him to sit on the couch. When there is regression with loss of ego control, the patient fears the couch. Linn added to Ostow's remarks that the couch functions not only as an indicator of how regressed a patient is at a given time, but, more important, it is a potent instrument which promotes regression.

Summary of the Case

Furst proposed that C.D.'s course of treatment with the presenting analyst should be seen as a progressive deterioration of his condition. The sequence of episodes, which occurred at successively shorter intervals are, therefore, parts of a general trend, as well as reactions to the specific external stimuli which immediately preceded each of them. The degree to which this deterioration is attributable to escape from the control of the drug, and the degree to which it represents a reaction to an increasingly stressful environment remained unclear to Furst.

Ostow summarized the case in the following way. Looking at the five crises together, he distinguished three processes. In some situations C.D. suffered depression with inhibition and incompetence. This condition was alleviated by the administration of Nardil with or without phenothiazine, or by increasing the dose of Nardil. On other occasions, the youth would attempt to cope with his depression by means of psychotic anger, gestures of independence, and an obsession with self-analysis. This syndrome was alleviated by Thorazine, which served to reduce his agitation. The third process, which emerged at the very end, was a psychotic depression with delusional hypochondria. This last state might have been aggravated by the Thorazine.

Furst added that sometimes the second and third processes were observable together. Roose, Winkelman, and Furst doubted that the third process was intensified by the Thorazine. Rather, they felt that the somatic delusions were present all along, but were masked by the patient's agitation. When the agitation subsided, under the influence of Thorazine, the delusions were expressed more openly. Linn observed that it is difficult to assess the role of the Thorazine in the last episode because of the uncertainty as to how much of it the patient was taking if, indeed, he was taking any at all. Loomis suggested that, by impairing self-perception, the Thorazine might have contributed to the somatic delusions. Winkelman cited the case of a patient of his in whom the onset of a very acute and violent paranoia was not in any way affected by the administration of a phenothiazine. Generally, he felt that somatic delusions are far less likely to respond to a phenothiazine than, for example, persecutory delusions.

Klerman saw the patient's experiences during his course of treatment as the gradual emergence of a latent schizophrenia. The fact that another member of C.D.'s family suffered a similar illness makes this interpretation particularly likely, though Klerman emphasized that he did not mean to imply a genetic cause for the similarity of the illnesses. If the patient had not been in treatment with the presenting analyst, the psychosis might have erupted earlier. The considerable fluidity of C.D.'s symptoms in the early episodes, and especially the depressive, apathetic, and paranoid elements, can indicate neurosis or the early stages of schizophrenia. Loomis added that, in evaluating the course of this patient's treatment, one must consider the resistance of the patient's family, as well as C.D.'s own personal resistance to changes in his condition. Ostow disagreed. He understood the patient's deterioration, and that of his sister, not as the gradual emergence of a latent schizophrenia, but as a series of episodes, each triggered by a specific precipitating incident.

Ostow proposed that two conclusions might be drawn from this discussion. The first conclusion describes the limits of the effectiveness of interpretation as therapy. Interpretation is ineffectual whenever function deteriorates, that is, when behavior is determined by drug influence; in the presence of some habit or addictive states (e.g. obesity); and in the natural evolution of a mental illness.

The second conclusion concerns the influence of drugs on a schizophrenic depression. Anti-depression agents will alleviate uncomplicated depression. Phenothiazines can relieve angry, agitated psychotic states which seem to defend the patient against depression. Paranoid conditions, by contrast, respond to different drugs, depending on the basis of the paranoia. The comparative response of depressive hypochondria to phenothiazines on the one hand, and to anti-depression drugs on the other was left unresolved. Linn added, and Ostow agreed, that, although the case of C.D.'s illness and the course of his treatment illustrate the limitations of the interpretive use of psychodynamic insight, a psychodynamic formulation of the case is nevertheless of critical importance to the therapist in making important therapeutic decisions such as the advisability of hospitalization rather than ambulatory treatment.

EDITOR'S NOTE: Although the outcome of this case was unsatisfactory, it was instructive. From the point of view of the phenomenology of mental illness, the case demonstrates, as does Case 1, the susceptibility to breakdown of young people who are too frightened to accept the challenges of adult life. It also demonstrates the frequent association between pure depression and schizophrenic decompensation.

From the point of view of drug therapy, it demonstrates the clinical problem of choosing medication when depressive and psychotic states coexist.

From the point of view of the dynamics of drug therapy, we see the mutual influences of the drug therapy and the transference. The phenomenon of escape from anti-depression control is also nicely demonstrated.

In retrospect I believe I can explain one phenomenon that occurred twice, that is, the patient's prompt recovery from depression after the addition of a small amount of Thorazine to an anti-depression regimen which had not yet become effective (September 1960), or to an inadequate dose (February 1964). I have observed recently that phenothiazine and thioxanthine tranquilizers, in low dose, can often alleviate depression, literally overnight. When these drugs are added to a subthreshold dose of anti-depression agent, they may promptly and vigorously elicit the anti-depression effect. Rereading this account now strongly suggests that that mechanism explains the two incidents mentioned.

The case demonstrates that when a young person collapses in the presence of a frightening challenge, drug therapy may reverse the collapse, but it does not really help him to deal with the challenge. There then ensues a contest between the pathogenic influence of the stressful challenge, and the protective influence of the medication.

It was this contest that I believe formed the basis for the course of illness described here. I suspect that the disappointing outcome may have been avoided had the therapist pressed antidepression therapy harder, giving no more than very small doses of phenothiazine, rather than attempting to deal with the psychotic state by increasing the dose of the latter, and diminishing the antidepression support.

CASE 3

Introduction—Fall 1962

On November 21, 1962, E.F., a fifty-six year old man, was referred to the presenting analyst for treatment of depression. His specific complaints were that recently he had been depressed, he had not been drinking (though he usually did), he had been sleeping more than usual, and he had no sexual desire. He told the doctor that this depression was the latest in a series of recurrent depressions, that he had suffered for many years, and that he had previously been in psychoanalysis and in other forms of psychotherapy with well-known practitioners. During one of his earlier episodes of depression, a psychiatrist had prescribed Tofranil (imipramine) for him. Although he did not remember how much Tofranil he had taken, he recalled that it did not help him. E.F. had never taken amphetamines, and he had never had electric shock treatment.

There had been a number of suicides in his immediate family. E.F. did not expect to live beyond sixty. The patient had been married for thirty years, and he assured the analyst that his relationship with his wife was harmonious. The reporting group member prescribed, at the outset, Niamid, 200 mgs a day, and suggested that E.F. start analysis. The patient responded that he would think about it.

Tuesday, November 27, 1962 A few days after the first visit, E.F. telephoned the analyst, and made an appointment for a second visit. He reported that he had been taking the Niamid regularly, and that he had also tried Deprol (meprobamate plus benactyzine), which had only made him sleepy. To the list of complaints presented in the first visit, the patient added that he was having trouble making decisions. At the end of the session, E.F. asked whether he could return on the following day. When the analyst said "Yes," E.F. exclaimed: "Oops, I just got an electric shock." The analyst assumed that the man must have been describing a body sensation that he was experiencing, and asked the patient when he had felt it before. The latter responded that he remembered having a similar flashing pain in his tenth year, when one of his brothers told him that their mother had just died.

Background

E.F.'s father was descended from a distinguished family and was himself a distinguished clergyman. Because he had an alcohol problem, he had never had a pulpit, and had never held a steady job. He was nonetheless a brilliant and popular speaker. E.F. suspected that his father was unfaithful, drank a great deal, and siphoned off for himself a large proportion of the funds he collected for the church. The patient told the analyst that when in the past he used to visit his father, the father would greet him by shaking hands and saying: "Glad to see you. What train are you taking back?"

The patient's mother was a daughter of one of the oldest and most distinguished Jewish families of Providence, Rhode Island. After her marriage to the Protestant clergyman she lost contact with her family, and she died when E.F. was ten years old. The patient once brought the analyst some letters that his mother had written to his aunt. From these letters the presenting analyst learned that, because E.F. was a sickly child, his mother used to take him to doctors. The doctors would ask about his bowel movements, and would prescribe cathartics and enemas.

E.F. remembered an incident in which he and his mother were riding together in a horse-drawn carriage. The horse bolted, and started to run wild. His mother jumped out of the carriage, leaving him inside. Although E.F. refused to see this act as abandonment, he once remarked to the doctor that, in his family there were so many children, when they moved from place to place, they always left a child behind, and did not notice that one was missing until they were part way to their destination.

When E.F. was two years old, the family was living in Cleveland, and his younger brother was born. A sister was born a year later, and a year and a half after that, when E.F. was four and a half years old, there was another brother. The patient was enuretic as a child. He remembered being very much affected by the sinking of the Titanic, which occurred when he was six, despite the fact that no family member was associated with it. When E.F. was seven, his family moved to Montreal. Two years later, when the boy's mother died of tuberculosis, family life became disorganized, and the children were assigned housekeeping chores. A year and a half after that, one of the older brothers died. Shortly thereafter, his father remarried.

In E.F.'s twelfth year his father had him and his two brothers circumcised. In the early part of this century, group treatment was common, and in E.F.'s family, many of the medical services obtained for the children were performed for several at once. Six months later, E.F.'s tonsils were removed. When E.F. was eleven and a half years old, his father caught him lying on top of, or, in his own words, "dry fucking" a sister, an activity in which, he said, his brothers often indulged as well. On this occasion his father warned him sternly: "If the neighbors saw what I have just seen, they would rip you from my arms."

When the boy turned twelve, he began compulsive masturbation. At that time, another brother died, and the family moved to New Haven, Connecticut, where E.F. spent most of his adolescence, and where he now lived. Four years later, at the age of sixteen, the patient was sent to prep school, and his father left New Haven. By the time E.F. was graduated from prep school at seventeen and a half, his father was divorced, and the household had broken up. Around the time the youth turned eighteen, he met his future wife and her family, and moved into their home, quite informally, as a friend.

The patient entered college when he was nineteen years old, and, three months later, he became seriously depressed. This was the first depression he recognized as an adult. For a while, the youth dropped out of college, and went to live with one of his brothers. This arrangement, however, did not work, and E.F. returned to college and completed his studies in more or less the usual length of time. At the time of E.F.'s first depression, another brother entered a mental hospital, where he died.

E.F. had relatively little interest in sexual intercourse; he had his first experience of intercourse when, in his twenty-second year, he was taken by one of his brothers to a house of prostitution. The patient found the experience repulsive, and never went to a prostitute again. When E.F. turned twenty-two, he entertained suicidal thoughts. A year later, the woman who was to become his wife married someone else. Within a few months she became pregnant, and left her husband.

When he was twenty-six, the patient was fired from his first job, and, almost immediately thereafter suffered what he described to the presenting analyst as acute anxiety. The next year, his father suicided, and E.F. was married.

E.F.'s mother had been wealthy, but his father, having no steady job, earned little, and lived off the mother's capital. The family of the patient's wife, the people with whom he was living in his mid-twenties, was also in poor circumstances. A year after E.F.'s marriage, his father-in-law died, leaving behind a small dry goods store which was then on the verge of bankruptcy. The patient invested some money in the business, and began to manage it together with his wife's brother. This enterprise prospered. At about this time, E.F. invested a modest sum, which he had inherited from his father, in common stocks. By 1962, this investment had built up into a fairly large sum.

When E.F. was thirty-four years old, his wife insisted on having her own bedroom; the patient was hurt by her demand. Two years after the birth of his only child, a daughter, he suffered another depression.

After recovering spontaneously from this episode of depression, E.F., then thirty-nine, became involved in a deal which, to the presenting analyst, seemed to have been a stock swindle though the patient denied it. E.F. returned the stock. He described to the analyst that, as soon as he had mailed the stock certificates, "I got a pain in my balls. I ran downstairs to the mailbox, but I couldn't get it out again." At this point, E.F. was dismissed from the family business by his brother-in-law.

This incident precipitated another episode of depression. A doctor whom he consulted at this time told E.F. that he had a peptic ulcer, and he went to the hospital to have it treated. The patient was then in therapy with one of the many psychoanalysts, authentic and inauthentic, whom he had seen.

In 1948, at age forty, E.F. retired from work. Since then he had not held a responsible job. In the same year, his wife informed him that she was having an affair. Although the affair itself did not bother E.F., he was angry and offended that his wife told him about it.

In 1950 a brother died of alcoholism and in 1962, E.F., then fifty-six years old, began therapy with the presenting analyst.

Group Discussion on Constitution and Suicide

The presenting analyst's enumeration of the multiple suicides in E.F.'s family led to a discussion of suicide and genetics. Klerman mentioned that suicide in the family renders an individual statistically more prone to suicide. Ostow believes that there is genetic determination for susceptibility to manic-depressive illness and schizophrenia, each of which may eventuate in suicide. Whether suicide will be elected as a resolution to the above states seems to be determined by cultural and family influences.

Wednesday, November 28, 1962*   "I felt better after I left yesterday. I took Librium last night, and it made me sleepy and somewhat more relaxed. My wife said I look better this morning. I don't know how to take New Haven. There is nothing here for me. I went riding this morning. I'm going to see Dr. Z. (another psychiatrist); that will get me more mixed up than ever. I'm afraid of you, like I would be afraid of a surgeon. When I was twelve, I was circumcised; my father thought we were masturbating. I'm against being anti-Semitic. My mother's family was Jewish." (The reporting analyst is Jewish.)

---

*The reporting analyst presented to the group selections from E.F.'s analytic hours. The passages are selected and arranged to emphasize what the presenting analyst considered the basic mood of each session, and its important events; the arrangement of passages does not necessarily coincide with the order in which they were actually spoken. This format is used consistently throughout the presentation.

Comments of the Presenting Analyst

To the reporting analyst, this man's depression was evident in his sleepiness, his inability to do anything or go anywhere, and his pessimism about the future. The doctor added to the patient's account that, when E.F. spoke of remaining in New Haven, he was referring to the fact that he and his wife own a home in Westport, Connecticut, where he had bought some property, and started to build houses. Although E.F. has not worked at a regular job since 1948, as a hobby he builds houses and then rents them out at generous rentals. He has refused to sell any. At this point, the analyst felt that E.F. resented having to remain in New Haven to see him.

Group Discussion

Linn, impressed by this man's extensive acting out, his chicanery, and his brilliance wondered whether E.F. could be accurately described as a psychopath. The presenting analyst felt that what differentiates E.F. from a psychopath is his anxiety. This patient was always anxious and fearful of the outside world; this is why all of his questionable activities occurred within the family. Moreover, E.F. had elaborate justifications for his dubious practices, and his idleness was not a matter of predilection, but, rather, the result of his fear of the world of business. In his object relations, E.F. was interested only in his wife and family, but in a narcissistic and infantile way. He was dependent, but with absolutely no fidelity: he would shift his allegiance, depending on where he saw benefit to himself.

Linn and Klerman pointed to the difference between E.F.'s character structure and that of more classical depressive patients. Abraham* describes depression-prone individuals as generally compulsive and law-abiding. The reporting analyst responded that E.F. was an extraordinarily meticulous man, and, in his own way, law-abiding. To the best of the analyst's knowledge, E.F. has never en-

---

*Karl Abraham, "A Short Study of the Development of the Libido Viewed in the Light of Mental Disorders" (1942) in *Selected Papers of Karl Abraham,* translated by Douglas Bryan and Alix Strachey. London: Hogarth, 1948.

gaged in frankly criminal activities. Even in his "stock swindle," no one was deceived, and there were no false signatures or other appurtenances of crime. E.F. merely persuaded members of his family to give him the stock he wanted.

To Klerman, this patient's expectation of complete care suggested an unresolved relation with his mother. Moreover, E.F.'s remark about his father's circumcising him for masturbating implies a fear of what the analyst might catch him doing, and what kind of punishment the analyst would inflict on him, once he learned of the patient's misbehavior. The remark also indicates a wish to confess.

Linn thought that the patient was trying to placate the doctor, as a Jew, and that by confessing he was seducing the analyst by producing material which he thought the doctor would like. Ostow inferred that E.F. feared he would die, and was looking for someone to protect him against death. He hoped to find in the doctor a loving parent, not a punitive one. The presenting analyst confirmed Linn's observation, and added that, throughout his treatment, this patient consistently resorted to confession as a strategy to disarm him.

In response to questions by members of the group regarding the prescription of Niamid, the presenting analyst explained that he had chosen Niamid for E.F. because he felt that the man was clearly depressed, and, at that time, he was using Niamid for treatment of depression.

Thursday, November 29 "I took the Librium; I guess it helped me to stay relaxed. In the morning I find myself far apart from everybody, as if in jail, hearing the world go by. I saw Dr. Z.; he was very nice. I found myself confused and frightened in his elevator. He told me to go to you. Then I found myself wandering down the street. I am where I was twenty years ago. I keep hoping my brother-in-law will let me go back to work for him. I was afraid of being late coming up here. I would say that I loved my mother-in-law more than anyone. When my father died, I didn't even want to go to his funeral. My mother wrote a letter once and said I was her favorite child. I have no picture of my mother. I am terribly frightened of sudden noises."

Group Discussion

Furst understood the patient's mention of his mother as an expression of his need for someone to love him. Linn was struck by E.F.'s almost romantic longing for his brother-in-law.

Monday, December 3   "I got through O.K. I am about the same, but, at moments, I feel better. I may as well confess that I am figuring out how to get out of New Haven. I am claustrophobic. New Haven frightens me. I keep wanting my brother-in-law to help me, to give me a job. I see my mother reaching out her hand to help me. I see my mother's face, and she wants to help me. Sometimes I see a child's face near hers, like the infant Jesus. One time I had a vision of my mother and Jesus Christ both reaching out their hands to help me. The only happy time in my whole day is when I get into bed. It's killing me to pay that much money, but I have to do it. I think I am better in some ways; the panic is less. The thought I choke back is, 'Thank God I got you to come to.' At least you gave me the Niamid, in which I have great hopes. I would like to go out and screw someone else's wife, someone nice. Too many people, fire engines, noise; it terrifies me. Christmas terrifies me.

"I have just gotten to be a big, fat slob. I worry about cancer all the time. I have been making up lists for my wife, my safe deposit keys, etc. I suppose I have a fear of homosexuality. I used to sit in the office with my factory manager, and I would get a pain in my balls as I spoke to him. I'm in a state of fury that this should happen to me. I have lived a fairly decent life, except that I screwed a few women and evaded the draft." (This last sentence was spoken very gently.)

Comments of the Presenting Analyst

The reporting analyst interpreted E.F.'s reference to the infant Jesus as basically a death wish, representing a wish to join his mother in the grave. Years later, this man was very much affected by the film *Dr. Zhivago,* which contains a scene in which a mother is being buried next to her dead child. The analyst also pointed out that this patient characteristically expressed his ambivalence towards the doctor through the juxtaposition of statements of appreciation and hostility to him. The analyst felt that E.F.'s last declaration, that he had always lived decently, was particularly important because, despite this patient's frequent gestures of confession, his draft evasion and his sexual misbehavior are the only events in his life about which he feels guilty, and they are his explanation for his depression. During this entire session, E.F. spoke quite a bit more slowly than was usual for him.

To Linn, this patient's worries about being sick suggested a feminine identification. The presenting analyst confirmed this observation. Furst was impressed by the ambivalence of this man's anaclitic longings, that is, his wish for support and his fear of rejection. Klerman commented that this session contains a considerable amount of material; he wondered whether this copious production could be attributed to the effects of the Niamid. The presenting analyst ascribed E.F.'s statement that he felt hopeful to the transference. He related the abundance of material to the fact that this patient had already been in treatment with several psychiatrists. He therefore knew what he was expected to say, and was obliging the doctor by behaving in the way he was supposed to.

There was some discussion about E.F.'s apparent ability to involve women in relationships which one would expect them to find unacceptable. The reporting analyst noted that this patient is an extraordinarily appealing man. As a child, he learned that the best approach is a sweet smile and, wherever he goes, people tell him how nicely he smiles. Moreover, as E.F. becomes more anxious, his smiling becomes more automatic.

Feder and Bressler commented on the fact that, before coming to the presenting analyst, E.F. had sought treatment with several female psychiatrists as well as a male psychiatrist. For a male patient, who has such strong and unresolved feelings for his mother, and who so eagerly seeks physical contact with women, to be in psychotherapy with a woman might generate very strong transference and counter-transference problems. The presenting analyst explained that none of the female consultants, some of whom are distinguished psychiatrists, attempted to treat E.F. He did invite one of them to dinner, however, and after dinner, when she invited him in for a few minutes, he attempted to seduce her. This incident notwithstanding, when the patient became depressed again recently, the first thing he did was to call up this woman to ask for assurance that the presenting analyst is a good doctor.

Ostow proposed the following summary of the December 3 session. The material describes a particular depressed patient's approach to treatment. First, he needed protection against death. Second, he feared that the therapist to whom he applied for treatment might castrate him as punishment for his sexual misbehavior. Third, he felt he therefore had to appease the analyst through obedience and confession. Finally, the patient yearned for the restitution of early protective relationships with his mother and with his brother-in-law.

Tuesday, December 4   E.F. reported feeling no change in his condition. "Librium makes me feel heavier. I feel better when I leave here, but it doesn't last very long. I tried to read a book, but I can't. I wrote to Dr. M. (a New York therapist with whom he had once been in treatment): I told him I didn't know whether I could take New Haven. I may come busting down there. I have a side effect—my muscle (he referred to his left forearm) is jumping. That's happened before, but it's a little bit worse now. I'm afraid I won't be able to come over here in the snow. I haven't taken a bath in the last three or four days.

"I'm looking for a white-haired old gentleman, preferably a Jewish gentleman." E.F. then proceeded to tell the analyst about a Jewish lawyer who had once been engaged by his family. The family had trusted this man because of his respectable, philosophical, and judicial image, but it turned out that he was dishonest.

"I am afraid of losing my teeth. I have terrible teeth. They used to give me hell for grinding my teeth at night, and for wetting my bed. I should have cured myself years ago. I can see myself as a woman, and you screwing me. My father caught me trying to screw my sister. His attitude was *so* tragic. (Here the patient imitated his father's ministerial mien, which was evident even in talking with the family.) He was very tragic, and he would say: 'If the neighbors saw what I have just seen, they would rip you from my arms.' My father was making too much of a fuss about it."

Comments of the Presenting Analyst

The therapist understood E.F.'s story about the white-haired Jewish gentleman as a description of the kind of doctor this man would have liked, and his disappointment that the presenting analyst did not project that image.

Group Discussion

Bressler remarked on the large quantity of candid, and, in some respects, regressive material produced in this session, and he questioned the appropriateness of this kind of data to what was only the patient's sixth visit to this therapist. The reporting analyst saw the associations from this session as a recapitulation of issues E.F. had already discussed with previous therapists. E.F. is a very obedient person, particularly on the surface. Although behind the doctor's back he is devious, on a superficial level he will behave as he is expected to. This is his way of being a good analytic patient.

Bressler further questioned the patient's apparent fantasy of seeking out a dishonest therapist. Perhaps, as a man who was circumcised at his father's will, E.F. felt that only a circumcised man could understand him. Ostow felt that the patient was basically describing his search for an ideal figure, his previous betrayal, and his hope that the analyst would not also fail him. The presenting analyst added to Ostow's observation that, during this time, E.F. was checking out the doctor's reputation with several other people to reassure himself that he had made the right decision. Bressler then suggested that the patient might have been producing the above material as another way of testing the doctor. E.F.'s analyst stated that he had the same impression and therefore did not use this information as a basis for psychoanalytic interpretation.

Roose and Klerman suspected that E.F. felt most comfortable with a therapist he could not trust, because the doctor's dishonesty absolved him from the obligation to give factual, honest data about himself. Linn was impressed by E.F.'s disparaging remarks about his father and about other male parental figures. The presenting analyst responded that this man's expectation of disappointment from a parent figure can also be seen as an evaluation of himself as a parent. This patient takes little interest in his daughter, and denies completely the emotional obligations of his own paternity.

Furst remarked that E.F. is not really close to anyone. The presenting analyst confirmed this statement, and added that, once he recovered from this depression, E.F. immediately attempted to seduce the doctor by offering him money. He asked whether there was any charitable foundation in which the doctor was interested to which he could contribute. The analyst was aware that it was through this kind of proposal that E.F. had seduced a female consultant into going to dinner with him; he therefore did not accept the offer. Furst thought that E.F. might belong to a category of individuals who seek disappointment in their object relations because they find that knowing they will be disappointed is more tolerable than the uncertainty of fearing that they will be betrayed. Ostow thought that, to the contrary, such people look for someone dependable, but then find they cannot tolerate relationships, and manipulate their objects into leaving them. Feder suggested that some people, in initiating a new relationship, can feel safe only by assuming that the object is untrustworthy and setting up their defenses. These maneuvers necessarily preclude the possibility of getting close to anyone. Ostow observed that many distrustful patients remember only situations in which they were betrayed; they do not remember relationships in which other people proved reliable.

Roose commented that this man seems to harbor a profound and general hatred: he does not like anyone, and he views everyone as an adversary. The presenting analyst specified that E.F. does not have a decent relation with any man. If he has any loyalty at all, it is to women. Bressler added that E.F. not only does not like other people, he does not respect them either. There was some discussion of whether a patient who talks about this kind of misbehavior, and who reveals so much suspicion in such an uncontrolled manner, might be schizophrenic. Feder responded that an important indicator of schizophrenia would be a tendency to regress. E.F. shows no signs of movement in this direction. The reporting analyst also stated that, in the six years he had treated E.F., he had seen no evidence of schizophrenia.

Bressler and Roose described E.F. as an "impulse-ridden" individual, that is, a person who becomes depressed when he is unable to act out his impulses, and in whom neurosis represents a denial of and flight from this depression. Impulse-ridden people are usually infantile, narcissistic, oral types, who are consistently active, and who are always manipulating people. Such characters become involved in pseudo-object relations for fear that they might devour or be devoured, and to deny their tremendous sadism, with which they cannot cope.

Wednesday, December 5   "I woke up this morning, and felt pretty good all morning. I sat down to do my income tax work. I'll have to go to Westport. My father said I mustn't look at him undressed. My older brother Adam tried to bugger me. I don't remember it. Nobody in my family lives to be more than sixty. I have a feeling that I am rapidly becoming an old man. My body looks badly caved in. My teeth are bad. I feel that I am a complete outsider.

"I can't believe that I had an impulse to hit you yesterday, when you opened the door to let me out. All the outsiders say, 'For God's sake, why do you go to a Jewish psychiatrist?' "

Comments of the Presenting Analyst

When E.F. speaks of "income tax work," he is actually referring to bookkeeping. Building and renting houses requires a considerable amount of detailed bookkeeping, all of which E.F. does himself. The patient's statement that he was instructed not to look at his father is an allusion to an incident in his childhood. E.F. woke up one day, while the father was changing clothes, and found himself staring at his father's penis. His father said, rather indignantly, "Turn your eyes to the wall!"

The presenting analyst asked the patient about his remark that his older brother tried to "bugger" him. The patient informed the doctor that a previous therapist had concluded that this must have happened. E.F. then tried to figure out which older brother it could have been, and decided that it was Adam. He once asked Adam about it, and, when Adam gave him an evasive answer, the patient assumed that his guess was correct. The analyst interpreted the patient's remarks about aging as a classic depressive expression, and he reminded the group that, though E.F. asserted that no one else in his family had lived to be more than 60, in 1969 at the time of his presentation, E.F. was already sixty-two years old.

In connection with the patient's reported wish to hit the doctor, the analyst explained that E.F. always used indirect expression for any embarrassing or hostile thoughts. There is a similar story behind the patient's declaration that his friends asked why he was going to a Jewish psychiatrist. At that time E.F. would approach people he knew, and announce that he was seeing a Jewish psychiatrist. His acquaintances would respond by saying "Why?" and then E.F. reported to the analyst; "All the outsiders say 'For God's saké, why do you go to a Jewish psychiatrist?' " This man constantly manipulates people in this manner.

Group Discussion

Klerman was impressed by the recurrence in this analytic session of the theme of E.F.'s positive yearnings for his mother. The discussion turned to the patient's voiced mistrust of Jewish psychiatrists. Loomis and Ostow pointed out that E.F.'s mother and at least one of his former therapists were Jewish. Loomis wondered specifically whether the white-haired, Jewish man might be E.F.'s maternal grandfather. The presenting analyst did not think that this was the case. Since his mother had run away from home, the patient never met her father.

Linn again emphasized the disparaged father figure and the patient's announcing to all of his acquaintances that he was involving himself with an unreliable person who would betray him. Feder suggested that E.F. might have employed this maneuver at times when he was feeling positively towards the analyst and wanted to reinforce his guard.

Ostow agreed: he thought that this announcement should also be seen as a request to his friends to provide protection in case the analyst should deceive him. E.F. seems to be a man who hoards protectors. Perhaps what he really feared was his homosexual desire and his wish to be taken advantage of. The patient began the session by talking about buggery, and he spoke quite openly about his feminine identification. Roose observed that

E.F.'s disparagement of the doctor reflects his low self-esteem, and is thus in keeping with the feeling of hopelessness and futility that marks this man's depressive trend.

Thursday, December 6   The patient began the analytic session by announcing, "I did move back. I called Dr. D. (the woman psychiatrist who referred him to the presenting analyst) to get assurance from her that you were the right doctor for me. Judgment Day is catching up with me. I see myself as an old man, deteriorating. I had a pretty bad night. I kept waking up. I forced myself to go down and have lunch with my wife and a few other people. I feel in competition here with a woman, who would get right to work in the analysis.

"I take about twenty Gelusils a day. I had some stomach pain yesterday. I equate you with Dr. A. (the physician who, six years previously, had hospitalized E.F. for a peptic ulcer. This doctor, who was an internist, did not see that the patient was really suffering from depression, but he told the patient that he had a homosexual problem). I wish you were an old man. With a female doctor, I'd end up screwing her; but not a man.

"I hate Christmas day. My father would make a party, and, in the middle, he would tell us 'Children, take your toys, and put them away. I had to sell another bond yesterday to pay for these presents.' I felt like when I took ether for my tonsils—going down a well full of pitch, with electricity running through it."

Comments of the Presenting Analyst

E.F.'s opening statement, that he moved back, refers to a decision he had made to return to the city for the winter rather than remain at his home in Westport, despite his phobia about living in New Haven. The doctor added to the patient's remark about checking out the analyst's reputation with his former psychiatrist; that this was the third or fourth time that E.F. had sought this kind of reassurance from Dr. D. in his two or three weeks of therapy with the reporting analyst.

The presenting group member also emphasized the juxtaposition of the patient's comments; first, that he was placing himself in the analyst's hands, that is, by moving back to the city, and then, that he was checking up on the physician. E.F.'s comment about competing with a woman was sincere. This patient does feel competitive with women. Finally, the stomach pains that E.F. complained of had occurred at the beginning of one of his earlier depressions, though no such pains were ever reported between depressions.

Group Discussion

Ostow noted that E.F.'s reference to himself as an old man was a sign that there had been no movement of the depression. Feder asked whether the remark about Judgment Day should be seen as a hint that the patient was considering suicide, and should therefore be hospitalized. Ostow responded that, at this point, E.F. appeared unlikely to suicide; though he was depressed, he was neither active nor agitated.

Klerman wondered about this patient's sleep pattern; the presenting analyst explained that this man usually sleeps very well. Indeed, when anything at all goes wrong, he goes to bed and sleeps without difficulty for hours and hours. E.F.'s doctor saw this readiness to sleep as the adolescent pattern of depression, which most people give up at age nineteen or twenty, but which this man retained.

Friday, December 7   "My daughter's husband has the mumps. I'm afraid to visit: I might become infected. I'd like to avoid coming in over Christmas week. I had a pretty good weekend, but the same old sinking spells. I'm feeling better today. I wonder whether I'll be able to stay in New Haven once I get well. It's obvious that I have my tongue in my cheek about this whole process. When I get into bed, I feel secure; I sleep pretty well. I am terribly afraid of doctors.

"I am afraid my marriage may break up. I used to let my brothers lead me, and I would string along with them. I want an older brother."

Comments of the Presenting Analyst

The reporting group member emphasized that, despite the

fact that the analytic material continued to reflect depression, the patient would begin each session by stating that he was feeling better. E.F. thought that the analyst would like him more if he would recover, and he was therefore trying to deceive the analyst.

What the analyst considered most important in this session, was the patient's expression of fear that his marriage might break up. Before this, E.F. had denied having any difficulty with his wife. Another new development in this session was the patient's attempt to relate to the analyst as to an older brother. E.F. has no fidelity to any role in the transference: therefore the therapist played different roles at different times. He represented variously E.F.'s mother, father, grandfather, brother, and others.

Group Discussion

Some members of the group expressed concern that a patient who attempts so regularly to deceive the doctor about his condition might be likely to suicide, possibly to spite the therapist. Roose and Feder agreed with Ostow's earlier suggestion that, at this time, E.F. was depressed, but was feeling too passive to attempt suicide.

Linn noted that what seems to save this patient, when he is depressed, is his ability to seduce others into supportive relationships. Feder and Ostow warned that, since this man depends on such reassurance, this would be an inauspicious time to attempt to analyze with him the nature and motivation for these relationships. To Roose and Ostow the shifting nature of the transference, as it was described by the presenting analyst, indicated that E.F. is a man who is always in search of a transference, but who cannot accept a real relation with any other person.

Tuesday, December 11   "My wife would like to see you. She's not going to be able to take this much longer. Just before I reached your office, I had the desire to turn around and go back. What's he going to do to me now? I have a constant desire to get out of here—out of New Haven—but I have a fear of going." At this point the physician's telephone rang, and E.F.'s reaction was, "When that phone rang, it went through me like an electric shock. I'm afraid I might have a brain tumor."

"I feel like coming up here and taking a crap. I feel relieved, and I go off. For years I wondered what a woman's vagina looked like. It's not a very pretty sight. I feel I don't deserve this. I've led a fairly decent life. I asked my wife to come into bed with me. She said she wasn't in the mood."

Comments of the Presenting Analyst

Mrs. F.'s reported impatience resulted from her husband's depression, which unnerved her. The reporting group member was particularly impressed by E.F.'s more extensive remarks about his wife. Mr. and Mrs. F. had not been having any sexual relations for quite a while, and the analyst understood the patient's approach as an attempt to appease her lest she abandon him.

Group Discussion

Linn interpreted E.F.'s sexual approach to his wife as a defense against his own homosexual fears of the doctor. The sequence of remarks about having a bowel movement in the doctor's office, the female genitalia, and his renewed advances toward his wife point to a confrontation, on the part of the patient, with his own feminine identification in relation to the doctor. The presenting analyst agreed, though he was more impressed by the fact that the patient was beginning to face his problems with his wife, that is, his sexual aversion to her, his need to cling to her, and her turning away from him. This situation forced E.F. to deal with his castration anxiety.

Ostow saw E.F.'s remark about having a brain tumor as a sign of persisting depression. Feder asked about the behavior of the analyst during these sessions. The reporting group member responded that, during this period, he asked questions mostly and gave assurance.

Wednesday, December 12   "I always hit my lowest point before I come here. In some ways I'm better. I keep feeling that, within a month, I'm going to head out of here. I can't take New Haven. I want partial treatment with you and partial treatment with Dr. M. This morning I tried intercourse. I couldn't get an erection. She was very nice. I've given up all desire to masturbate. Tonight I'm going to force myself to play tennis with a nice fellow.

"I almost had several accidents while driving home. Those large trucks . . . I became apprehensive that my wife was out screwing a guy. I thought, 'If she would practice fellatio, at least I would get an erection, but she's not the fellatio type.' I never wanted to have children. I had a vision that once I lost my temper, and threw a hatchet at my brother, and almost killed him."

Comments of the Presenting Analyst

E.F. again began the session by stating that he felt better, though this time he also let the doctor know that their relationship was only temporary. He was not planning to continue the treatment. The fantasy of throwing a hatchet at his brother is a recurrent one. Though the doctor doubted that such an event ever happened, he felt that the story does reflect a real sadism on the part of the patient, and a murderous attitude towards men, probably in response to his homosexual attachment. Thus the fantasy might also be interpreted as this man's indirect way of informing the doctor of the need he feels to defend himself in the transference.

Group Discussion

Feder was impressed by the way E.F. habitually juxtaposes good and bad reports to the doctor. Ostow suggested that the patient may be afraid to say anything that might offend someone without preparing the way first. Feder further saw E.F.'s advances towards his wife as an attempt to rise above his inertia to a level of greater activity. Perhaps this man sees all activity as murderous aggression, and feared that he would lose control of his hostility. The presenting analyst agreed with this suggestion. Feder added that this aggression might be a result of the drug. In his own practice, Feder had observed that some anti-depression agents, and Tofranil particularly, tend to elicit aggression in patients, which is expressed in their dreams and in analytic material. E.F.'s therapist was not convinced that E.F.'s aggression was elicited by the drug though he recognized that it was a possibility.

Thursday, December 13   "I still get that small electric shock as soon as I hear the door to the waiting room open. I tried to play tennis after twenty years; I just can't function at all. I seem to clear up a little at night after I see you, and I put my problems aside. There's a numbness of body and mind. I had it before the pills. I don't function too well. I couldn't put my matches in my pocket this morning. I'm envious of my wife's social success. I'm going to bring my wife up here on Tuesday. I'm going to live twenty years—and be depressed the whole time.

"I told my friend that his wife was pregnant. He said: 'Only about a month.' I said: 'It will probably be a girl.' I have an instinct for that. Several times in my life I have told a woman she was pregnant. I was holding the cat. I felt his windpipe. I thought I could choke him; I want to kill my wife's dog. I want to die. The only funeral I ever went to was my father's. I always duck funerals. I'm thinking of myself being born out of my mother's vagina."

Group Discussion

Linn asked why E.F. wanted the analyst to meet his wife. The presenting analyst felt that the wife wanted to speak to him, and the patient wanted the doctor to tell Mrs. F. to behave. Linn wondered whether the patient might be bringing his wife to the doctor as an offering. E.F.'s analyst doubted that this was the case, because the patient seemed to have no respect at all for his wife, and was aware that others also found her difficult to get along with.

Linn and Feder expressed concern that the patient's allusions to death and rebirth might indicate a suicidal proclivity. The reporting analyst did not feel that E.F. was any more suicidal in this session than he had been previously, though his hostility was becoming more and more open. Ostow suspected that this more overt hostility might be a result of incipient drug action.

Friday, December 14   "I feel better this morning. By the time I get here, and get mixed up in this maze of problems, I get low again. Last night my wife really gave me the works. She said she wouldn't let me pull her down. I keep saying 'Judgment Day is here.' Her constant demand for service irritates me."

As this session marked the end of the fourth week that E.F. had been taking the Niamid, the presenting analyst ended the session by saying: "Maybe you will have a surprise for me on Monday." The patient answered: "A baby." The analyst responded: "You will be the baby."

Group Discussion

The presenting analyst explained that this man's wife really does treat him with disrespect: E.F. prepares breakfast for her, washes the dishes, mails the letters, and does most of the household errands. He performs these tasks because he is afraid that Mrs. F. will leave him, and he cannot live without her.

The group then discussed the analyst's final remarks to the patient. The reporting group member elaborated that these remarks were meant to encourage E.F. by letting him know that the doctor expected him to be well. Feder and Linn felt that, by speaking in this way, the analyst was contaminating the experiment, that is, by making a suggestion which the patient was likely to accept. Linn cited an article by C. Fisher* which described how a suggestion made by a psychiatrist to a patient is typically received by the patient as an oral impregnation fantasy and birth. E.F.'s response, "a baby," corroborates this thesis. Ostow pointed out that this response can also be seen as a reference to the approaching Christmas holiday. He felt that encouragement is important for depressed patients.

Monday, December 17 "I feel better in a doped up kind of way. Question of whether you should see my wife; as if I want her to look at you. Dr. M. said there would be nothing in it for me—a long ordeal, expensive. This is a gray world. I guess I'm afraid to uncover my troubles between me and my wife. Now she wants me

*Charles Fisher, "Studies on the Nature of Suggestion: Experimental Induction of Dreams by Direct Suggestion," *Journal of American Psychoanalytic Association* 1:2 (April 1953) pp. 222-255. Also see "Studies on the Nature of Suggestion: The Transference Meaning of Giving Suggestions," *Journal of American Psychoanalytic Association* 1:3 (July 1953) pp. 406-437.

to take up art. She tries to encourage me. I keep thinking the only way out is death. I'm rubbing my stomach because I have a lot of pain, like ulcer pains. I'm going to have dinner with my brother-in-law tonight (the brother-in-law who fired him twenty years ago). I have a desire to ask him to help me get back to work.

"As I came into town today, I got lower and lower. I jerked off with the idea of someone else screwing my wife. For the first time in months, I woke up with an erection."

Group Discussion

The presenting analyst reported that E.F.'s mention of Dr. M. was an allusion to a conversation some time ago in which Dr. M. had apparently told the patient: "There is no point in going any further in analysis. You've got to get off your behind and do something. If you do any more analysis, you'll be wasting your time." To Ostow the most significant element of this analytic hour was the patient's statement that he had masturbated. The two previous sessions revealed a return of E.F.'s aggressive impulse, and this visit marked the revival of his sexuality. Linn remarked that the erotic feeling occurred in a setting where the patient was playing a voyeuristic role. The reporting analyst added that, when E.F.'s wife had had an affair several years earlier, and had told him about it, he had intercourse every day for months, and he masturbated with the fantasy of seeing his wife having intercourse with her lover. Feder commented that, in the last week, E.F. had begun to talk about himself in a much more realistic way.

There was more discussion about whether, by bringing her to his analytic session, the patient was offering his wife to the doctor as a gift. Linn and Loomis thought that such a gesture might serve as a defense against E.F.'s emerging homosexual feelings toward the psychiatrist. Feder and Loomis suggested that, in this case, perhaps E.F. felt that, as an untrustworthy Jew, the analyst deserved her.

Tuesday, December 18   "I think those pills are working a little. I feel a little steadier. I couldn't remember whether I took one this morning, so I took another one at noon. I feel that I'm going to bust out of the city in January, and go to Westport.

Yesterday I bathed, and cleaned myself up. My brother-in-law and his wife are coming for dinner. I asked whether he could talk to me sometime, and he said he would.

"I'll never make love to my wife again. I won't be able to. I wouldn't be able to get along if my wife died before I did. I always guess that people are going to die when I hear they're sick. Like my guessing when a woman is pregnant."

At this point the physician increased E.F.'s dose of Niamid to 300 mgs. He felt that 200 mgs had sufficed to start the patient moving, but that it had stopped working, and E.F. was not progressing any further.

E.F. then spoke of his wife's family; he described them as "dumpers," because they "dumped people"—specifically him. The doctor asked the patient whether he felt any guilt about his mother's death. E.F. replied that he thought that the trauma incident to his birth might have set in motion the pathologic process that resulted in her death.

Comments of the Presenting Analyst

It is significant that on this day E.F. forgot whether he had taken the medication. Frequently, when patients begin to recover, they resist the pills, and cannot remember whether they have taken them. E.F.'s bathing and cleaning himself up is another objective indication that he was feeling better. The doctor understood the patient's reference to his wife's death as an expression of his wish for her death, and of his conflict about it.

The analyst interpreted E.F.'s statement that he guesses people will die when he hears that they are ill, as meaning that the patient is afraid of losing people through death. He anticipates their dying in order to minimize the trauma that their possible death might cause.

Group Discussion

Loomis noted that this man consistently associates pregnancy with illness and death. Ostow suspected that E.F.'s ambivalence toward his mother may have been related to her frequent pregnancies.

Wednesday, December 19   "Everything's in place—just the same. I have all kinds of pains in my stomach. I wonder whether I'm working up an ulcer." The analyst suggested that E.F. see a physician about his stomach pains, and the patient responded: "I'm afraid of having more x-rays: I can't take any more. I feel that the pills are failing. I want to go to Dr. D., and ask her to take me on. I see a little boy running in all directions, not knowing which door to go through. I am steadier, and I am steadier in my driving."

Group Discussion

Linn and Ostow found it surprising that, as E.F. was recovering, his stomach pains were increasing. Ostow attributed the pains to the transitional stage, specifically to the agitation associated with being half in depression and half out of it, and to the patient's renewed attempt to deal with conflict. Feder and Ostow mentioned that recovery from depression almost always includes minor relapses. The presenting analyst agreed, but he thought that what was observable in this man during this visit was not a minor relapse, but a real regression. He had expected E.F.'s recovery to proceed more rapidly. Ostow understood the patient's final remarks as an attempt to reassure himself, and as a simultaneous expression of disappointment and mistrust of the doctor.

Thursday, December 20   "I hit my lowest spots on my way here. I had a beautiful sleep last night: I woke up feeling fine; I felt pretty good all day. As soon as I get here, I feel lower." E.F. then wondered aloud whether he could masturbate in the analyst's presence, without the doctor's knowing it. He added: "I feel weird here—that big dog, this old, gray building.

"I was thinking that people see me coming out of here, and think, 'There's a nut.' I don't want to admit to any anti-Semitism. My father had my brother and me circumcised to prevent masturbation. Give me the power to get an erection."

Comments of the Presenting Analyst

In this session, the patient elaborated his homosexual anxiety in the transference: as E.F.'s condition was improving, his relationship with the doctor was becoming a more serious problem. The request for an erection particularly marks the resurgence of this man's initial fear that the Jewish analyst might castrate him.

Group Discussion

Feder added to the presenting analyst's interpretation that he had once treated a Protestant clergyman's son, who expressed the same conflict about seeing a Jewish therapist. Loomis saw E.F.'s request for an erection as an expression not only of fear of the doctor but also of the wish that the analyst would be able to help him achieve an erection. Feder and Ostow thought that, by making this request, the patient was actually asking the physician for permission to have an erection, and, more generally, to be a man.

Ostow remarked that, as in the two previous case histories, this patient, as he comes out of depression, encounters again the original pathogenic situation. E.F.'s basic problems seem to be his conflict with his wife, and his inability to maintain a relation with another man.

Friday, December 21   E.F. brought the analyst a drawing of what New Haven looked like to him. After showing the drawing to the doctor, the patient remarked: "I had a bad night last night. Some noise kept me up. I worried about getting up in time to come here. I have a feeling that New Haven is very dangerous for our marriage. My wife loves it, and I can't take it. We seem to be really drifting apart. My wife is giving me real hard looks. She looks like a Mongol, wearing that fur hat of hers. My brothers used to say, if they couldn't screw, they'd rather be dead. I hate vaginas. I used to go to sleep with a hard on, holding it. I felt my penis this morning; it just seemed as if it was shriveled up—nothing."

Group Discussion of E.F.'s Drawing

Feder described the drawing as a conglomerate phallus. Linn remarked on the obsessive-compulsive character structure revealed in the painstaking way in which each detail is executed, and he suggested that the drawing might point to an identification of this

patient with his wife. The presenting analyst confirmed both of
Linn's observations, and added that E.F.'s identification with his
wife was quite open. He would frequently say: "As I am lying
here, I imagine that I have breasts." He would start to rub his
chest, and say: "This is like masturbating." Feder commented
that, for this man, identification with his wife both recaptures his
mother, and takes him out of competition with his father.

Group Discussion of the Analytic Session

Ostow saw the patient's elaboration of the threat to his
marriage as a result of the increase in his medication. E.F. was
again struggling with his depression and encountering castration
anxiety with his wife, as well as his homosexual anxiety with other
men. These difficulties were continuing to impede his recovery.
Feder pointed out that, with E.F., as with the two patients
previously considered, though his depression was lifting, the
contents of his thought were still depressive. There is a time lag before a person's thinking catches up with changes in his affective
state.

Wednesday, December 26   "Those pills seem to be working.
Lately I have had shock dreams:

> Something is coming at me quick. A man with a machine
> coming up to my face. Very frightening.

I wake right up. I told you I was working on the idea of getting out
of New Haven. The strain of New Haven is very rough on our marriage. New Haven is too crowded and rushed. I can't stand wearing
a coat. Westport is lovely. My apartment looks to me like an
empty hole. The thing I've always loved is a home. I love my home
in Westport. No apartment has ever been a home. The summers
there are delightful, but after the summer I can't stand it. A friend
of mine noticed that, when I get to the city, I get twitchy and nervous. I wish I had been brought up with a quiet life on the farm.
I've been much less suicidal. My wife is really getting tough with
me."

As previously related, the patient then told the analyst, for the first time, about the incident that, when he was five or six years old, he was with his mother in a buggy, and the horse bolted. This story was presented in two versions: the first was that his mother jumped out when the horse bolted. The variant is that he was not there, and his mother did not jump out, but he was very frightened.

Comments of the Presenting Analyst

The presenting analyst elaborated on E.F.'s aversion to wearing a coat. The dislike is genuine, and, even in the coldest weather, E.F. comes to his analytic session lightly clad. The analyst understood E.F.'s dislike of coats as primarily a transvestite fantasy. E.F. also does not like to wear a belt or any other tight garment. He says that, if he had his way, men would dress like women. He dresses as often as possible in formal wear, because it is looser than more casual wear, and he does not wear a belt with a tuxedo. The doctor later learned that, when E.F. goes to the opera or to a concert, he frequently opens his trousers as soon as he is seated.

Group Discussion

Linn noted that it was Christmas time, and wondered whether E.F. was identifying with the baby Jesus. The reporting group member responded that this patient does identify with the baby Jesus. His Jesus fantasies notwithstanding, however, E.F. expresses contempt for religion. Ostow, responding to the story of the horse and buggy, pointed out that both versions depict situations of great danger. Linn added that both versions also suggest the idea of loss of control of impulse.

Ostow proposed that, in this session, what is evident is mainly that the patient, in a state of being half well and half depressed, was reaching out, more than ever before, to other men, and particularly to the analyst. This movement intensified the homosexual challenge to the patient, and he was defending himself against this threat. E.F.'s expressed need to get away from the city should be understood in the framework of his earlier drawing of the city as a multitude of phalluses.

Roose, noting how the patient utilized his illness to seduce others into taking care of him, wondered what would happen to E.F. once he became well. The presenting analyst noted that when E.F. is well, he does not need people. He becomes independent, does not reach out to others, and therefore has no need to defend himself. Moreover, once recovered, the patient becomes enamored of New Haven, and cannot leave it: there is enough narcissistic investment for object love to become irrelevant, and his object relations become even more superficial.

Group Discussion of the Increase in the Patient's Dose of Niamid

Ostow proposed that, when a patient's dose of anti-depression drug is increased, the patient must have at least one night's sleep, and often two, before a result óf the increase is observable. Loomis agreed, and added that, for this reason, he usually recommends that patients take their largest dose of medication at bedtime. Klerman wondered whether this phenomenon could be attributed to the effect on sleep-dream mechanisms. Ostow thought that this effect might result from either the sleep-dream mechanism itself, or from physiological factors reflected in the sleep-dream mechanism.

Bressler observed that patients on tricyclic drugs require less sleep generally, and asked whether anti-depression drugs affect the REM cycle. Feder said that many of his patients have reported that, as they recover from depression, their dreams change; specifically, as their condition improves, they remember their dreams better, and hostility in the dreams becomes more overt. Feder speculated that the four weeks required for recovery from depression, after beginning an anti-depression drug, may be tied to biological rhythms.

Linn mentioned that slow wave sleep tends to be deficient in depression, but becomes more normal as depression lifts. REM sleep, however, is influenced by anti-depression drugs: Parnate, for example, will produce a reduction of REM sleep. The various anti-depression drugs affect a person's clinical state similarly, and yet have very different REM effects. Klerman commented that, when patients report that they are having difficulty sleeping, they may be perceiving a real physiological change. Ostow felt that any drug or situation which makes it possible for a person to have enough good, deep sleep, will increase REM, and conversely, a drug which interferes with length or tranquility of sleep will decrease it.

Thursday, December 27   "I am trying to set a deadline at the end of January (this deadline refers to when he expects to leave the doctor). I'm very grateful for what you've done, in case I do go (that is, to Westport). I'm scared. I don't see myself ever adjusting to New Haven. I got upset with my wife last night. She told me she had bought a painting for $200; when I got the bill, it turned out to be $2,000. She does that sort of thing; we'll go broke.

"I didn't sleep much; at a quarter of twelve I tried intercourse. I couldn't get an erection, and finally I just jerked off. My wife said this morning: "Your heart is shaking.' She's kind of nutty. Over the week-end, she filled the house with people. I can't stand it. I can't bear to fight with her. Then I had the old suicidal thing. I feel like I'm in a runaway car. When I drive over here, I drive very slowly."

Comments of the Presenting Analyst

The reporting group member emphasized that E.F.'s description of his ambivalence towards his wife occurred immediately after his reference to suicide. The analyst further likened the patient's feeling that he was in a runaway car to his story about his mother in a runaway carriage, which Linn had interpreted as loss of control of impulse.

Friday, December 28   "I felt a little dizzy last night in my right upper section, a constriction in the head [he meant the right upper part of his head]. Maybe I could faint, so I didn't take the pill this morning. I worry about my driving. I had another restless night. I've never had them before.

"My wife said she is going to stay in New Haven and build a career. She's not going to let me hold her back. I thought, 'You're making yourself into a widow.' I can't bear to fight with her. I was

wondering whether I could go to Westport alone. I thought more
and more of suicide. I feel pretty low again. I felt nervous about
the police on the highway today. Maybe I was driving too slowly
(sic), so I slowed up a little. I keep thinking that I've tried to lead
a good life. The first time I took ether for my tonsils, I kept going
down, down."

Comment of the Presenting Analyst

At this point, E.F. appeared somewhat depressed, but was
feeling better than before.

Wednesday, January 2, 1963   Although, the previous
evening, the patient had telephoned the doctor to cancel his appointment because some pipes had burst in his house, he appeared
for his scheduled session anyway, and announced: "I'm going to
stick it out for a month at least to see. The Niamid is working, and
I suppose you would say that most of the credit goes to the
Niamid.

"I had a good week-end, except for the nights. I had flash
dreams that woke me up:

Someone was coming at me.

When I came into New Haven, my spirits just drooped. I had intercourse the other day, and I had a premature orgasm. Later I
masturbated. I'm losing my temper with my wife. There's tension
every minute.

"I had a feeling just now that you were going to hit me. The
faces of the people in New Haven are depressing. I feel like a ship
heading into a thick fog, with no sense of direction. I just don't
feel so panicky, but I feel drugged, as though the Niamid has
calmed me, but has not solved my problems.

"I felt much surer of myself in everything I did this week-
end; I did a good drawing; I ate better; things were much more in
focus. But I didn't sleep well, which is unusual for me. If you drop
dead, I could get out of New Haven tomorrow.

"I slept beautifully last night, for the first time in three
nights. I wish I was born in 1860, and died in 1914."

Comments of the Presenting Analyst

The reporting analyst had previously maintained to the patient that, from the psychotherapeutic point of view, the progress made so far was not sufficient to justify recovery. Therefore, any improvement in E.F.'s condition would have to be attributed to the drug. The analyst considered the patient's remark about the Niamid as protest against this point of view. The appreciation of the doctor supports E.F.'s extension of the amount of time he expects to devote to the treatment.

E.F. has also become significantly less timid about quarreling with his wife. E.F.'s expressed wish to have lived for the fifty-four years from 1860 to 1914 should be seen as a longing for a less complicated world. E.F. was then fifty-six years old, and the doctor later learned that the patient's father had committed suicide at the age of fifty-four.

Group Discussion of the Patient's Reported Insomnia

Ostow found it significant that the patient reported his insomnia without any distress at all. This is a good example of Ostow's observation that, generally, when a patient is profiting from drug therapy, the side effects are tolerated with considerable equanimity, and complaints are kept down. The insomnia is a manifestation of E.F.'s improvement, and not merely a side effect of the drug. The patient was sleeping less, because he was beginning to have more available energy.

Feder warned that when patients make very general statements about their sleep patterns, the doctor should press for particulars, as these evaluations are largely based on the patient's very subjective views about his usual sleep habits. For example, someone who claims that he is "sleeping all the time" may mean that he is now sleeping five hours a night, whereas he used to sleep only two or three hours. Feder observed further that, although in this session the patient repeated much previous depressive material, he seemed no longer as troubled by it as he was earlier. Feder wondered whether E.F. was really beginning to sound different, or whether the apparent change in his mood was merely a reflection of the analyst's own enthusiasm.

Klerman then suggested that the insomnia might be an indication that the analyst should consider reducing the patient's dose of
Niamid. The presenting analyst explained that he did not think of
lowering the dose at this time, because the patient was still not
entirely free from depression. He agreed, however, that sleep
manifestations can serve as indicators of a change in the patient's
condition that might warrant alteration of the drug dosage.

Furst commented that, in this session, what seems to be a
remnant of depression, may actually be an expression of this
man's fear of the consequences of his incipient recovery in terms
of hostility and difficulty in interpersonal relationships. For this
patient, depression is a safe position, even if it is a more uncomfortable one. Ostow and Roose responded that, although E.F. uses his
illness to cling, once he is well, he gives up his dependence.

Friday, January 4   E.F. brought the analyst a check and
some pictures that he had drawn. He told the doctor: "I had an
argument with my wife yesterday. I told her, 'You're going off
like a fucking cannon.' She got furious. She has a very fast mind,
and she interrupts. Then I said something to which she replied: 'I
have a fantasy that you will tell me that you are a great guy.' I
had my old fantasy:

> I was dead, and my brother-in-law said: 'How sweet he is;
> we should have done more for him.'

I had the idea of committing suicide on his doorstep."

Group Discussion

E.F.'s analyst added to the suicide fantasy that when the patient was ten years old he had a similar fantasy:

> He was lying stretched out in a funeral parlor. All the
> townspeople were gathered around, reflecting on how un-
> justly they had treated him, and feeling sorry.

Ostow remarked that this is a classic Tom Sawyer hero fantasy.
Furst mentioned a Japanese tradition that, if you have a terrible

enemy, you hang yourself on his front porch; he then has the obligation to support your family for the rest of his life.

Linn questioned the presenting analyst's apparent hostility to E.F.'s wife. The reporting group member responded that, from the point of view of the patient's well-being, she is a destructive element. Winkelman commented that E.F. has hardly proven to be a kind, loving, husband. Ostow added that the patient and his wife appear to be hostile to each other.

Klerman wondered whether it might be beneficial for Mr. and Mrs. F. to enter psychotherapy as a couple. The presenting analyst explained that these two people have had all kinds of treatments, with different types of therapists, as individuals and as a couple, but these earlier courses of treatment do not seem to have made any impression on them at all. Feder speculated on the possible beneficial effects for the patient of a separation from his wife at a time when he was not depressed. The presenting analyst felt that E.F. could not tolerate living alone, and that it was the threat of divorce that precipitated this depression.

Monday, January 7 "I have my city clothes on now. I hate city clothes. There's something binding about them—tight coats and collars. I feel good. I really have my feet on the ground. For two or three days now, I felt like myself for the first time in months. I saw my brother James off today; he's gone to Europe. I asked my brother David whether I had ever been buggered as a child. He said there was no homosexuality.

"New Haven doesn't seem nearly as bad today. Things are much more in focus. I tried to jerk off the other day, and I couldn't even get an orgasm. My wife and I decided that we should feel free to go out separately with others. I love to have women rub my head. I am a genius at getting women to rub me. My head is very sensitive. Our new house is beginning to shape up, and I'm beginning to get a thrill out of that. I shit six times between Friday evening and Saturday night. I get constipated in New Haven, but I shit in the country."

Group Discussion

To the presenting analyst, this session evidenced clear-cut recovery on the part of the patient. Linn wondered what had become of E.F.'s plan to leave the therapist, and go to his homosexual peers. The reporting group member replied that the patient was no longer driven to leave him. Since E.F. was feeling better, he was less dependent on the analyst, and the homosexual threat was correspondingly reduced. Indeed, it is because the doctor no longer seemed so threatening that E.F. was, at this point, able to say overtly that he wanted the analyst to admire him. E.F. could not acknowledge this feeling earlier in the treatment.

Recapitulation of E.F.'s Recovery from Depression

November 21 – The patient began to take Niamid, 200 mgs a day.

13 days later – The patient was still feeling depressed, dependent, fearful, guilty, and afraid of the homosexual transference.

19 days later – E.F. acknowledged his marital difficulties for the first time.

20 days later – E.F. admitted that his wife was impatient with him. He made his first sexual approach to her, and she refused.

21 days later – The patient made his first attempt at intercourse, but had no erection. He reported aggressive fantasies and a greater interest in object relations.

22 days later – The patient began to play tennis for the first time in twenty years (and he continued to play, almost daily until his next episode of depression, six years later). E.F. described sadistic and omniscient fantasies, though he was still fearful in the transference.

23 days later – E.F. reported feeling better, and complained, for the first time, of his wife's hostility.

26 days later – E.F. acknowledged both the problems in his marriage, and his fear of facing them. He had his first morning erection in several months, and masturbated, for the first time, with a voyeuristic fantasy. His other depressive symptoms continued.

27 days later— The patient felt steadier. He forgot his medication, and cleaned himself up, but maintained his threat to leave the analyst. He reported, for the first time, fantasies of Mrs. F.'s death. The analyst thought this was significant insofar as it meant that E.F. could begin to imagine being independent of his wife. E.F.'s sexual desire was beginning to be diverted to other women. At this point the Niamid was increased to 300 mgs a day.

28 days later— E.F. complained of abdominal pains and discouragement.

29 days later— The patient felt better until he saw the analyst. He seemed threatened by the doctor, and spoke of defying him.

30 days later— E.F. reported insomnia for the first time. He was concerned about the threat to his marriage, and seemed to be experiencing castration anxiety.

35 days later— The patient reported homosexual fears. Though he continued to complain of depression, the analyst saw fewer external signs of it. E.F. expressed displeasure with his wife, and noted the first definite improvement in his mood. Moreover, the doctor noticed a reduction in the patient's externally-directed hostility.

There was some discussion of the extent to which this patient's experiences are generalizable. The group agreed that time-tables for recovery from depression are different for different patients, and vary, even for the same patient, from depression to depression.

January 1963 to June 1968   Following his recovery, E.F. remained well for five years. He saw the presenting analyst five days a week, and took Niamid, 350 mgs daily. At one point, E.F. became a little high, and the doctor added Mellaril, 25 mgs a day. This medication was never altered. The patient spent his time with his friends who are unsuccessful artists. During the winter, he invited these friends to his apartment in New Haven, and attended concerts and the opera. Week-ends and summers were spent at his home in Westport, also in the company of many friends and sycophants. Mr. and Mrs. F. continued to maintain little of what would traditionally be called "family life."

Spring 1968   E.F.'s relationship with his wife began to suffer severe strains. One major problem was that Mrs. F. wanted to go to London to visit friends. The patient opposed this project, because he has a chronic fear of becoming poor, and cannot stand the idea of spending any money unnecessarily. (In fact the clothing which E.F. wears to his analytic sessions is twenty-five or thirty years old, and he rarely throws anything away.) Mrs. F. insisted on the trip, despite her husband's objections, and the patient finally decided to follow her a week later.

Tuesday, June 11, 1968   (second to last visit before E F.'s departure) "I lost eleven pounds in the last three weeks. I decided that I must have a quick cancer. I had a mental struggle about intercourse with Mrs. A. (a neighbor with whom the patient was having occasional sexual relations). I called my wife in London last night, and had a terrible time with her on the telephone. I made damn sure to get down to the hospital today for a chest x-ray and blood tests."

Comments of the Presenting Analyst

The analyst noted the patient's close association of a cancer and an affair and he reminded the group that this man could be potent, only if he had intercourse very quickly, and then got out of bed immediately. E.F. could not spend the night with a woman. Mrs. A was divorced and was quite crazy. Moreover she was very attractive, and welcomed men in general, and E.F. in particular. The patient and the analyst had spoken at length about the consequences of extramarital affairs in terms of ultimate catastrophe within the family. E.F. was tempted to have an affair with Mrs. A., but, as a result of his discussions with the analyst, he felt he ought to abstain. The chest x-rays and blood test had been suggested to the patient by his internist on the basis of some trivial complaints.

Group Discussion

Bressler asked whether the approaching separation from the doctor was generating any anxiety in the patient. The reporting group member felt that E.F. was caught between separation from his wife, on the one hand, and from the analyst, on the other. Given the choice, the patient would have preferred to remain with the doctor, except that his wife was so insistent that he follow her. The patient had been planning, in any event, to interrupt the analysis for the summer.

Roose remarked that a quick cancer might be E.F.'s only legitimate excuse for not going to London. Ostow noted that, as a child, E.F.'s major claim to his mother's attention seems to have been his illness. He may have thought that, by being ill, he could force the analyst to take care of him, to keep him in New Haven, and to persuade his wife to return home. The mention of a "quick cancer" also suggests that, if E.F. should become sick, he wanted it to go quickly.

Klerman speculated that the patient may also have seen his separation from the doctor as a form of illness, or death. Bressler thought that the illness could serve a further function: as a form of resistance to dealing with the real problem of the impending separation from the analyst over the summer. Ostow suspected that, more specifically, E.F. was anticipating losing both the therapist and his wife, and was defending himself by withdrawing cathexis from external objects, and reinvesting it in himself in the form of a hypochondria. Furst commented on how this man resists coping with the decisions and problems implicit in his circumstances. Instead, he reacts to stress by placing himself in a completely passive position, where others have to take care of him.

Thursday, June 13   E.F. had persuaded his wife to alter her plans in such a way as to permit him to remain in New Haven for an extra week. On this day he told the analyst: "I was hoping all along that you would cancel. Mrs. A. was over last night. We stayed up until 5:00 a.m. I do feel depressed today. I did demonstrate that I could get an erection and maintain it. I did many times during the course of the night, but I could not have an orgasm. I have never had an orgasm with this woman yet. She

238 PSYCHODYNAMIC APPROACH

mentioned something about incompetence, and that concerned me. Immediately I thought I'd be punished. For example, the doctor would tell me that my chest x-ray showed something. I did look at her sexual parts, and found it quite exciting. It excited me to rear up on my knees, and watch myself screwing them. That's when I almost had the orgasm. I said, 'If I had an orgasm, I'd lose my fire.' "

Comments of the Presenting Analyst

E.F.'s mention of looking at Mrs. A.'s "sexual parts" was a response to a discussion he had had with the analyst that, though he was then sixty-two years old, and had been involved in affairs with many women, he had never looked at a woman's genitals. He had assured the analyst that he did not know what the clitoris was, or where it was; he had never seen it.

Group Discussion

Ostow was impressed by the amount of narcissism involved when this man has intercourse. He tries to justify and rationalize his impotence by saying that it is a deliberate device to preserve his vitality. Furst and Roose thought that what was involved was not merely narcissism, but also castration. Many patients want to watch their penis go in and out in order to be sure that it comes out again. Linn wondered whether this man's watching himself have intercourse might have primal scene implications. He cited an article by Kanzer[*] that describes how, for many depressed patients, the recollection of exclusion from parental intimacies is a core memory. Perhaps, through watching himself make love, E.F. was trying to create a primal scene experience. Ostow confirmed that he had encountered this phenomenon among his own patients.

The presenting analyst observed that the complexity of this analysis makes it difficult to tell whether, for this man, the primal scene is an important element. E.F. has been in psychotherapy for most of his adult life: he knows most of the

*Mark Kanzer, "Manic Depressive Psychoses with Paranoid Trends," *International Journal of Psychoanalysis* 33(1952) pp. 34-42.

theoretical formulations, and can recite personal memories that substantiate most of them. E.F. did say he thought that he had slept in his parents' room, though he was not sure. At one point every baby in his family slept in his parents' room, but was later bundled off to the nursery.

Linn asked whether E.F. had expressed concern about his wife's sexual adventures in London and the reporting analyst replied that he had. Bressler noted that, for this man, an ejaculation is equivalent to a loss. It temporarily empties him, and emptiness is one thing he cannot tolerate. Ostow found that many depressed patients, and especially men, feel depleted, guilty, and ashamed after an orgasm. Furst added that depressed men often experience retarded ejaculation and even failure of ejaculation. Loomis remarked that these men fear that they possess a limited supply of vital energy, which will not be replenished.

Summer 1968   After this session, the analyst heard nothing more from the patient for quite a while. E.F. spent two weeks with his wife in London. They returned to New Haven at the beginning of July, and then went to their home in Westport. At the end of July the doctor received a phone call from Mrs. F., complaining about her husband's compulsive cleaning and excessive drinking.

Group Discussion

Feder commented that the patient's obsessive need to put things in order might be a reaction to a feeling of dissolution within him. Klerman wondered whether this was an obsessive compulsive reaction or an early manic phase. Loomis remarked that E.F. may have been competing with Mrs. F. by playing housewife. Ostow added that, for this man, housewifely behavior also represents another way of identifying with his mother. Klerman asked whether the presenting analyst had ever seen E.F. this high before, and the reporting analyst replied that he had not.

Klerman then remarked that this manic behavior, on the part of the patient, could be interpreted as a signal to reduce E.F.'s dose of Niamid. E.F.'s analyst understood this high as a defense against depression; under these circumstances, decreasing the dose of the anti-depression drug would push the patient even higher.

There had been incidents earlier in the therapy in which this patient had become hypomanic on too low a dose of Niamid.

Monday, July 29   After receiving Mrs. F.'s call, the therapist telephoned E.F., and questioned him about the activities his wife had described. Over the telephone, the patient sounded quite intoxicated, and the analyst strongly urged him to come into the office so that they could talk together about his summer. An appointment was made for the next morning.

Tuesday, July 30   "I'm glad you put the pressure on me to come in, because I know I should have, and I have been resisting it. There is no question that I have been on a high. I also have been drinking too much. I think I am going to give it up. My plans are: no more drinks. Check me out in September."

As E.F. was speaking, the analyst noticed that he was hoarse, very high, and very cheerful. At the doctor's suggestion, it was agreed that E.F. would come in for three visits, of which this was the first.

Wednesday, July 31   "I felt better after I left here yesterday. I had lunch with one of my friends, and then I had dinner with him and his wife at their home. They noticed the constant talk and annoyance about interruptions." When the analyst asked E.F. about his cleaning, the latter responded: "I used to help my wife's mother clean the ice box."

The doctor then inquired about the trip to London and the patient replied: "I got the shittiest bed in the house. I was fearful about being on the top floor. I studied the fire escape four or five times. I got tired of wandering the streets of London. I was bored. The trip meant nothing to me. We didn't fight. On the plane back, she said to me: 'You are a homosexual.' I had no compulsion to screw."

The doctor asked when the overactivity had begun. E.F. said: "About three weeks ago (this would have been a week after their return from London). I suddenly realized that this was my summer to clean up the hundreds of things I never get to. Since she has been back, she has been away from nine to six, and I love it. I hid from her the other day. Whenever she sees me, she gives me hell. I had a large number of bad dreams in early July. I lost this bottom tooth in a bad dream."

Comments of the Presenting Analyst

The reporting analyst confirmed that E.F. does become very angry when interrupted, though one has to interrupt him to get a word in. From the patient's report of his trip to London, the doctor understood that, although E.F. had gone there to be with his wife, once he was there, Mrs. F. ignored him, and banished him to the periphery of the company, in effect, leaving him to wander the streets. The analyst interpreted E.F.'s studying the fire-escape as a wish that a fire would destroy the whole house, which his wife had rented, and where she was also lodging her daughter, her secretary, several relatives, and some of her friends.

The reporter was impressed by the intensity and overtness of E.F.'s controversy with his wife, during this manic period, and he suspected that Mrs. F.'s accusation that he was a homosexual might have been the precipitating trigger for mania.

Group Discussion

Roose was surprised that E.F.'s dream of losing his bottom tooth occurred in the context of a manic episode. Ostow saw the mania as a defense against the depression signified by the bad dream. There was some discussion and elaboration of the general experience of many members of the group, that almost every manic episode contains elements, or signs, of depression. Bressler noted that when manic patients feel threatened or pushed to any significant degree, they drop immediately into depression, and Feder added that manic patients tend to weep. Loomis cited the case of a patient, who, when he becomes manic, works harder and harder, until he begins to succeed, at which point he becomes depressed. Furst and Ostow felt that, generally, mania is an extremely fragile state. It turns into depression if the individual either succeeds, or becomes frustrated.

Ostow wondered whether the only time one can see a mania free of depressive tendencies is when the mania develops as the result of too large a dose of an anti-depression drug. As an example of a pure mania that is not chemically induced, Furst brought up the case of hypomanic individuals, who are not clinically ill, but who are extremely active, and have a low tolerance for frustration. It was Feder's experience that such people also lapse easily into depression. Ostow wondered whether everyone can be chemically induced to mania, or whether some people have a particular susceptibility to mania and depression.

Linn was impressed with the infrequency of mania induced by overdoses of anti-depression agents. He cited Lewin's* formulation that mania is a state in which a person has, in fantasy, achieved union with his mother and fusion with his id. Depression results from the loss of this happy fusion. Although mania and depression frequently appear as alternating states, the alternation is not necessary, and the fusion, or mania, is not a defense against depression. Roose added that unity with the mother can be achieved through a fantasy of success, or through death.

There was some discussion as to whether a drug should be prescribed to treat a patient's clinical manifestations, or whether it should be directed at the patient's underlying dynamic state. The group agreed that, to the careful observer, a patient's clinical symptoms reveal his dynamic condition; therefore the conflict between these two levels of analysis is superficial.

Roose suggested that, as this patient was trying to achieve the idyllic state of being reunited with his mother, he seemed to be experiencing increasing anxiety that he would be completely engulfed by her. Bressler remarked that E.F.'s constant activity, upon which mania depends, enables him to maintain the fantasy that it is he who is doing the devouring. Furst added that hebephrenic schizophrenics, who are similarly euphoric, express delusions that they have multitudes of people inside them.

Thursday, August 1   "I think you are wrong. I should not run away from a crisis. I had a dream last night:

A guy said: "Don't cut in on me. It isn't done anymore." Later he said: "Don't tell me to fuck my wife, because I can't."

*Bertram Lewin, *Psychoanalysis of Elation*. New York: W.W. Norton, 1950.

The analyst asked E.F. about the origins of his concern with cleaning up. The patient responded: "In 1916, when I was ten years old, we had no help, because it was during the war. All the children were expected to help keep the house clean. Nobody did it, except me."

Comments of the Presenting Analyst

E.F.'s first remark, about running away from a crisis, was a response to the doctor's advice to refrain from creating more difficulty at home. The new material about E.F.'s childhood suggests that, for this man, cleaning up is both an attempt to please people by being a good boy, and an identification with his mother, who, by 1916, was dead.

Group Discussion

Klerman wondered what, in his current situation, was making the patient feel like a child again. Ostow suggested that it was rejection by his wife. Loomis suggested that the patient was trying to be a better wife to his father than the new one.

Friday, August 2   E.F., at his own initiative, extended his stay in New Haven to four days. He began this fourth analytic session by stating: "I always wanted to go out and clean up that mess outside your office building. I had a fantasy that you died, right in the middle of my treatment. I felt tired last night at dinner. I dreamed last night:

Some woman was going through my room, into the next room, tidying up things.

I got up to see, and there was no one there but my window. There wasn't any next room.

"Today I feel a little low. Not on my high by a long shot. I haven't had a drink since Monday night. It's been no effort. I like to smell my wife's perfume." The analyst instructed E.F. to increase his dose of Niamid to 400 mgs, and to keep in touch by telephone.

Comments of the Presenting Analyst

The reporting group member explained that E.F.'s street is frequently left messy, and he always wants to go out and clean up. At one point he started to bring trash into the analyst's office, and to throw it into the doctor's waste basket. The analyst felt that the dream was ominous: during his prior depression, there was a time when E.F. would wake up in the middle of the night and find himself at the window.

The patient's comment that he was feeling "low" represents a response to the analyst's endeavors, during the previous days, to impress E.F. with the seriousness of his condition, and to distinguish between reasonable behavior and manic behavior.

Group Discussion

Ostow and Loomis observed that though, on many occasions, this patient prefers to remain passive and to avoid decisions, at this point, he was quite active and decisive. Ostow thought that the patient wanted to spend extra time with the doctor because he was frightened. Bressler suggested that E.F. may have been trying to recover the week of analytic work that he had lost by going to London.

Loomis was puzzled by the dream of going to the window. Roose speculated that, if the words "Don't cut in on me" in the dream of August 1 meant "Don't cut me out of my mother's womb," perhaps this reference to a window should be seen as an expression of the fear that complete fusion with his mother would dissolve the patient's identity. There would be no way out. Ostow felt that the dream was about suicide. The person tidying up was E.F.'s mother. When the patient would become his mother, he too would die. The presenting analyst added that, before he left for London, E.F. had rearranged his life insurance policies, and had written an inventory of his estate. When he told his wife what he had done, she had asked: "Are you preparing to die?"

Feder suggested that E.F. may have been communicating a fear that, if he gave up his manic behavior, a terrible depression would result.

Wednesday, August 21   Mrs. F. kept an appointment with the presenting analyst. She explained that she was seriously considering leaving her husband, because he was such a difficult person. The analyst replied that E.F. might not survive her departure, and that she might find it less easy to live alone than she thought. The doctor further informed Mrs. F. that a good deal of the patient's misbehavior could be averted if she would accommodate his needs for patience, gentleness, and affection. She promised that, though she found it difficult to tolerate her husband's idiosyncrasies, and felt that she must escape him from time to time, she would make every effort to devote herself more to him.

Friday, August 23   One of E.F.'s neighbors telephoned the doctor to complain that he was "overactive" and seemed "disturbed mentally." Obviously distraught, she was weeping over the telephone.

The analyst called the patient to hear his account of this most recent incident. E.F. realized that he might have been overactive. In response to the analyst's questions, E.F. claimed that he had not been drinking, but he acknowledged that he might be a little high. The analyst suggested that E.F. increase his dose of Niamid to 450 mgs a day, and his dose of Mellaril to 50 mgs a day, and the patient agreed. It was also decided that E.F. would come to New Haven to see the doctor for at least one and possibly two sessions some time during the coming week.

Tuesday, August 27   The reporting analyst, not having heard from the patient, telephoned him in the evening. E.F. reported that things were going quite well: he had increased the medication as the analyst had suggested, he was sleeping well, and he saw no need to come in to see the doctor. Although the patient maintained that he would not be able to be in New Haven that week, at the analyst's request, he promised to keep in touch by telephone, which he did not.

Thursday, September 5   Although E.F. had promised to come to see the analyst that week, he remained in Westport and sent Mrs. F. to see him in his place. The patient's wife described how her relationship with her husband had deteriorated considerably. She told the analyst that E.F.'s behavior continued to be bad, but was no worse than when the analyst had seen the patient at the beginning of August. E.F. was no longer drinking alcohol, but he held a glass of iced coffee in his hand at all times. Moreover he was busy constantly, digging some things up and moving other things around. Specifically he was carrying dirty objects from attics and cellars into the kitchen. Most recently her husband had become somewhat more extreme than usual in his dress, and he was avoiding people most of the time.

Mrs. F. emphasized that personally she was feeling very gloomy about the situation, and she thought that she might need help. She was not consistently despondent, however, nor had she dropped any of her usual activities.

At ten o'clock that evening, E.F. telephoned the doctor, and, once more, tried to assure him that everything was going well. The patient maintained that his work in the country required that he stay there an additional two weeks. The analyst elaborated to E.F. his deep concern about the situation, and added that E.F.'s sense of well-being was not reassuring, and might in itself be a symptom. The patient then promised to come to see the analyst no later than Wednesday of the coming week, and possible sooner.

Wednesday, September 11   As E.F. entered the analyst's office, obviously chewing something, the doctor began the session by asking "What are you chewing?" The patient responded: "I got candy in my mouth. Last time I was here, I was high. I'm glad I'm over the high.

"I don't like the feeling of urgency which you expressed over the telephone. Everything has been going very well, except my relation with my wife. As far as she and I went, it was a bad summer. I have been gathering up excess stuff, and putting it in place. She has been constantly going to pieces. She analyzes me, and she irritates me. I haven't had a drink since we spoke. I had one drink when I strained my back. I lost twenty-five pounds. I do drink. I have one drink of Italian Vermouth a day, maybe four ounces. I suddenly see my mother's face leaning over the balustrade. I see her complete body—not so fat, and quite pretty. I also believe that my wife attacks me all the time."

Friday, September 13 E.F. came quite late to his analytic session, which he seldom did. He said he thought the appointment was for 1:10 instead of ten of one. Since he had been coming every afternoon for six years at ten of one, it is unlikely that this confusion was undetermined.

"I was one of the first people to revolt against men's clothing. If I were the doctor, I would cut down on the dose. They may be harming me physically. You have got to fight this rushing in the city. I think I am comparatively calm. My mouth is really dry. My wife said that she has cancer."

At this point, because the physician felt that the patient was becoming seriously depressed, he told E.F. to discontinue the Mellaril, and to take instead Taractan, 100 mgs a day.

Comments of the Presenting Analyst

Because E.F. is usually compulsively prompt, the analyst felt that his lateness to this session indicated considerable disturbance. The doctor saw the patient's complaint that the dose of medication was too high as both an extension of his hypochondria, and as resistance to the physician. Depressed people frequently complain of dryness in the mouth.

Monday, September 16 "We had a nice, quiet week-end. I have been out collecting things for our new studios. There wasn't much occasion for our clashing. My wife invites me to anger. My mouth gets so dry. Friday or Saturday night I had a dream. You were in it.

I said: "You are scaring the hell out of me by telling me about depression."

Even if I were on the verge of depression, it wouldn't develop, because I am coming here. I don't think I have been very high in August; I *was* in July. I think less and less about death."

Comments of the Presenting Analyst

The presenting analyst emphasized this patient's magical

reliance on contact with the doctor and with his wife to protect him against depression. At this session, E.F. seemed somewhat slowed down. The reference to death, even in the negative, signified to the physician incipient depression.

Group Discussion

Ostow wondered whether 100 mgs of Taractan is more depressing than 50 mgs of Mellaril. He suspected that E.F. might have responded better to Navane or Stelazine. Stelazine particularly might have produced less motor impairment and more inner tranquility. Bressler felt that, compared to Mellaril, Taractan has less of a depressing, or tranquilizing effect, and acts more to slow down motor function. Feder agreed that Taractan affects a person externally more than internally, but he thought that Taractan can slow a person down much more than an equal amount of Mellaril. Linn suggested that lithium might have been effective had it been given in the spring, at the first evidences of strain in the patient.

Linn related E.F.'s excessive cleaning to the pre-menstrual syndrome. The group discussed the accumulation of fluid as a sign of pre-menstrual depression. Ostow maintained that the accumulation of fluid is characteristic of the state of narcissistic tranquility, which may be associated with hyperaldosteronism.

Tuesday, September 17   "Last night my wife said: 'Why don't you devote all of your time to me?' I don't think it behooves me to be her pansy. I goofed last night: I should have bought her an orchid for the opening of the opera, but I didn't. I would like to straighten out this anti-Semitic thing. I stopped losing weight, and I presume I've gained a few pounds."

Comments of the Presenting Analyst

The history of E.F.'s remark about being his wife's "pansy" is as follows. When the family became wealthy, the patient's mother-in-law had, what she called her "pansies," that is, a circle of homosexuals whom she fed and supported. The doctor understood that E.F. feared he would become his wife's pansy, because she had the money. This man's failure to bring an orchid for his wife is hardly unusual; he never gives her a present on any occasion.

The patient's comment about anti-Semitism refers to an occasion on which he had expressed some anti-Semitic feelings in talking about some of his neighbors.

Wednesday, September 18   "My wife said that I've been walking with my head down and to the right. I feel that's a psychological thing. They used to call me "turtle" because I pulled my head down. This morning she had a masseuse come to massage me. It didn't do any good. I don't like a professional masseuse. I did notice how calm I was. I sat, and chatted with my wife. I didn't do any work, and I felt sleepy. She was very calm last night We had dinner together, and we both liked it. Suppose I refuse to take the added dosage."

Comments of the Presenting Analyst

E.F.'s remark about walking with his head down should be seen as a reference to periods of depression in the past. In emphasizing his calmness, the patient was pretending that it was an indication that he was recovering from his mania. E.F. refused to acknowledge that his tranquility was actually a symptom of incipient depression. The defiance likewise should be seen as still another bad sign: the patient was resisting the drug because it was not helping him.

Group Discussion

Linn commented on the negative influence of E.F.'s wife on her husband's condition, and he wondered whether the patient might be able to manage better without her. The reporting analyst explained that he had tried, on every possible occasion, to introduce this concept to the patient, but the idea of living alone was intolerable to him.

Thursday, September 19   "There is no doubt that I have slowed down compared to last week. The thing that haunts me is

the picture of my brother and sister-in-law eight feet underground.
I dreamed last night:

> There was some reason to dig up my brother. I didn't
> want to because I was afraid he had started to rot. Some-
> one said: 'No, he is just like he was before he was buried.'

I see my mother looking at me very angry."

Group Discussion

The reporting group member explained that E.F.'s older brother had died the previous spring of a stroke, and his sister-in-law
had thereupon committed suicide. The dream expresses the
patient's identification with his dead brother; when this man is depressed, he feels that he has started to rot. Ostow commented that
many depressed patients feel that they are decaying inside. Loomis
noted that such patients seem to be eating themselves up. Cancer,
which is almost always on this patient's mind, can also be seen as
an eating up of oneself. Klerman observed that the patient's identification had shifted from his mother to his younger brother.

Furst felt that the dream expressed E.F.'s depressive
tendency and his simultaneous wish to deny it. There seems to be
a dialogue between the thought that the brother can be exhumed
because he has not deteriorated, and the feeling that the brother
has indeed started to rot. This dialogue suggests a depression that
is incipient, but that can be averted. Ostow suggested that the
dream can be understood as the patient's desire not to look at himself and not to be aware of his own feelings. Furst responded that
the desire not to look at oneself may spring from a fear of what
one might find.

Feder wondered whether E.F.'s memory of his brother's
death might have revived unresolved conflicts about his father's
suicide. The presenting analyst told the group that, earlier in the
treatment, a sister had committed suicide after E.F. had refused to
lend her money, but this experience had not precipitated
depression.

Ostow brought up the problem of the cause for this new depression, or E.F.'s escape from the influence of the drug. He

attributed the recent deterioration of E.F.'s condition to the exacerbation of the patient's controversy with his wife, which had already begun in the spring, and which was brought into the open when she told him: "You are a homosexual." The presenting analyst mentioned that E.F. had experienced low periods before, but he usually came out of them quite well. This time his accustomed resilience was absent. Bressler felt that maybe the fact that the brother had died at age sixty was important.

Winkelman pointed out that this course of treatment represents an unusual kind of therapy. The reporting analyst seemed to be using some drug therapy, some psychoanalysis, and was giving the patient some general support and lots of good advice. Given E.F.'s age and chronicity, this may be all that can be expected. Perhaps at this point the doctor was trying to do some intensive psychoanalysis, and the patient was resisting.

Roose wondered whether E.F.'s most recent depression might have developed from the transference. The patient may have been feeling low because the analyst failed to protect him from this unfortunate trip to London, and had abandoned him over the summer. The presenting analyst responded that he in fact kept after the patient over the summer, and did not give him permission to go to London. When the patient had asked for permission to go, the analyst had replied that he would not prohibit the trip, but he did not encourage it. In retrospect the reporting group member feared that the patient might have fared worse had he remained in New Haven for a month without his wife.

The presenting analyst described his general approach to the treatment of this patient as follows. When E.F. is manic, the doctor can only show him what is symptomatic behavior, as opposed to realistic behavior, and give instructions about what to do and what not to do. When E.F. is depressed, the doctor analyzes the ambivalence, and tries to make conscious the patient's hostility to his wife, to the analyst, and to everyone else. Attempts to work through infantile material are made only during intervals of relative calm. Although a considerable amount of this last kind of work has been done, the analyst has not reported it to the group because he felt that it was irrelevant to the purposes at hand.

Ostow summarized the discussion by describing it as a study of pre-depressive mania. Among the causes discussed were neglect of the patient's anaclitic needs, abuse by the love object, and abandonment by his therapist. The manifestations of the mania were overactivity, and, in this case, compulsive cleaning and equally compulsive soiling (i.e., when E.F. cleaned, he brought dirty things into the kitchen). In addition, the patient drank excessively (both alcohol and other beverages), talked excessively, and adopted a managerial attitude towards others. The concurrent depressive elements were hypochondria, thoughts about death, and dreams of loss. The onset of the patient's depression was marked by weight loss, hypochondria, fear of being poisoned, denial of the incipient depression, and obsession with death.

Friday, September 20   "My wife and I had dinner alone for the second time. It was very nice and quiet. Last night she said: 'You seem very hopeless.' I had two dreams:

1. I was in the army, and there was snow all around. The enemy threw spears. Our group gathered them into piles. We didn't know what to do with them. How could I get behind the lines and escape. Everything has disintegrated. There was no attack.

2. I was feeling very lonely, unwanted, and useless."

E.F. referred to his second dream as "a flash of sensation which I call 'Little Boy Lost.' " The patient reported further that he was very relaxed at the opera the previous evening, and, following instructions, did not undo his trousers.

Group Discussion

Ostow remarked that, by not undoing his trousers, E.F. was trying to be a good boy. The first dream seems to represent the patient's understanding that he was being attacked and did not have the energy to fight back. This feeling might have been elicited by the Taractan. Ostow commented further on the cleaning element in the first dream. The snow probably refers to feces, and the spears are being picked up and put into piles. The presenting analyst noted that E.F. habitually picks up and puts into piles the dirt he finds in the street.

Linn thought that the patient was describing how he was receiving one barb after another from his wife. Again, he may have been complaining of the doctor's failure to protect him. Feder added that, in response to these blows, all E.F. could do was to try to behave like a good boy. To the patient, sitting in the opera and not opening his clothing might represent a defeat and capitulation to the analyst. Ostow agreed, and observed that this man seems to be willing to do anything for protection against depression, even to the point of surrendering his masculinity.

Monday-Tuesday, September 23-24   The analyst was unable to see the patient.

Wednesday, September 25   "Thank heaven I had those two days off. I had a thousand trees to plant. Those guys just can't get organized without me. I almost decided to call and say I wouldn't be in today. I was bossing the boss. It was a lot of fun watering and organizing."

E.F. then started to review the conflict with his brother-in-law, which had occurred about twenty years previously. When the therapist asked "Why are you bringing this up now?" the patient responded: "Because it is there; it changed my whole way of living. I would like to know where I fell down. I haven't settled this question yet.

"I never dared to clean up my wife's room. It's a hell of a mess. I see my mother with a sad look on her face, almost crying. I am concerned about being left by my wife." The analyst then, feeling that the Taractan might have been too strong, reduced E.F.'s dose to 50 mgs a day.

Group Discussion

The group agreed with Ostow's interpretation of this episode as a reassertion of the patient's mania.

Thursday, September 26   "I woke up with a stomachache last night—gas pains relieved by a good healthy crap. I feel dizzy today. My hands are numb. I felt claustrophobic in the bathroom this morning. I felt that way also in the car today. I assume it's a little indigestion. By 9:30 last night, I felt exhausted. I slept from 9:45 last night to 9:30 this morning. Several times this summer, when I bent over, I felt momentarily a slight dizziness."

E.F. then began a long monologue about his financial problems. At the end of this discourse, he told the analyst: "I came up early today because I felt the pressure of my wife. I like to go watch the children in the park across the street from your office building. Friday I am going to the auction of my brother's furniture. My wife thought I should go.

"Yesterday was a bad day. I felt so much better after I left here. It was the first time in three years that I couldn't get a tennis game. I found yesterday that I had sold the same stock twice. The broker hadn't notified me. It was very embarrassing. I was driving down the road, and I had a flash that I would get into an accident. I also had a flash that I would feel guilty if my wife and daughter had a car accident. I had a fantasy that my brother and sister-in-law were joking in their graves. I was impressed by the complete lack of sound of the grave. It terrified me. Last night I was trying to blame you for my lack of sexual desire. This morning, I was remembering my mother. I smile at her and amuse her. My right breast is sensitive, not my left. I used to rub it while I was masturbating."

Comments of the Presenting Analyst

In this session the patient was contending with his depression. Although E.F. had been taking Niamid for six years, this was the first time he complained about its side effects. The doctor emphasized the patient's disinclination to attend the auction of his brother and sister-in-law who had died the year before. The reference to their joking should be seen as E.F.'s attempt to make the idea of death seem less frightening. In his evocation of his mother, the patient was again identifying with her, and joining her in the grave.

Monday, September 30   "Basically I had a good week-end. I think I untangled my financial affairs. I didn't see much of my wife, so I can't say we got along well. I went down to the meadow alone, and I said to myself: 'Some day my ashes will lie here.' I bid on my brother's house, but I didn't go to the auction."

Tuesday, October 1   "I have difficulty doing concentrated work in my apartment. I think I am going to make a rule that when I am working at home, I am not to be disturbed, except in case of emergency. I am going to the country tonight. I am not afraid of going alone.

"Today I was wondering, justifying my coming here. You have let me down. You haven't helped me. I had a vision of Mrs. A. this morning. I still feel bad about intruding upon my week-end guests. I am very happy that I have given up my drinking. I found out that it was not really necessary. I was thinking today about my sister-in-law. She's rotting; probably her eyes are caved in. I want to be cremated. I wouldn't even give my eyes to the eye bank. I wonder why you lock the door. I have a fantasy of being cornered in the bathroom by Miss Stone (one of the hated nurses of E.F.'s early childhood), and jumping out the window."

Comments of the Presenting Analyst

Although E.F. was complaining that others were distracting him from his work, it was actually the patient himself who was spending a considerable part of his day making telephone calls. E.F.'s decision to go to the country should be seen as a reaction to an announcement by the doctor that he would not be able to see the patient on Wednesday.

The therapist explained further that the patient's pretense of having given up drinking discounted the four ounces of vermouth that he was taking every evening. Finally, E.F.'s antipathy to the idea of donating his eyes to the eye bank constituted a refutation of his previous interest in the eye bank.

Group Discussion

Ostow attributed the patient's accusations against the doctor to his current depression. The recurrence of depression during the course of psychotherapy frequently revives a patient's original resistances to the doctor. E.F. seemed to be identifying the analyst with his former nurse. In order to escape from the doctor, the patient thought he had to die by throwing himself through the door and the window. Ostow wondered why the patient wanted to run away.

Feder felt that the Taractan may have been overwhelming the patient, who, quite correctly, saw his sense of defeat as a result of having entrusted himself to the analyst. Ostow added that the therapist had put an end to the patient's manic defense. Moreover, by prohibiting some of E.F.'s activities, and by giving him a drug which slowed him down, the physician was, in effect, castrating him.

Furst interpreted the claustrophobic fantasy as a request for maternal care and support from the analyst as E.F. was facing his new depression. Ostow agreed, and classified this fantasy as a typical intruder nightmare. Children frequently express their need for their parents by dreaming of an intruder breaking into the room. The child's anger at his parents is projected onto the intruder, who is seen as fierce and dangerous.

Feder emphasized the importance of distinguishing a patient's drug-induced change in his sense of himself from the merely verbal pressure of the analyst's instructions. It is much more difficult for a person to cope with an unknown chemical action than to deal with another individual. E.F. seemed to be feeling more helpless now than at any earlier period in this course of treatment. For the first time in six years the patient noticed the bolt on the doctor's door. Furst felt that it was still uncertain which of the two assaults on the patient was the precipitating factor. Linn suspected that the patient was identifying the therapist with his mother, whom he wanted to love and join in the grave, and, for this reason, was becoming increasingly fearful of him.

Thursday, October 3   "Your dreary old neighborhood. I've been coming here so many times. I'm not steaming about anything today. It makes me sort of empty as far as this hour goes." The patient then told the analyst that his wife "wanted out" and that he was carrying his head to the left and pulled in a little.

"I had a peaceful, pleasant time, a busy time. I am getting a desire for sweets and candies. I have picked up five pounds and then stopped. I constantly want to have something in my mouth; I am glad I don't have a compulsion to drink. I had a quart of

Cinzano last week. Last night I felt that it really is necessary to have a woman around. I have been thinking of cunnilingus—bury my face in pubic hair. My daughter's dog is bigger than yours."

Group Discussion

Ostow commented that E.F. seemed to be retreating to tranquility. Roose wondered what had happened to the patient's rage. The reporting analyst mentioned that, during this session, he had several times tried to confront E.F. with his anger and with its source, that is, his murderous feelings towards his wife. The therapist interpreted the material of this session as the patient's denial of his fury. Feder and Loomis saw the remark about the dog as an intimation to the doctor that E.F.'s rage was even stronger than the analyst's description of it, and as a warning to the physician not to push this anger too far.

Friday, October 4   "We were very peaceful last night: we had just one guest. After dinner my wife wanted to play cards, and I let her play with him. I had two dreams:

A group was hiding from a bunch of cut-throats. They never quite escaped from them: they would torture us.

I looked down a huge tank, and I was afraid of falling in. A nice little boy was there. I saw him cling to the wall. It was a dangerous place. I yelled to the father to grab him: it was too late. He dropped down another large hole, and he was gone.

I went to sleep again and the dream started again. I had two fantasies.

A train is running over me.

I was dying happy and joking about it."

The analyst told E.F. that he was frightened by his wish for the doctor's love.

Comments of the Presenting Analyst

The two dreams should be understood as the patient's prediction that he would succumb to the depression. The cut-throats in the first dream represent the analyst, from whom E.F. was trying to escape. The boy falling down the hole is E.F.; the father had to grab the boy, but he was not fast enough.

Monday, October 7   "I wonder why I said my daughter's dog is bigger than yours."

Thursday, October 8   E.F. reported the following dream:

I suddenly sat up in bed and thought there was another person on the couch. I said: "Be careful," and then I looked and there was no one there.

"The thought which dominates me these days is my unconventionality and inability to adjust. I see that all my life I have offended people without knowing why I was doing it. Last night I brought opera glasses to the concert, and I studied the faces of the people in the orchestra. It seemed much more enjoyable without the liquor. At least on the surface my wife and I are getting along much better. I have to appear this afternoon at a deposition. This morning I seem to be a little discouraged. My thoughts are negative."

Comments of the Presenting Analyst

The couch in the dream is the analytic couch. The patient frequently expressed the conscious fantasy:

If you would lie down on the couch next to me, I would get up and smack you in the jaw.

The analyst understood E.F.'s unconventionality and inability to adjust as a form of defiance. This was the first time that the patient spoke of this trait with self-criticism.

Group Discussion

Feder observed that the lawsuit supports the idea that E.F.'s references to the dog were expressions of his rage. Roose felt that during this time the patient's anger was being suppressed by his constant desire to submit. Ostow commented that the fury was being projected onto the analyst, who was being seen as an intruder, and was also being directed at the patient himself, as expressed in the self-criticism.

Wednesday, October 9   "I seem to resent paying your check. I feel much better today. I had a very good sleep from 2:00 to 10:00 a.m. I gained back about eight pounds." The therapist asked about the deposition, and E.F. responded that it had been postponed.

Comments of the Presenting Analyst

The patient's description of his sleep should be seen as his indirect way of telling the doctor that he could not fall asleep before 2:00 a.m.

Thursday, October 10   "I went to a party last night. My wife was sick with a cold. I was dancing with an attractive woman. I wondered what kind of family life Dr. Y. has (the presenting analyst). My father was not very jovial. Since I have come here, I have learned to like my father more, and to question my relationship with my mother. I would like to see the doctor naked, with a big hard-on."

Group Discussion

The reporting group member remarked that this is as close as E.F. has ever come to requesting physical affection from the analyst, though this wish was previously expressed negatively in the patient's claustrophobia and in his dream about the cutthroats. Linn noted the prominence of the primal scene theme in this session, and Ostow related the desire to see the doctor undressed to E.F.'s earlier memory of seeing his father naked.

Friday, October 11   "If it wasn't for the goddamn psychiatrist I could see the moon shot in ten minutes. It is very thrilling to see that thing take off. I had a fantasy:

You came into the room and said: 'I'm going to fuck you.'

Monday, October 14   "New Haven is getting so busy, you can't depend on anything any more. It must be prosperity. I had a fantasy:

I'm dry and I have nothing to say here.

I'm so glad I can come up here. The week-end was just the same. My wife was very calm and cooperative. The whole family gets along much better since her mother died."

Comments of the Presenting Analyst

E.F.'s final remark was the opposite of the truth. His mother-in-law, while she was living, kept the family together, and acted as his protector. In fact, E.F. had married his wife to please his mother-in-law, and, since her death, he has been on the outs with all of Mrs. F.'s relatives.

Tuesday, October 15   "I feel closer to depression now than when I resumed here two months ago."

Group Discussion

Ostow understood E.F.'s final remark as both an observation and as a reproach to the analyst. Roose added that this is as close as E.F. has ever come to expressing his anger at the therapist.

Wednesday, October 16   "I guess the message I got yesterday was that I am pretty stubborn about letting anyone get close to me, including you. All my life I have been fearful and constantly on guard. When I see someone attacking me, I feel guilty. My wife said last night; 'You never squeeze me any more.' I had a fantasy last night:

I was dancing with a beautiful girl. I said: 'I love you, but it is much better if you remain untouched. Sex would mar it.'

Group Discussion

Ostow attributed E.F.'s refusal of intercourse to his impotence, and to the contribution of the impotence to his depression. Roose noted that the patient's sexual inability is consistent with the infantile relationship he maintained with the analyst, and with others. The presenting analyst emphasized that E.F. has always been able to have intercourse only under very special circumstances, and, after intercourse, the patient always returns to his own bed immediately.

Thursday, October 17   "Lately I have been more conscious of past depressions. Today I have the feeling that, underneath, I was a little depressed. I have to raise a good deal of money to pay taxes because I took profits this year.

"My wife and I seem to be getting along much better. Last night she didn't serve dinner. I thought I would like to be home alone. At 6:00 p.m. I noticed that I was beginning to panic, so I called my sister-in-law. She invited me for dinner, but I refused." E.F. then called three other people, and obtained three invitations, but turned them all down. He explained: "It was too much trouble to get dressed and go out. I'm not upset that the dentist has to rip out some teeth to fix a cavity, and then put them all back. I need a change of life, of scenery. Where would I go? Yesterday I transferred one of my life insurance policies to my daughter."

Comments of the Presenting Analyst

For E.F. to admit that he felt even a little depressed represents a significant concession. He expressed serious concern about his financial status and feared bankruptcy.

Group Discussion

Ostow saw the patient's reference to his past depressions as an example of what Ostow calls the "palimpsest phenomenon": when an individual becomes depressed, memories of his previous depressions become more vivid. In fact, in any state of mind, memories of previous, similar states of mind occupy one's thoughts. Loomis added that these depressive memories also represent screen memories. Linn suggested that the patient's preoccupation with past depressions might be an expression of the hope that he will recover from this depression just as he recovered from the earlier ones. Ostow remarked that, in his practice, it is usually he who adds this note of hopefulness. His patients do not make this observation spontaneously. Ostow emphasized further the accumulation of depressive elements in this session: the patient's financial fears, memories of other depressions, conflict with his wife, and dental problems.

Summary of E.F.'s Deterioration from
Mid-September to Mid-October 1968

Ostow proposed that the change in the patient's condition during this month be thought of as "descent into depression." The clinical manifestations of this phenomenon are:

1. the feeling of loss of energy and hopelessness; (This feeling is expressed in E.F.'s dream in which his team is attacked by people throwing spears, and cannot retaliate.)
2. thoughts about death, including fantasies of reunion with his dead mother;
3. ambivalence towards the objects of his anaclitic needs;
4. difficulty in concentration;
5. the feeling of emptiness;
6. anger, in the form of self-criticism and accusations, against the doctor;
7. discouragement;
8. acknowledgment of his depression;
9. recollection of previous depressions;
10. fear of bankruptcy.

Also significant is the great number of apparent causes for these troubles. When a person becomes depressed, suddenly a multitude of different reasons appear to justify his low spirits. For this patient, the apparent causes are:

1. his troubles with his neighbors;
2. his fears of financial reverses;
3. a lawsuit;
4. his difficulties with his wife.

When people come out of depression, these same circumstances often remain unchanged, but lose their urgency.

Friday, October 18 "It is certainly obvious to me that I am in a worrisome period. When I went to sleep last night, I started going over and over anything that would worry me. My wife had four men in last night. They played cards; I read the paper. I thought I hurt her feelings by going to bed early. I began tossing when I got into bed. It is not hard to see that my relationship with my wife is deteriorating. I felt this morning that, if I was not coming here, I could easily get depressed. I think I am getting so afraid of having trouble with people, that I am tending more and more to live alone.

"Yesterday my daughter gave my wife hell about being too close to Richard (one of the men who came to play cards). Last night I was wondering whether my wife had an affair with anyone. But, I thought, 'Many people do that.' "

The analyst, in an effort to halt E.F.'s rapid deterioration, reduced the dose of Taractan from 50 mgs to 25 mgs a day.

Comments of the Presenting Analyst

On this day, E.F. acknowledged the depression and insomnia which he had previously referred to only indirectly. The patient's reluctance to admit to the exacerbation of his conflict with his wife should be seen as a response to the doctor's interpretations and emphasis of this conflict. The analyst understood that E.F. went to bed early because he was angry with his wife for spending the evening with other men.

E.F.'s therapist noted further the patient's denial of his depression and renewed tendency to withdraw. Furst suggested briefly that the withdrawal, which is characteristic of depression, should be seen as this man's effort to control his hostility.

Monday, October 21   "The last few days I have been in a depression. You were right. I had a dream Friday night:

> I was a stowaway in the Apollo. It was very frightening, especially as it came down. It scared the hell out of me. I hit the water, and the damn thing began to turn over.

It's the first time since I came here that I feel shaky. It's hard to believe that it's my wife who makes me depressed. I want to be near her in a dependent way. I am glad I am able to come here. I desperately seek help. My body doesn't feel the same. Yesterday morning, while starting to shave, I thought, 'You are back in depression.' I fell to the floor as if in a faint. The blood rushed to my head. That never happened before. It comes in waves, and, when it does, I break out into a sweat. Then I feel cold.

"I spent most of yesterday in bed because I felt grippy. I worry about my wife. I want to say 'I'm sorry I have been such a lousy husband.' I even have the fear of being hospitalized this morning. I have been thinking how terrible it would have been if my wife had died of appendicitis."

At this session the analyst increased E.F.'s dose of Niamid to 500 mgs a day, although he had virtually given up hope that it would help.

Comments of the Presenting Analyst

Again the patient was acknowledging his depression, this time in an even more serious way. The analyst related E.F.'s dream to one of his earlier fantasies:

> I was going through a tunnel, and, although I saw a light at the end, as I progressed through the tunnel, it became narrower and narrower, until finally I could not get through.

He interpreted the patient's falling to the floor while shaving as a kind of hysterical helplessness. The feeling of coldness is also a common manifestation of depression, as is the retreat to bed. The background of E.F.'s concern that his wife might die of appendicitis is that, when Mrs. F. was hospitalized for appendicitis, E.F. had let the doctor take her to the hospital, while he himself remained at home. At this point he was feeling guilty about this incident. The analyst emphasized however that E.F. feels guilty only when he is sick or depressed. At other times he feels no guilt at all.

Group Discussion

Ostow was impressed by the dream of the Apollo. He explained that many of his patients who are on the verge of schizophrenic and hysterical detachment, or who are becoming depressed, find the Apollo flights especially upsetting, and often use it for their imagery. The blast-off particularly dramatizes their fear of detachment from the world. Furst added that his patients' interest in the Apollo usually relate to anal wishes: they are intrigued by the idea of shooting garbage and feces into space. Roose added that, in this dream, the return to the water represents E.F.'s depression.

Ostow saw the patient's expressed guilt as another reflection of his hostility redirected inward. Loomis wondered whether, by attributing to Mrs. F. the qualities which make her actions depress her husband, the analyst was actually naming her as the agent responsible for his distress.

Thursday, October 22   "Last night I got mad at this depression. I said, 'I won't have it again.' I had a beautiful sleep. I felt OK when I woke up this morning: later I felt faint in the bathroom. My wife suggested that I walk down the street with her. I didn't want to, but I did it reluctantly. Then I was working on my tax figures. I was sort of working at half pace. I finally lay down, and read a financial report.

"I feel cold. My wife said that my lips were white. I had a desire to be near you and near my wife. I just can't bear the thought of my wife being dead. I got in bed with her last night for the first time. Nothing happened in the world of sex. I am frightened. I hear myself yelling, 'Help me! Help me!, I have a headache. I am sweating. I have a feeling of usefulness. (He meant "uselessness," and, when questioned on this point, the patient corrected himself.)

"I'd like to pull my nuts right off. Westport has suddenly lost its charm for me. I'm admiring my wife much more than before. I keep saying, 'Dr. Y. must be wrong.' My wife says that Philip (Mrs. F.'s suspected lover) thinks that the studio needs decoration. That means that he must have been up there."

Group Discussion

The presenting analyst saw E.F.'s taking a walk with his wife as an effort to be a good boy. Mrs. F.'s remark about her husband's lips is characteristic of her faithful reporting of every possible negative observation. Klerman wondered whether the patient's faintness could reveal a state of hypotension, or a drop in blood pressure, caused by the medication. E.F.'s therapist responded that, at this point, the patient had been taking large doses of drugs daily for at least six years. Ostow was struck by the patient's tiredness, which is common in depression. Loomis asked about E.F.'s possibly overdramatized description of his fear. The reporting analyst thought that, though E.F. was then too embarrassed to express himself eloquently, his fear was genuine.

The discussion then turned to E.F.'s feelings of uselessness, which Ostow considered very central and important in depression. In this sense, being a parent complicates depression by precluding this feeling. It is perhaps for this reason that some adults kill their children before committing suicide. Roose and Ostow added that the slip of the tongue should probably be seen as a form of denial. Furst suggested that the patient may have meant that his new symptoms might be "useful" to him in gaining the needed support of other people.

Ostow saw E.F.'s mention of self-castration as a gesture to appease the fates, and he related it to the terrible pain in his testicles which E.F. had experienced thirty years previously, when he returned the stock certificates to Mrs. F.'s family. Bressler remarked on the bisexual nature of testicles and their ability to serve as ambiguous objects, either a penis or a breast. Several of his male patients, when they are becoming depressed, have dreams about breasts without nipples. These dreams always concern the return of repressed oral sadistic rage, redirected against the self.

Roose proposed that this patient was attempting to cope with his depression primarily through denial, and through maintaining a vigorous aggressiveness. This oral sadistic aggressiveness, however, was aggravating the conflict. Bressler suggested that the patient was trying to modify this conflict by longing for an oceanic reunion, or a non-ambivalent relationship, as symbolized by his need to be constantly drinking.

Wednesday, October 23 "Well, I feel a little better today. I am wrestling with this damn thing. I am trying very hard not to give in to it. I hope I haven't goofed about that checkbook. I had a very good sleep last night. Yesterday, I forced myself to play tennis. I bought too much furniture when I was high. My wife put on her new coat, and she said that a man tried to pick her up in the street. This morning I felt a thrill about imagining her screwing another guy. I feel guilty about not being a good husband. I can't honestly say that I want her dead." E.F. then wept.

"I wondered why am I not better after five years here? I said last night, 'I think it is time to pray. You haven't been religious, but when you are in a jam, you've got to pray.' I don't think that I have been contemplating suicide. I have been thinking of running away; taking a voyage, or going to the West Coast."

The analyst again increased E.F.'s dose of Niamid, this time to 600 mgs a day, and telephoned the patient at home that evening.

Comments of the Presenting Analyst

In this session, for the first time, E.F. expressed concern about making mistakes in his bookkeeping, although he is normally very careful. The remark about not wishing his wife were dead represents another protest against the therapist's interpretations in that direction.

The reporting analyst emphasized the patient's first open protest against him and his desire to pray. E.F. is a minister's son who never took religion seriously. In his family no one was interested in

religion except his father. Finally, E.F. characteristically announced his suicidal thoughts in the negative. It was this mention
of suicide that prompted the analyst to telephone him.

Group Discussion

The group was impressed by E.F.'s fantasy of his wife's
affair. Klerman felt that this patient liked to think of himself as his
wife's lover. Ostow thought that, on the contrary, E.F. enjoyed
imagining himself as his wife. Furst added that, perhaps it is for
this reason that the patient was finding all kinds of things to
admire about Mrs. F. Ostow emphasized the juxtaposition of this
man's admiring his wife aloud, and then reporting that men were
trying to pick her up on the street.

Klerman asked whether the presenting analyst had considered
changing to another drug instead of merely increasing the dose of
Niamid. Bressler suggested decreasing the Niamid gradually, and,
at the same time, starting a new drug and slowly increasing its
dose. He reported a case in which he had obtained good results by
shifting a patient, in this manner, from Nardil to Elavil. During
this procedure, however, there was a point at which, on 45 mgs of
Nardil and 80 mgs of Elavil, the patient had alternated between
moderate sleepiness and mania. Ostow responded that well-regulat-
ed patients tend to react to the events of daily life up and down
around a base line. The drugs give the patient this resilience.
The problem with Bressler's procedure is that it contains the risk
of an accident for which the physician could be held responsible.

Thursday, October 24   "I was quite touched that you
called last night. I got into my wife's bed after she left. Later I
loved her up a little, and I did cunnilingus. I tried intercourse, but
I soon lost my hard-on. I tried to sleep in her bed, but I couldn't
get to sleep. I went back to my own bed, and slept there. I stayed
in bed from nine to eleven this morning; I tried to shorten the day.
Then I got up, and did some perfunctory work. In a sense I am
better, but I still feel shaky. I keep saying, 'I've got to listen to the
doctor; he knows.' I am feeling kind of broke. I want to go back
and apologize to my gardener if I created trouble for him.

"I played tennis, but it was very difficult. I felt weak. When I did get up this morning, my wife was gone, and I missed her. I even wondered whether she had a date with Philip. She said, 'At last my husband is back.' " The doctor asked whether E.F. was concerned that his wife might have an accident. The patient answered: "Yes, you would say that it's a death wish. I thought I would make love to her again tonight. I want to stand up, and look at you. I wanted to tell my wife, 'Don't tell me that I married you to please your mother.' I feel a little better when I leave here, but it doesn't last long."

Group Discussion

Ostow commented that E.F. was, at this point, using sexual activity and looking as methods of clinging. This clinging by looking might be based on the prototype of the infant's looking into its mother's face while nursing. Furst saw the patient in this session feeling desperate and confused as to whether he should cling to his wife or to the analyst, and feeling ambivalence with both.

Friday, October 25   "I haven't taken a crap for three days. My appetite is way off. I have lost five pounds in the last ten days. I have a hope that these pills are working. I sleep well. After I wake up, I feel free for a moment, and then it moves in on me. Last night my wife gave a birthday party for my daughter. I sat, and tried to smile, and I felt like hell. I take two aspirins when I go to bed, and it seems to help me get to sleep.

"These sessions with the doctor are sheer hell. I noticed how my wife makes our home comfortable in her own quiet little way. I am afraid to get mad. I was even doubting you. I feel like I meant to apologize to everyone I've hurt. I had a fantasy:

Some mother figure was putting me to bed—'Now we are going to put you to bed and keep you going.'

The only peace I find now is when I am in bed and asleep. I think of Dr. G. (one of E.F.'s first therapists) who said, 'Get out of here, you are no good.' I feel humble, weak, and guilty; I see a frightened little child."

Comments of the Presenting Analyst

E.F. began this session with a recitation of common somatic components of depression; constipation, anorexia, and weight loss. The patient's comment on his wife's home-making should be understood as a continued denial of his hostility to her; in fact, Mrs. F. is a noisy individual, who ignores the house completely. The story of E.F.'s quote from his earlier analyst is that he was in treatment with this doctor for several years, and then left. When he later became depressed, he returned to the psychiatrist and asked for help. The latter responded that he could do nothing for the patient. The analyst interpreted this recollection as indicating that the patient contemplated being thrown out by his current doctor also. This idea is probably a projection of thoughts of leaving the analyst which E.F. was entertaining in connection with suicide.

Group Discussion

Ostow commented that the patient's waking up in the morning, as he described it, is common among depressed people. The moment they wake up they feel fine, but, as they take cognizance of reality, they become depressed. This suggests that it is the reality which demands the depression. Electric shock treatments help depressed people by impairing apperception, and thus making reality seem more remote. Furst noted that Ostow's suggestion contradicts the group's earlier observation that depressed people see the world through their depression. Ostow responded that the depressive view of the world seems to be non-operative when the patient first awakens. Furst then suggested that it may be increasing wakefulness and consciousness, rather than perception, which reinstitutes the depression.

Roose observed that the patient's awareness and insight had increased in the most recent sessions. Roose and Ostow agreed that this heightened awareness is characteristic of depressed patients, and usually takes the form of self-condemnation and self-disparagement. Indeed this awareness serves as a form of self-depreciation and as a call for help. Ostow emphasized the ominous import of E.F.'s fantasy of the return of his mother and his claim that he could find peace only in sleep.

Monday, October 28 "I haven't taken a crap for a long time. I better take a high colonic. I think the pills are working, but everything is working against me. The last hour I began to feel low again. I just get something in my head, and turn it over and over. I have trouble taking a leak. It is sort of hell to be half alive."

The analyst increased E.F.'s dose of Taractan to 75 mgs a day, and began to talk to him about the possibility of electric shock treatment. The patient responded by saying: "That scares the hell out of me, electric shock treatment."

Group Discussion

The reporting group member noted the patient's continued expression of ambivalence toward his wife, and the anxiety it was causing him. Furst, referring to the patient's constipation, suggested that many depressed people try to retain feces and urine to combat their feeling of emptiness and their fantasies of being drained.

E.F.'s therapist explained that he had increased the dose of Taractan because he thought the patient was becoming agitated and restless. In retrospect he considered this a mistake. He was planning, at that time, to change the anti-depression medication, and he hoped to use electric shock treatment during the latent period, before the action of the new drug would start. Because the idea of electric shock treatment was very frightening to this patient—indeed, E.F. had come to his current therapist partly because he thought this doctor did not use shock treatment—the analyst introduced this idea very gently and carefully, pointing out that it would serve as an expedient in the transition to a new drug.

Tuesday, October 29 "I'm probably kidding myself, but, in some ways, I feel much better. All of a sudden I feel good. Can you give me any formulas to fight this? I don't seem to have anything to do that I can do. I did take an extra red pill as you suggested (i.e., the Taractan). I finally went into a deep sleep. This morning I felt just wonderful when I woke up, but, just before I went to the dentist I broke out into a sweat.

"I suppose I ought to force myself to go riding with my wife. I don't know if there is any formula for fighting this. I took the enema, and it didn't do any good at all. My wife has been very nice. I did sell some stocks yesterday. I've got a big loan at the bank. You get these desires to run away to Westport or the West Coast. I have a great desire to see Dr. D. I know my wife will stay with me."

The doctor instructed E.F. to discontinue the Niamid.

Comment of the Presenting Analyst

E.F.'s therapist was particularly impressed by the patient's renewed turning against him in this session.

Wednesday, October 30   "I got my bowels open last night. The doctor told me to take M-O and prune juice. Now they are pretty definitely going to cut the dividend. I get definitely worried about money. I sometimes think I am getting nearer to the hospital than I thought. I feel so futile coming up here. How did I get myself into such a financial jam? I look at the checkbook, and I just hate it. I tried to play tennis yesterday. I just don't function well at all. I got nervous in the dentist's chair today. I keep saying in my mind to my wife, 'Stand by me.' I sold some more stocks. I feel I wronged my wife more than she has wronged me. I keep seeing my mother. Boy, I really feel lost. I want her to be home when I get home, and she won't be. I have a desire to move up here to this place."

Thursday, October 31   "I went home yesterday, sat down, and paid my bills, and, for some reason, I felt better. Then my wife came home, and confirmed that the company was cutting the dividend off. When I am in my condition, everything looks bad, and I really haven't felt so terribly badly—none of the hot sweats and headaches.

"I have an awful fear of being broke and using up my last money. I did get into bed with my wife last night. I did some cunnilingus. I couldn't get a hard-on. I tried to sleep with her, but I couldn't. I had a hard time getting to sleep. Tonight she has to go to an opera. I don't see why she shouldn't go. It faces me with more hours of being alone. I can't occupy my time. I can't read. Television makes me nervous. All that has to happen now is for her to die." At this point E.F. struck his head with both hands. The doctor said: "What are you doing?" The patient answered: "I did that unconsciously. I suppose I am angry with myself. I get that desire to pull my balls right off."

Group Discussion

Bressler commented that Taractan acts with some people as an anti-depressant. Ostow suspected that Taractan reduces autonomic activity, and thus makes people feel better. With this patient, however, the Taractan seemed to be exacerbating the depression. Klerman suggested that E.F. may have been previously obtaining partial support from the Niamid. Ostow responded that this patient's condition also deteriorated during the time in which he was taking high doses of Taractan and Niamid. Bressler and Klerman felt that even 100 mgs of Taractan is a low dose. When Taractan is used as an anti-depression drug, up to 250 mgs a day are prescribed. The presenting analyst explained that the motor weakness that E.F. was reporting at 75 mgs a day discouraged him from increasing that dose.

Friday, November 1   "Everything is just about the same. Every once in a while, I feel as if I am going to get well, and then I feel bad again. I stayed home again last night and felt very lonely. This morning I crawled into my wife's bed. I loved her up a little. I couldn't get an erection. I told her that one good thing about this depression is that it makes me love her more. I kneeled down to her.

"The secretary of the company told me that the dividend cut hasn't been decided yet. The few times I do something productive, I feel better. I am building up more constipation. You go into the hospital for some light electrical shipments—I mean treatments."

Monday, November 4   "I suppose if I put the past few days through a machine, it would come out a little better. Last night the whole thing lifted for an hour. I felt great. I had actually taken the first crap in two or three weeks—a small one. Last night I had such a beautiful dream:

I was a child in fairyland. I visited people who have eternal happiness. Everything is beautiful and peaceful there. It is full of pleasant surprises. At the end, I came back to the hard world, and the childhood place disappeared. We just seemed to float down among these beautiful trees.

I was desperately looking for my wife at the opera this morning. I have been toying with the idea of letting you do with me what you want to do. I have no appetite, but I force myself to eat. I don't think I am getting suicidal. New Haven looks dreary again. The noises bother me. I see terrible anger against my mother for giving birth to me."

Group Discussion

The patient's remark about putting himself in the analyst's hands is a reference to the shock treatments. Furst pointed out that E.F. sees the shock treatments as a rape. Ostow added that the dream E.F. reported is a classic depressive dream, a denial of anguish.

Tuesday, November 5   "I should say everything is just the same. I am depressed now. This morning I thought I could get through each day by sleeping until noon, and through the afternoon, by coming here. The tough period will be noon to twelve at night. I begin to worry about my wife's getting sick of my depression. My wife wants to go to the horse show, and insists that I go with her. I paid off $50,000 in bank loans by selling stocks last week. I have a great desire to be with my mother-in-law. How strong she was. It is almost as if each hour I have to get through that hour. My bowels won't work at all. I don't doubt that not being able to get an erection makes me feel very badly. This is no time to be aggressive. I am sorry I was ever born. I resent my mother having given birth to me. I haven't even opened up your bill yet."

Wednesday, November 6   "I am doing medium. I went to the horse show with my wife. It carried me through the evening. It was much less of an effort than I thought. I was very silent. My talking ability is way down, and my worrying ability is way up. I found work to do, and it keeps me from worrying. Every day seems to bring some new disaster. All of my daughter's jewelry was stolen, but that is not my disaster. It's insured. I did sell some stocks. I thought I would be better with my bank loan. Last night I had a dream:

> It was about a small boy. His father gave him a shock treatment. He was tied to an outdoor water pump. The lower part of his body was immersed in electrically-charged water. The neighbors thought it was cruel.

I had a great desire to see Dr. D., and to have her assure me of being in the hands of a very capable person. I see my mother's voice—I mean face. I make a great deal of ice water, and drive with it. I am in hot water. It is not as hot as I think. Today was the first soft crap I have taken. I had another dream:

> I was a sergeant in the army. I kept worrying about how I could learn to dress snappily and fast to make a good appearance. I couldn't seem to get my coat buttoned right. I had no fear of fighting."

When the analyst asked why E.F. had thought of being in the army, the latter responded: "So I could have a soft job. I am very unhappy that I was ever born. I worry that electric shock treatment will make me flabby mentally. I wish you would beat the hell out of me."

Group Discussion

Ostow noted that E.F.'s first dream confirms Furst's suggestion that, for this patient, electric shock treatment amounts to a rape. More specifically, the rape occurs in the womb, and the analyst is the attacker. The patient's final remarks express his masochistic wish to be filled up by pain, or stimulated, which is another aspect of his view of the shock treatment. Roose asked why the patient had not yet been hospitalized. The reporting analyst stated that E.F. had not yet agreed to go to the hospital, and, in this matter, the patient's acquiescence was most important.

Summary of E.F.'s Condition from Mid-October to November 6

Compared to the four weeks from mid-September to mid-October, which could be described as the process of becoming depressed, Ostow proposed that the period from mid-October to November 6 be thought of as a fairly intense form of depression. During this time the patient alternately acknowledged and denied his depression. In the therapeutic sessions, he expressed both through:

1. ambivalence towards his love objects, e.g., his wife, mother, and analyst;
2. an oral craving for food, love, and protection;
3. clinging, the need for proximity, confession, self-humiliation, begging, making love, wishing to be useful and needed, and regressing, going so far as to assume a religious attitude from time to time.

Moreover, the patient was furious, and wished to kill others, to kill himself, and to castrate himself. The ego changes observed in the patient during these weeks consisted mainly of increased self-observation. The somatic changes included constipation, anorexia, weight loss, insomnia, weakness with spells of faintness, and coldness.

Thursday, November 7 "I got through yesterday and today without any great pains. How could I possibly leave my wife? Yesterday I noticed that my sacroiliac hurt. I slept well from 11:00 p.m. to 11:00 a.m. I have given up the aspirin. To wake up and see stormy weather scares you. I am sort of numb, as if I had been whipped and it hurt, and now I'm numb. I don't seem to thrash about as much as I did. I have a feeling that I am coming out of this thing like an old man. I had a desire to yank my balls off." The analyst, hoping to elicit E.F.'s repressed hostility, asked him: "How would you kill your wife?" The patient responded: "I'd kill us both together. I think of our inevitable family history."

Group Discussion

Ostow remarked that feeling old is characteristic of depressed persons. Linn added that depressed patients tend to look old and poor. Feder suggested that, for this patient, the feeling of aging might also result from the motor impairment caused by the Tarac-tan. Feder thought that the Taractan interfered with playing tennis, which, for E.F.,was a defense against depression. In this way, the drug made the depression more apparent.

Friday, November 8   The analyst had planned to leave town for the week-end. Although normally he would have left Thursday night, he arranged to see E.F. very early Friday morning, and to leave immediately thereafter. The patient appeared for this early appointment, and began the session by announcing: "I am furious with you because this is my escape period when I sleep so well. If I had a choice, I wouldn't have kept this appointment. I wonder how much I am faking this depression. Last night I drew pictures of things in the apartment. My wife praised me and said I did so well. I'll get through the week-end: it looks grim."

The doctor, then suspecting that the Taractan might be exert-ing a deleterious effect, instructed E.F. to discontinue it.

Group Discussion of he Analyst's Departure over the Week-end

The reporting group member emphasized that he had made special arrangements so that E.F. missed none of his regular sessions as a result of the analyst's trip. The patient had also been informed that provisions had been made so that, if necessary, he could reach the doctor by telephone, and the analyst had told E.F. that he would return on Saturday night so that there would be no day when the doctor would not be available to the patient in person.

Feder cited the case of a patient who, after having always been informed of his doctor's itinerary, attempted suicide on the one week-end that the analyst left town and would not disclose his destination. Feder also questioned the wisdom of the analyst's discontinuing the medication on a day when he would be out of town. E.F.'s therapist responded that, at that time, not only did he feel the medication was harming the patient, but E.F. also did not like the drug. Moreover, when he directed E.F. to stop taking the Taractan, he explained that he thought it was hurting the patient by taking away his energy.

Sunday, November 10   E.F. telephoned the analyst in the evening to announce that he was willing to go to the hospital for shock treatment. The doctor told him to take 100 mgs of Tofranil immediately and another 100 mgs the next morning.

Group Discussion of Different Ways of Dispensing Drugs

Roose asked how the new drug was dispensed to the patient, and the presenting analyst explained that E.F. was told to go to a drugstore and have the pharmacist telephone the doctor. At that time the analyst could not actually *give* the Tofranil to the patient, first, because he was speaking with the patient over the telephone, and, second, because he had no Tofranil.

Ostow stated that, occasionally, when a patient is in serious trouble, and needs a dramatic gesture of support, he will give the patient something himself, but he usually expects patients to buy their own medication through the normal channels. Roose described how one of his patients would frequently walk over to the analyst's desk, rummage through the drug samples that were lying around, and ask the doctor: "What have you got for me?" This same patient refused to admit that his medication was having any pharmacological effect. Linn remarked that that case seemed to represent a very negative transference situation, and demeaned the therapeutic procedure. Roose responded that this patient's condition was serious enough to warrant such flexibility on his part.

Monday, November 11   "This week-end was worse: it was horrible. I just slept most of the time. When I was awake, I really felt desperate—thoroughly depressed. The time has come to do something. My wife is panicky, and wants to see you."

The analyst asked the patient about a recent meeting of the family company to discuss omitting the dividend. E.F. answered: "Nothing happened. They were all concerned about me, and they want to put up a plaque in the factory thanking me for what I did. The dividend is only going to be cut in half, not completely eliminated. There is much less closeness or clinging to my wife than in the past few weeks. She wants me to give my proxy to the lawyer, as if I was gone forever. There is much less closeness than there was. I am sweating like a horse. I have to make a payment on a loan on the 15th of December."

The therapist explained that he would make arrangements for E.F.'s hospitalization.

Group Discussion of the Patient's Reported Sweating

Ostow saw the sweating as resulting from E.F.'s final struggle against his depression. Patients generally report sweating, especially of the back, the back of the neck, and the back of the head, just as they are beginning to fight depression actively. The sweating usually occurs in the morning and at night, and it appears whether or not the patient is on medication. Klerman suggested that sweating might be especially strong with Tofranil. Ostow cited the case of a patient on Tofranil, who complained of sweating, but who stopped sweating when the dose of Tofranil was increased.

Tuesday, November 12   When the reporting analyst saw him at the hospital, E.F. appeared quite phobic and eager to leave. He did not like being locked up in a ward, and he had telephoned his wife and said: "Get me the hell out of here." The therapist started the patient on Elavil, 25 mgs intramuscularly, four times a day; phenobarbital, half a grain, twice a day, to prevent any possible convulsant effect of the intramuscular Elavil, and Tarac-tan, 25 mgs orally four times a day, to control the patient's phobic agitation and desire to run away. At the time, the analyst thought that phenobarbital might also facilitate the action of the Elavil, an effect he had seen described in the literature though he no longer believes that it does to any significant extent.

Wednesday, November 13   The reporting analyst again saw E.F. in the hospital, where the latter was trying to sleep as much as possible. At first the doctor thought that this excessive somnolence was caused by the intramuscular Elavil, but he then decided that the patient was retreating into sleep as a substitute for, and defense against suicide. E.F. frequently employs this strategy when he is depressed. The patient continued to be phobic about his hospitalization, and still wanted to escape, but he seemed less agitated than he had been the previous day. He had almost nothing to say to the doctor.

Group Discussion

In response to questions by other members of the group, the presenting analyst explained that E.F. was no longer sweating, and was no longer taking oral Tofranil. He actually took only 100 mgs of Tofranil by mouth on Sunday night, and another 100 mgs by mouth on Monday morning. The reason the Tofranil was given on those two occasions was to help the patient over Sunday night and to prepare him for the intramuscular Elavil. E.F.'s therapist emphasized that he does not like to start a patient on an intramuscular drug without first checking out his reaction to a smaller oral dose of that drug.

Thursday, November 14   Forty-eight hours after beginning the intramuscular Elavil, E.F. seemed more cheerful and a little more relaxed in the hospital. Although he was still apprehensive, he was thinking positively about the future, which the doctor saw as a slight improvement.

Friday, November 15   The patient's condition remained stable. He was feeling better, but he seemed apprehensive about a relapse, and he reported the following dream:

> You urge me to have an electric shock treatment. I feel horrified by the suggestion.

The analyst understood this dream as a contradiction of E.F.'s conscious declaration that he was feeling better. If the patient were really feeling better, he would not have been dreaming about having to undergo shock treatment.

Group Discussion

Linn wondered whether, in the dream, the patient might have been expressing resentment that the doctor had first left town, and then locked him up in the hospital. The presenting analyst confirmed that E.F. was quite distressed about his hospitalization.

Saturday, November 16   Although E.F.'s apprehensiveness continued, on this day he was feeling more vigorous, and most eager to leave. In talking with the analyst, he seemed cheerful, and denied having suicidal thoughts. The doctor prescribed 25 mgs of Elavil intramuscularly, half a grain of phenobarbital orally, 75 mgs of Taractan orally, and 200 mgs of Tofranil orally. He then discharged the patient from the hospital.

Sunday, November 17   "I feel pretty well today, not so much depressed, as shook up. I had a hard week, or ten days. Strange that I should feel that I need a rest. I can't tell you how glad I am to be out of that place. It was so depressing. This morning, for the first time, I was able to feel angry with my wife. She kept asking interminable questions. I had a small amount of diarrhea. I noticed a tendency to a little unbalance, sort of floating like a drunken sailor. I didn't drink Dubonnet, or anything else." The analyst then asked E.F. to stand up, and walk. He also noticed some deviation in the patient's gait; also, E.F. was less stable than usual in the Romberg position.

The patient continued: "I didn't take my pills this morning. I will take them when I return." The doctor, then noticing that E.F.'s speech was unclear, asked: "Why is your speech slurred?" The patient answered: "I wondered about that too. Maybe my teeth aren't secure. Could I spend some time in bed today?" The doctor responded in the affirmative. E.F. then said: "I am building up some jealousy of my wife and Philip. I wonder what right I have to expect her to be celibate. I certainly feel a little drugged. I have a great desire to see Dr. D., though I know she will say, 'You are in the hands of a good man.' When I turned on the cold shower, I thought 'suppose you had to stand under it for ten minutes as part of your care.' I had a fantasy:

You are standing up with boxing gloves on, and I am going to hit you in the solar plexus.

I notice occasionally a muscle jerk." During this hour, the patient tended to fall asleep on the couch, which is very unusual for him, and he reported the following dream:

The god Woden was having an affair with his daughter.

E.F. then exclaimed: "I want to go out, and cry my heart out, because, after five years of coming here, I find myself in this condition." The analyst then reduced the dose of Taractan from 75 mgs to 50 mgs a day orally, and discontinued the phenobarbital. As the patient left the office, the therapist told him to be careful about his unsteadiness, and not to drive to see the doctor, but to be driven or to take a cab.

Group Discussion

The reporting analyst saw the patient's somnolence and slurred speech as a result of the medication. Linn wondered whether E.F.'s use of the word "celibate"—as opposed to "abstinence," which seems to be the more appropriate work—suggests a homosexual attachment on the part of the patient to his wife's lover. E.F.'s analyst saw no evidence for that hypothesis. Ostow understood the patient's reference to his former therapist as a continuation of E.F.'s denial of his ambivalence toward the doctor.

Monday, November 18   The analyst had to be out of town, and was unable to see E.F.

Tuesday, November 19   "It is pretty rough. I guess I am terrified about going back to the hospital for electric shock treatment." The doctor asked about E.F.'s muscle jerk and slurred speech. The patient answered that the jerk had stopped and that his speech was better. The analyst also noticed that the patient showed less swaying in the Romberg position. E.F. was, at this point, taking 100 mgs of Tofranil orally and 50 mgs of Taractan a day, and the analyst discussed with him the possibility of a toxic effect of these drugs.

The patient then continued: "I have very little appetite. I feel sort of numb with, occasionally, a great desire to see Dr. D. I had a dream:

I was trying to play tennis and I just couldn't hit a thing.
I was completely out of control.

Group Discussion

Ostow commented that the dream seems to reflect the

beginning ataxia caused by the medication. The group then discussed the advisability of speaking openly with a patient about the possible effects of the drugs he is taking. Roose felt that the patient's condition and circumstances are important elements in deciding how, and to what extent, drug effects should be discussed. He usually tells patients that there might be side effects, a warning which he considers particularly important when there are significant negative elements in the transference.

Feder thought that such an exchange was particularly important as a form of reassurance to this patient, who was feeling so fearful. Ostow considered it useful for E.F. to be able to distinguish the side effects of the drugs he was taking from their principal effect, in order to tolerate the side effects better. It was also important for this patient at this time to know that the doctor understood what was happening to him.

Wednesday, November 20   "This is a hellish period for me. Sleep is my only retreat. My wife said that she wants me to go to New York to see Dr. M. She said she can't drive me here everyday. When Mrs. A. visited us, I thought, 'If I could just screw her, I would feel better.' I feel numb, no motivation at all: a dim bulb, like a real mental case. As for my work, there is nothing there. I feel like a little boy, shriveled away.

"I was looking at my wife last night. She looked so pretty, and I was so proud of her, the way she keeps her chin up. Suddenly I see my mother's face. There is a resemblance between her face and my wife's face. I have been feeling like I am sad, going into old age."

The therapist instructed E.F. to discontinue the Tofranil and to take Vivactil, instead, 30 mgs a day.

Group Discussion

The reporting group member explained that 30 mgs of Vivactil is equivalent to 150 mgs of Elavil or Tofranil. Klerman found that Vivactil causes extreme dryness in the mouth, and he cited the case of a patient for whom Vivactil caused severe gum problems. Ostow saw in this session signs of both the toxic effects of the drug and a simultaneous return of E.F.'s depression despite the action of the medication.

Thursday, November 21   During this period so many drugs were being administered, and the dosage was being changed so frequently that, to minimize the patient's confusion, the analyst each day wrote down instructions regarding the medication for that day. On Wednesday, E.F. had taken the wrong drugs. He said: "Everything is the same. I read your Sunday instructions, and that is where I goofed. I think I can drive over OK tomorrow. Is it very complicated getting transportation?

"I don't expect to go to the country over the weekend, and I don't see much difference between today and yesterday. I keep thinking maybe I am hanging on to this disease. I got up and went out to dinner with my wife and a friend. I was very silent. I felt like a wet blanket. I am afraid of getting chilled. I wore my heavy coat today."

The therapist asked E.F. about the drug toxicity, and the latter responded: "I don't feel nearly as much like I am under medicine. My speech seems normal. I had a feeling of helplessness coming over here. I come here, and just spout a few words, and nothing happens. There is a meeting of the company board today at 2:30. I can see them saying, 'He'll be all right in a little while,' and then everybody will forget about it. I suddenly had the desire for you to hold my hand. At times like this, you feel you wish you had some kind of religion to fall back on.

"After I left here yesterday, I felt better, but it didn't last too long. I can't seem to think out my old thoughts. I felt for my cock, and it was practically gone. My nuts seem to be up in my stomach. I keep thinking of my mother-in-law these days, but she couldn't stand sick people. I wish I had died when I was young. I keep wishing I could just cry. I feel bloodless, cold, no sunshine, no warmth."

Group Discussion

Roose wondered whether this patient might have done better had he been transferred to another hospital, perhaps for a prolonged stay. Linn remarked that, in the same situation, he would probably have discontinued all medication for a while, and relied on the therapeutic effects of hospitalization. The reporting analyst thought that, at the time, the pressure of being hospitalized was having a negative effect on E.F., and that the patient was more likely to improve out of the hospital. Moreover a transfer to another hospital under these circumstances might have discouraged the patient more.

Ostow proposed that what went badly for this patient was, not so much his release from the hospital as the toxicity of the drugs. When the dose was reduced, and he started on Vivactil, E.F.'s condition changed from a non-depressed toxic state to a non-toxic depressed state. Feder, impressed by the rapid appearance of these most recent toxic effects, suspected that some of them might be attributable to the combination of intramuscular and oral drugs.

Ostow observed that this patient seems to be particularly sensitive to any drug that has a sedative effect. Winkelman mentioned that frequently toxic side effects of drugs are really manifestations of negative feelings in the transference. Roose noted that this is especially true with anti-depression agents. Winkelman and Ostow agreed that although mild physiological reactions might be magnified as a result of negative transference, in this instance the toxicity seemed organic enough.

Feder suggested the following formulation. A state of negative transference is a particularly stressful situation for a very dependent person. It has been demonstrated that ACTH, when administered to a patient, facilitates the conversion of norepinephrine to epinephrine. Many of the psychically active drugs seem to act through their effect on metabolism. Here one finds a physiological mechanism whereby a state of negative transference, in an extremely dependent person, can alter metabolism so that drugs are handled differently, and thus could have different effects. Ostow objected that the toxic effects in question did not occur when the patient was taking MAOI drugs.

Linn referred to Lewin's observation* that the feeling of a shrunken body together with clinging and somnolence represents a return to the womb. This tendency should be seen as a result of the patient's psychodynamic state, and not as an effect of the medication. Ostow agreed with Linn about E.F.'s body image and clinging, but he felt that the somnolence was produced by the drug. E.F. never reported overwhelming somnolence before he

*Lewin, *Psychoanalysis of Elation*. New York: W.W. Norton, 1950.

entered the hospital. Feder and Linn responded that in the case of such a complicated person whose circumstances change in so many ways, it is difficult to assign one cause to each manifestation. Perhaps it would be more useful to think of the behavior as resulting from different forces operating in conjunction.

Summary

Ostow summarized the discussion as follows. The primary effect of a drug may be reinforced through an act of affectionate concern on the part of the doctor, or may be compromised if the patient is subjected to additional stress—for example, if he is discharged from the hospital before he is ready, or if the doctor goes away. In the same manner, toxic effects of drugs may be intensified by stress or by negative transference. Tiredness as a toxic effect may be augmented by defensive withdrawal, and several toxic symptoms, especially those that are associated with phenothiazines, might be better understood as physical postures of aversion. For example, torticollis, that is, a vigorous turning away, may be a physical expression of psychic aversion, which would be expressed more directly by depersonalization or "de-realization."

The mechanism of a toxic effect may also be based on a stress reaction which intensifies metabolic derangement, such as the balance between norepinephrine and epinephrine in the brain. Finally, drug toxicity may have the effect of intensifying negative transference, sometimes to the point of accentuating the depression. Ostow suspected that this was the case with E.F. There are times when, though the drug choice may be correct, the toxic effects of the medication will upset a patient coming out of depression to the point of precipitating a relapse.

Bressler commented that some patients see the toxic effects of the medication as part of a punishment for recovering. Moreover, some patients react differently to the same drug, depending on whether it is administered orally or parenterally. Drugs are unlikely to be effective in patients who have a high level of metabolite in their blood. Bressler had observed that, at least with the parenteral Elavil, the sleepier the patient becomes, the better the primary effect. The reporting group member felt that this observation has limited application to the case under consideration because when E.F. is depressed, he sleeps most of the day, no matter what the medication. Feder suggested that the method of administration of the medication might influence the rate at which the drug is absorbed into the blood stream. Ostow did not notice a difference in his own patients between the effects of orally and parenterally-administered drugs other than latency of onset.

Friday, November 22   "Everything is the same except that every once in a while I think that I am coming out of it, but then it comes back, especially when I first wake up. Sometimes I feel like a helpless baby. I feel a little more solid: I try never to think about suicide. My wife called Dr. Q. (a friend of theirs who is an internist). She thinks I need vitamins. I don't know whether or not to conform to her wishes. The only safe place seems to be in bed. My wife wants to go riding in the country. I feel so futile here. I just pass the time of day. I suddenly had a desire to make you beat me, hurt me."

The analyst understood from this material that the patient's depression had returned. At this time, E.F. was taking 30 mgs of Vivactil and 50 mgs of Taractan a day. In order to recapture the patient's earlier progress, the doctor increased the Vivactil to 50 mgs for Friday and instructed E.F. to build it up to 60 mgs a day over the week-end. The Taractan was reduced to 25 mgs on Friday and none thereafter.

Monday, November 25   E.F. reported that his condition had remained stable, and that he had a young lady in the car, who had been trying to play around with him from time to time. "When I woke up this morning, I felt so good. I had a dream:

I bought a huge wagon—a horse wagon, but there were no horses. There were very comfortable pillows and seats in it. I got much pleasure from it, but then I told myself: 'You are spending money again.'

I woke up at 9:15 and felt good, but I began to move back about a quarter to ten. I wore myself out, and at about 10:15 the horrible scourge was back. I had a terrible desire to phone my friend Charlie (this man is a West Coast industrialist who keeps inviting

E.F. out to work with him). I wanted to call him and tell him I am very sick and he should come and get me. Then I had another fantasy of moving to the West Coast. I even took a large drink yesterday. It didn't do any good. It even affects my wee-weeing; I start and then I stop. This stuff I take makes my underarms smell."

Group Discussion

The presenting analyst felt that the patient's dream was ominous because it was about E.F.'s reunion with his mother in the grave. Ostow commented that many of his patients complain that both MAOI and tricyclic anti-depression drugs affect the odor of their perspiration. Loomis's patients who were taking these drugs also reported experiencing an unpleasant metallic taste in their mouth.

Tuesday, November 26   "Yesterday when I left here, I felt better, and all evening I felt better. I felt better again this morning, but I didn't have the energy to go riding because I felt dull. I can't help but feel that the pill is taking effect. I am reluctant to say it. I am still numb. Mrs A. rubbed my feet last night. I dread these holiday periods. I have to go visit my daughter for Thanksgiving on Thursday. They all want to go to Westport for the weekend. I seem to be out of touch. I feel drugged, but less so. My driving seems to be under good control.

"Today my wife said: 'You'll never know how much I missed you while you were in the hospital.' I almost got mad at her. I took a pretty good crap yesterday. I woke up much happier yesterday morning than this morning. I got chilled this morning. There is some question about whether I really wish to be dead. Sometimes I think it would be awful to be dead. I have gotten so that I hate the sight of my checkbook. I am thinking of going to the athletic club and doing some exercise. I compare coming here to going to the Wailing Wall, where you go to wail."

Wednesday, November 27   "Everything is pretty much the same, doctor. I felt badly today because it seemed as if I was being too dramatic. I tried to play tennis; I just couldn't coordinate. I tried swimming: I felt numb and overdrugged. I dread going home today because I want to crawl into bed. I woke up this morning feeling good again. I can relax as long as I can stay in bed, and maybe for a half hour after I wake up, and about ten minutes after I dress. I wish I could come here looking and feeling young or gay.

"I see my mother looking mad at you. Last night I woke up, and felt that my wife was making out with Philip or with the Frenchman who is visiting. I forgot to bring my wallet with my license. It is very hard to make decisions. I poured the bottle of pills into two bottles last night, in case I should drop one. This pen seems to be whistling while you are talking. I am down from 198 to 168 pounds: my hands are scrawny."

Comments of the Presenting Analyst

E.F.'s therapist observed that, on this day, the patient's speech was again slurred. The doctor understood this manifestation as a toxic effect of the Vivactil. The patient seemed once more to be resisting the drug because of its toxic effect and because it was not making him well. Moreover he was invoking his mother's wrath at the doctor for disappointing him and for causing his symptoms. The analyst added that the patient's suspicions of his wife seemed not unreasonable; in fact they were reinforced by later circumstances and events. In response to Klerman's question, the reporting group member explained that E.F. never uses the word "gay" to refer to homosexuals. Ostow commented that the Vivactil was failing to help this patient because of the recurrence of toxic symptoms.

Thursday, November 28   Because it was Thanksgiving, there was no analytic session.

Friday, November 29   "I definitely feel better this morning. I feel more solid on the ground, and I am more hopeful. I am sure I won't get depressed again. It is very hard to have faith when everything is so painful."

Group Discussion

Feder and Ostow remarked that depressed patients typically

volunteer that they feel better, and then deny it immediately. Feder suspected that many of these patients fear the responsibilities implicit in recovery.

Monday, December 2   "I didn't take three pills this morning; only one because I found I was a little wuzzy and out of touch with things. I am disappointed because I assumed that by Monday the depression would be further away, and today I felt I slipped back an inch. Friday night I had a funny dream:

> One of the houses in Westport would be occupied by an enemy. We would be beaten in a war. We were all supposed to be out at 5:00 a.m.

I woke up and started packing my bag. That happened a number of times. I had a hard time orienting myself. The decor didn't seem to be the same. Then I said: 'What am I doing?' and went back to sleep again and woke up again.

"On Saturday morning I found myself in the kitchen eating cereal at about 7:00 a.m. I thought I might as well cook my wife's breakfast for her. I took it up to her and woke her up at 8:00 a.m. instead of 9:00 a.m. Saturday night I had the same dream as Friday and a second dream:

> My wife needed a screwdriver upstairs, and I thought of taking my whole tool kit up there. I left the screwdriver at the foot of the stairs, and I thought: 'She always loses things.'

Sunday after lunch it suddenly got very gloomy, and I got blue inside. My wife went up to get her fanny rubbed, so I went to sleep, and dreamed:

> She and I had a hell of a fight. I wanted to make up with her.

When I got up I thought the dream was true, and I told my daughter to tell her to come to me as soon as she could. She told me it wasn't true. I saw my doctor, and told him what I had been through. I asked him to talk to my wife, and he gave me some vitamins because I asked for them." The analyst volunteered to contact E.F.'s internist if the patient wished him to. E.F. responded: "I think we ought to let that ride. Sunday night I had another dream:

J was in your office.

I got out of bed, and thought 'What should I do now?' I got back into bed, and went to sleep. This happened two or three times. One time there was a woman in the closet, and I said 'Doctors.' I wondered whether you were there. Again I got back in bed.
"Today I felt drugged again. It frightened me. I seem to be awake, and yet not in touch with reality. People say I look so much better today; my face looks firm. I have been so hopeful that this damn thing would pass, and not come back, and I feel so disappointed when it comes back, even a little bit." E.F. reported some renewed muscle twitching, which he had also experienced while on Elavil, and stated that he had dropped some cigarettes. He continued: "I see my father getting gloomy. I see myself getting gloomy." The analyst had noted that the patient was unsteady on his feet that day, and expressed his concern. E.F. responded: "I feel a renewed faith in you. I have had enough of this depression. It isn't fair. I have a constant fear that you will say that I have to have electric shock treatment."

For fear that the side effects, especially the confusion, apparently induced by Vivactil, were counteracting its anti-depression effect, the analyst decreased the dose of Vivactil. He also added 25 mgs a day of Taractan in the hope that it would combat nascent signs of delirium.

Group Discussion

The reporting analyst described E.F.'s visit to the internist as an effort to please his wife. Feder, having ascertained that E.F. was taking the Vivactil in two doses a day, remarked that his patients show less toxicity when they take Vivactil in doses of 10 mgs every two or three hours. Ostow observed that, under the influence of the toxic effect of the drug, the patient's dreams had become much more direct and open.

Ostow was surprised that, although E.F.'s hallucinations had previously been about his mother, on this day he spoke of his father. Feder thought that the reference to the father might actually have been meant as a statement about the analyst.

Tuesday, December 3   "I had a friend come up with me, but I drove. I am afraid I am in a very apprehensive state, and out of touch with things. I slept most of the time since I saw you last. I didn't feel up to going to the concert last night. Thank God I haven't got some cruel person in charge of me. I don't recall leaving the light on last night. I didn't have those dreams that I had over the week-end. It's quite frightening. I saw myself going to bed saying, 'I'm terribly sick.' I thought I was so sick you had to come see me in my room. Maybe I should have a nurse." The analyst asked whether E.F. was still experiencing muscle twitches, and the patient responded that there had been none since the previous night.

"Several times during the past few weeks I saw myself as a starving Jewish person in Dachau prison camp. If I had any sense, I would have left my family, and gone to live with my Jewish relatives, because they were so much more normal. I started getting mad at my wife, and she said that I had plenty of time. I had a momentary flash of anger at her."

The doctor decreased the patient's dose of Vivactil to 40 mgs a day, and started E.F. on 2 mgs a day of physostigmine, in the hope that it might counteract the toxicity of the Vivactil.

Group Discussion

E.F.'s therapist reported that, on this day, the patient seemed to have a particularly broad-based gait. E.F.'s analyst was, moreover, surprised that the patient was beginning to identify as a Jew, since E.F. had always felt great ambivalence about his mother's Jewishness. Ostow and Feder agreed that, at this point, the patient's condition seemed grim. The man was still suffering from the toxicity of the medication; he was becoming more depressed, and the doctor had disclosed his retreat by decreasing the dose of the Vivactil before there was any evidence of improvement.

Wednesday, December 4   "After I left here, I went to the
gym, but I couldn't make it. I just took a shower and went home.
I debate the efficacy of forcing myself too much. After that I slept
until about noon. I suddenly break out into a sweat, two or three
times yesterday, and now I think my loose bridge is affecting my
speech. Yesterday, I didn't drive up to my daughter or back. I let
my wife have it while she was directing the driving. During the last
few days, I had glimpses of the idea of going out to work for
Charlie on the West Coast. The first flash came to go back to work
for my brother-in-law, but that's out.

"I don't know what I can do about the marriage. During the
summer, I thought I was proving that I could be independent of
my wife, and walk out on her. I am talking more, and with a
much stronger voice. I had a fantasy:

You and I whispered to each other.

This morning I woke up at 4:30. I had a dream:

A friend of mine and his wife and children came in. The
children were off balance, as if they had to lie sidewise to
be normal, and I had to lie sidewise too. The wife said
that her husband had been very upset about my condition.

I got up several times to make sure they weren't there. In the
dream they didn't have their feet on the ground; they were leaning
way over.

"In the past few weeks I haven't felt the impulse to suicide,
but I could see it around the corner. I could see why my brother
and my sister-in-law both committed suicide. I am angry with you
because you didn't explain to me about the hospital. I had that
awful feeling of being locked in. My bowels are working a little
better. The peeing occasionally turns off like a faucet. If I had
twenty years to live, would I be willing to face such disappointments as my wife's leaving, sickness, or death? Will I press the
button and die now?"

Group Discussion

The presenting analyst interpreted the patient's reference to his bridgework as an attempt to account for his slurred speech. Ostow saw E.F.'s sweating as evidence of a renewed struggle against the depression. The dream expressed the patient's concern about the effects of the drug on his psychic functioning. This kind of hallucinatory dream with spatial disorientation and the difficulty in urination are signs of the drug's increasing toxicity.

Friday, December 6 "I think things are more solid. I woke up feeling pretty sorry. I took 1 mg of physostigmine at 9:30 this morning (it was then 12:30 p.m.). I went riding this morning. I am suspicious that this is just a momentary improvement. Last night I got up, and went to the bathroom to take a drink of water, and I wanted to go to the kitchen to get some fruit, but I didn't. Over the weekend I had a dream:

> I would suddenly find myself in the bathroom or in the kitchen.

Now I fear the long road back, wrestling with the marriage. The words that come to my mind are 'desolation' and 'isolation.'
"I got some relief by thinking of going to work for Charlie on the West Coast. I am going to a wedding today. I feel like quoting you to my wife, but I won't. I don't want to upset her. I had the feeling that old age has suddenly crowded in on me, as if someone would say, 'My God, how he has fallen off.' Suddenly I feel like an old man. I am so ashamed of whimpering." The analyst asked whether the patient's mouth was still dry. E.F. answered: "Yes, my bridge is still loose. I am sure I shouldn't feel as pessimistic as I do. Last night I dreamt:

> I was back in prep school. We had just arrived, and the children were getting acquainted. I was looking for my room. Should I straighten things out, or should I lie down and snooze."

Comments of the Presenting Analyst

E.F.'s plans to attend a wedding indicate some improvement, because this man rarely goes to social events. Generally, however, the patient seemed to begin each session with the wish to be well, only to realize that he was, in fact, no better at all.

Sunday, December 8   E.F. was taking 4 mgs of physostigmine and 50 mgs of Vivactil a day. He told the analyst: "I feel that I am headed for the nuthouse. I don't have the headache; it's just sort of numbness. I keep confusing the days. I felt fairly good on Friday, not so good yesterday. I got into bed at 5:30 or 6:00 p.m. yesterday. I had feelings of guilt. When my wife was sick, I didn't go to the hospital with her. Occasionally I have the feeling that I went through this as a child. I am very sick, and no one knows what it is all about, and everyone is worried. When I was twelve, someone hit me in the face with a basketball, and I had a numb feeling. Just like a living corpse at Dachau. I have decided to apologize to my wife for being in this condition." The patient then stretched, clenched his fists, and made agitated movements, wringing his hands.

"I feel guilty about going back to bed. My mouth is really dry. I am upset about having to sell stock to make the next payment on the real estate. I feel like calling out the reserves. Since I saw you, I have been in bed most of the time. I seem to sleep very soundly. I don't recall having any dreams. I feel like a little boy who has flunked his tests. I am awfully glad I am able to come here, but everything seems the same after I leave. I have to pay a note at the end of the week for $15,000. I don't know whether to borrow money or sell stock.

"Yesterday I had milk, cream, and a few eggs. I still don't have much taste: my taste buds are shot. If I could only get well by going out to the West Coast for a month.

"I feel as though I am climbing a cliff, and everything has come loose, and I can't hang on. I can't help but feel that things are a little more solid. Yesterday and today I took a fairly reasonable crap, and it seemed to me that that was a sign of being better, but it is the same old story. I wake up feeling good and ready to go. I lie there for a while, and then I make myself get up and go out for a walk. Yesterday I had a hell of a chill. I would like to assure you and my wife and myself that I am not hiding anything which would make me depressed. Coffee has lost its appeal. I know my wife is getting ready to go to the West Coast after Christmas. We haven't discussed it. I'm afraid to have her go away; I would be lost and lonely. In 1962 my wife was living in New York and I was alone in Westport. I have to make up my mind that I am not going and that I want my wife not to go.

"I think I should have gone to work for Charlie years ago. I think I am good only for menial jobs. I am so ashamed of my doubts and fears, and I am being punished for doing something wrong. Last night I had a fantasy:

My wife was being screwed by one of the visitors.

"There is some improvement each day. I keep on feeling that something will come into my life and save me, for example, a girl who was visiting yesterday. I think my driving up here is quite safe. I feel not really so close to my wife as I was a couple of weeks ago. She seems to be terrified of my condition. If it were up to me, I would leave the medicine at the same dose. No one asked me."

Group Discussion

Feder cited an article* which reported that physostigmine is being used to treat acute toxic syndromes resulting from anti-Parkinson drugs. The idea behind this method of treatment is that the acute toxic syndrome is an anticholinergic syndrome, like an atropine poison.

Klerman asked whether the reporting analyst was concerned about E.F.'s financial judgment at this time. E.F.'s therapist answered that he kept up with E.F.'s major transactions during this period, and was astounded at the acuteness of the patient's financial judgment despite his depression. Winkelman suggested that financial supervision by the analyst might compromise the transference. Feder stated that every transference is always modified by reality, and to the extent to which it supplies the patient much-needed support, this kind of interference is constructive. Ostow added that financial supervision can be carried out discreetly, and in keeping with the educational purposes of the

*R.D. Duvoisin, et al., "Reversal of Central Anticholinergic Syndrome in Man by Physostigmine," *JAMA* 206:9 (Nov. 5, 1968).

transference, and of psychoanalysis generally.

Ostow interpreted the patient's nourishing himself with milk, cream, and eggs as a regression to baby food, and the presenting analyst mentioned that this man seldom drinks milk. E.F.'s doctor explained further that, at this time, Mrs. F. wanted to go to the West Coast although her husband could not bear the thought of being away from either her or the analyst. E.F. was frightened by the idea that he doubted he would be able to persuade his wife to remain in New Haven. Loomis thought that, by making remarks discrediting their relationship, E.F. was preparing himself to leave her.

Friday, December 13   The patient was taking daily 6 mgs of physostigmine and 60 mgs of Vivactil. He stated: "I feel quite panicky. I feel pretty numb in my hands. I drove over OK. I went to my wife's party last night, and everybody said I looked all right. My wife came back with a group of people. One man said, 'Give me a kiss.' She said, 'Don't be foolish, my husband is in the next room.'

"My wife wants to go to Westport. I panic about leaving New Haven. I called my broker, and sold some stocks. I want to crawl into bed. I had to plead with my daughter last night to protect me against my wife's going away. I felt hopeless, like a little boy who knew his mother was screwing around, and couldn't do anything. I would like you to tell me whether to go to Westport today." The analyst made an appointment to see the patient at 9:00 a.m. Saturday morning. He meant, through this gesture, to tell E.F. that he could go, but not until Saturday. The patient responded: "OK. Then we can go tomorrow. Now I feel that the tiger has gotten cornered.

"I'm destroying everything, my home, my family, and my wife. There was something about my wife's voice last night. It frightened me. All the grim reality of life is evident to me now. My beautiful warm gloves are gone, and my hands are freezing. There are at least two plane crashes around Christmas."

The Presenting Analyst's Note to Himself

The presenting analyst read aloud the following note which he had made on the evening of Friday, December 13.

My patient is somewhat panicky, though I expected him to be
better because of the latest increase in the medication. It turned
out that he was especially disturbed because he felt pressure from
his wife to accompany her to Westport, and to the West Coast
over Christmas vacation. He was afraid to let her go, and to be
left behind. He asked me whether I would talk to her if she
called, and I promised to do so. She called at about 3:00 p.m., and
I tried to convey to her the importance of accommodating her-
self to his needs at the moment. She is not easy to reach, and she
told me she did not believe that one person should sacrifice him-
self for another. He has been sick before, and will be sick again,
and she has her own life to lead. There is an opportunity for her
on the West Coast, and she sees no reason to forgo it. Her
daughter will also be on the West Coast, and she would like to see
her there.

As far as this week-end goes, she said there is important business
to take care of in Westport. I tried to explain that this is a crucial
period for her husband, and that her cooperation is needed,
especially now. At about 4:00 p.m., E.F. called to tell me that his
wife was urging him to get out of bed lest he deteriorate further.
He asked for permission to remain in bed, and I advised him to
do so.

Saturday, December 14   "I felt terrible again. My immediate problem is whether I should go up to Westport with my
wife and her friends, or stay here. I feel like crawling back into
bed. I want to be able to stay in bed. I told you that I would like
to call Dr. M. Last night I told my wife that our lives are so inter-
woven. We are one parcel. I developed an antipathy to my
carpenter: he is so nice, he would do anything for me."

Comments of the Presenting Analyst

The remarks about the carpenter were actually a reference to
the analyst. After the patient left on Saturday morning, the doctor
telephoned Mrs. F., and suggested that she remain at home with
her husband. She replied: "I'm sorry, I have my own business," and
described how she had arranged for a niece to stay with Mr. F.
Later in the day the analyst, knowing that Mrs. F. was in frequent
contact with Dr. M. telephoned Dr. M., and told him what had been
happening in New Haven.

Monday, December 16   E.F. was taking daily 60 mgs of Vivactil and 4 mgs of physostigmine.

"I went out to get a haircut this morning. I had enough of the damn bed. I decided to walk down, and join my wife and her friends for lunch. In some ways I feel a little more solid on the ground. I have the feeling that maybe we should cut down a little on the medicine. She told me to tell you that she has definitely decided not to go to the West Coast, but she said that, if I am not well in two weeks, then we had better see Dr. M. The analyst understood from this remark that Dr. M. had spoken with Mrs. F. over the telephone.

"When I woke up, for a brief moment I thought, 'It is all gone now,' but then it sneaked back. I had a fantasy:

A tiger was chasing a monkey, and bopped it on the head.

I am the tiger and you are the monkey. This fantasy keeps going through my head, though one minute I'm the tiger, and the next minute I'm the monkey. I had another fantasy:

You talk about electric shock treatment, and I think of an undertaker cutting off my balls, and displaying them."

Tuesday, December 17   E.F. telephoned the analyst in the evening, and stated that he was ready to enter the hospital for shock treatment. To avoid a repetition of the anxiety experienced by the patient during his last hospitalization, the doctor arranged this time for him to enter a very small, private hospital, where he would not feel so obviously locked up. E.F. was to report to the hospital early in the morning, where he would have an EKG as an outpatient before going to see the analyst. After his analytic session, the patient would return to the hospital, and formally check in.

Wednesday, December 18   E.F. was taking 50 mgs of Vivactil and 2 mgs of physostigmine. He was seen at the hospital.

"My wife wants you to know that she intends to cooperate with you. No sense in kidding you or me, I am getting more depressed; I guess I am facing the fact that I have to have electric shock treatment. I called my doctor, and asked if he had any accommodations at the hospital he's affiliated with. I called another doctor friend, and he told me he was in favor of it. I went to bed fairly resigned, and I woke up feeling terrible. I feel that I am not in touch with the world. I told my wife that it looks like the pills are not going to work, and I feel panicky. This happened to me when I was a little boy, and I feel the helplessness. I suppose I want to faint. I don't know how to describe this fear." The therapist told E.F. that no treatment is completely safe, but that electric shock treatment is safe enough so that the analyst himself would take it should he ever need it.

The patient responded: "This is for real. You think about death and operations, and all of a sudden you're there. I like this hospital much better than the other one. I felt that I didn't trust you, so I called my friend Herbert. I have been talking to him now for about a week." The analyst asked what specifically frightened the patient about the shock treatments. The latter replied: "Brain or personality damage. It isn't fair to you or me for me to act this way. Yesterday I bought my wife a half dozen small handkerchiefs. I got so gloomy about it, I started crying. I sure got the blues." The patient then asked the doctor to be with him for the first shock treatment. Althought the presenting analyst would not ordinarily be present for such a procedure, he complied with this request.

Group Discussion: Review of the Failure
of the Vivactil and Physostigmine

Ostow thought that the physostigmine failed to relieve the toxic effects of the Vivactil because it was started too late, and because, by the time it was initiated, the patient's condition was already too complex. The presenting analyst responded that it is difficult to add physostigmine earlier because, at the beginning, it is unclear whether a given patient will become toxic. Feder felt that the group's previous discussion of the anticholinergic syndrome failed to distinguish possible differences in the effects of physostigmine given orally and intravenously.

Feder also wondered why the presenting analyst persisted so

long with the Vivactil, after its failure to help the patient became apparent. E.F.'s therapist responded that, during this time, he was considering possible alternatives to the Vivactil. He resisted the shock treatment for as long as he did, because he feared that it would provide only temporary relief, and that, after two months or so the patient would suffer a relapse. Linn commented that he would have used the shock treatment much earlier.

Friday, December 20   E.F. received his first electric shock treatment. Because he was so apprehensive, the analyst met him at the hospital, and accompanied him for the treatment. The doctor continued the patient on 40 mgs a day of Vivactil because he had observed with previous patients that, sometimes, the shock treatment will sensitize them once more to the medication if they are on an anti-depression drug to which they have not responded before.

Saturday, December 21   The analyst visited E.F. at the hospital, where he found the latter resting comfortably. The patient reported that he was no longer worried, that he was sleeping a great deal, and that his wife was visiting him from time to time. He also mentioned that his appetite was better, and that he was confused.

Sunday, December 22   The analyst again found the patient feeling comfortable. E.F. told the doctor that he was actually feeling bad, apathetic. He was thinking about the future, but not too courageously, and he had fallen asleep in the morning when he was supposed to arrange for his wife to join him for lunch. The patient also spoke of wanting to belong to a group; he wished for the good old days when everyone was working together in the business.

Group Discussion

Ostow noted that, on the second day after the first treatment, there was evidence of a return of libido and the return of a little bit of optimism. Feder wondered about the possible psychodynamic effects of the shock treatment as a kind of punishment. This patient's earlier remarks about the Wailing Wall and Dachau suggest a proclivity in this direction.

Monday, December 23   E.F. had his second shock treatment in the morning. The analyst visited him in the evening, at which time the patient reported that, immediately after the treatment, he had felt uncomfortable, though he could not say exactly how. At this time he was feeling physically comfortable, but somewhat more despondent.

Tuesday, December 24   The patient had his third shock treatment, and the analyst did not see him.

Wednesday, December 25   The doctor visited E.F. and found him feeling very sleepy. When he checked through the patient's chart, he saw that E.F. had sugar in his urine. The analyst informed the patient of this discovery, and advised him to have it followed up. It was later confirmed that E.F. has diabetes.

Group Discussion

Roose remarked that diabetes which appears in middle age is usually quite mild. Feder raised the question of whether the elevation of the patient's blood sugar might have complicated the action of the drugs he was taking. Because MAOI drugs tend to lower the glucose tolerance curve, they have, at times, been used to fight diabetes, while phenothiazines, and tricyclic anti-depression agents usually elevate the glucose tolerance curve. Ostow cited a case from his practice of a patient whose diabetes becomes more acute when he is depressed, and subsides as the depression lifts. Ostow attributed the aggravation of this patient's diabetes to the additional stress on the patient resulting from the depression.

Thursday, December 26   Two days after his third shock treatment, the patient appeared disoriented, confused, claustrophobic, and unable to remember much about the events of recent days. E.F. told the doctor that he thought a partition had been removed from the room, that he could not think ahead, and that he was eager to leave. The analyst, fearing that the patient might be continuing to suffer toxic effects of the Vivactil, reduced the dose from 40 mgs to 20 mgs a day.

Friday, December 27 Because E.F. remained somnolent, confused, and impatient to leave, the analyst discontinued the Vivactil, but retained the Taractan, now at 50 mgs a day, to prevent him from becoming too agitated.

Saturday, December 28 The patient felt somewhat less confused. He was eating a considerable amount of chocolate candy, but he was still fairly dysarthric, and he had a positive Romberg test. The therapist did a brief neurological examination.

Sunday, December 29 E.F. remained somnolent and eager to leave.

Monday, December 30 E.F. was better oriented, his talk was relevant, and he still wanted to leave the hospital. The analyst discontinued all medication, and discharged the patient.

Group Discussion

Ostow commented that it was probably the combination of the shock treatments and the Vivactil that was responsible for E.F.'s initial post-treatment confusion. The presenting analyst emphasized E.F.'s extreme sensitivity to any sedative drug. Linn wondered whether the patient's confusion might be considered possible evidence of organic brain disease. The reporting group member maintained that he had never seen any signs of organic brain disease in this patient. Moreover, when E.F. becomes confused and toxic, he does not make errors, but merely reports that he feels remote.

Tuesday, December 31 The patient stated that he was vague, and that he could not remember the shock treatments. "I was very depressed, and I'm not depressed any more, but I lost my continuity. I feel 'blah,' whatever 'blah' means. Was this treatment a way of jarring me out of my despondency?"

Group Discussion

Roose wondered whether the patient's feeling of discontinuity resulted from amnesia, or from some difficulty in mental functioning. The presenting analyst suggested that E.F.'s discomfort might arise from the sense of unreality which he mentioned from time to time.

Wednesday, January 6, 1969   Because E.F. seemed still somewhat depressed, the analyst started him again on 200 mgs of Niamid. The doctor had been impressed by this man's response to Niamid six years earlier, and, since he had not taken the Niamid for four weeks now, it seemed possible that, after a rest period, the Niamid might again prove effective.

Thursday, January 7   The patient complained of nausea. He said that he felt empty, he had no energy, and he had little to say. "I don't seem to be depressed any more." E.F. then described a tender spot in his epigastrium. The analyst asked whether this was the same pain the patient had experienced when he suffered a peptic ulcer, and the patient responded that, though it was in the same place, it was a different kind of pain. When the analyst inquired whether E.F. had any sexual thoughts, the latter replied "No," and added that everything seemed distant. "For some strange reason I get the impression that one of the doctors in the hospital was a quack. I know that it is not true, but it is just an idea that I have." The therapist asked why the patient was so upset about the shock treatment, and E.F. answered: "I had the impression that, when they give you a shock treatment, you have a little convulsion. It is not pleasant to contemplate having a convulsion."

The analytic material was generally depressive. The patient made some remarks about suicide, and complained further that his sleep was disturbed and that in his nostrils and in his throat there was a peculiar odor which he associated with the hospital. This constant odor led to a great deal of anal material, such as dreams that his face was near someone's crotch or near someone's anus.

The doctor increased the patient's daily dose of Niamid to 400 mgs.

Group Discussion of the Shock Treatment

Most members of the group agreed that this was not a typical course of ECT. Furst wondered why the analyst did not administer more treatments. E.F.'s therapist replied that he feared that further shock treatments might add to the patient's already considerable confusion. Klerman suggested that the analyst might have waited five days, and then given six more shock treatments. The reporting analyst felt that five days after the first series of treatments, the patient, though he was not entirely well, no longer seemed sick enough to require ECT.

Linn thought that this shock therapy was particularly difficult to evaluate, because it was complicated by so many other issues; however he generally associated confusional reactions with a poor response to further shock therapy. Roose was impressed by E.F.'s bewilderment, and the presenting analyst elaborated that the patient seemed puzzled by the fact that problems which used to preoccupy him so, no longer seemed important.

Sunday, January 10   The patient reported that he felt somewhat better, and was no longer remaining in bed during the day.

Wednesday, January 13   E.F. complained that he was depressed again.

Thursday, January 14   One week after resuming the Niamid, E.F. expressed sentimental feelings of attachment. He said: "I want to hold on to you. I want to cling to you."

Friday, January 15   The patient elaborated sexual fantasies about his wife, and achieved a semi-erection. He told the doctor; "The electric shock treatments merely got rid of the painful part of the depression, but a painless depression remains."

Saturday, January 16   E.F. was feeling better and was more thoughtful toward his wife. For the first time since beginning treatment with the presenting analyst, he reported homosexual dreams.

Wednesday, January 20   The patient seemed somewhat

better, and, for the first time in several weeks, criticized his wife.

Friday, January 22   E.F. mentioned that the odor had disappeared from his throat and nostrils.

Saturday, January 23   The patient was more active, more vigorous, more confident, and more hostile to his wife. He also reported insomnia. Mrs. F. told him to tell the doctor that he was too high.

Group Discussion

Klerman commented that, had E.F. been his patient, he would have given more shock treatments. He attributed this patient's confusional toxicity to the Vivactil, and he felt that the confusion was a temporary phase. The patient, most likely, would have come out of it spontaneously. Many of Klerman's patients have exhibited reactions to Vivactil of irritability, insomnia, confusion, and extreme dryness of the mouth. Vivactil seems to have a more intense atropine-like effect than the other tricyclic anti-depression agents.

Feder noted the amphetamine-like effect of Vivactil, and suggested that this drug is best used for individuals who can tolerate an immediate high. E.F. unfortunately seemed to feel threatened by this degree of innervation: perhaps the confusion he suffered is attributable to this heightening of activity. Ostow argued that E.F. showed confusion without any heightening of activity.

Linn was skeptical of the reporting analyst's heavy reliance on Vivactil. Feder mentioned that Vivactil had been used very successfully with patients who had previously been treated with heavy doses of amphetamines. The presenting analyst explained that he had chosen Vivactil because E.F. had ceased to respond to MAOI drugs. After E.F. had suffered a confusional reaction to Elavil, the analyst had hoped that a relatively smaller dose of another tricyclic anti-depression agent might produce the same therapeutic effect and avoid the confusional reaction.

Klerman brought up for discussion the question of the effect of the transference on the patient's response to the drugs and to the shock treatments. Ostow felt that this man's response to the shock treatment and to the drugs was not significantly influenced by the transference. Klerman then described how the electric shock treatment sponsored by the doctor, contributed to the patient's masochistic view of the transference. Ostow added that this was evident particularly in the dreams about being electrocuted and being abused sexually. The presenting analyst reminded the group that, although E.F. maintained unconscious homosexual wishes toward the doctor for years previously, the masochistic fantasies generated by the shock treatments brought a new emphasis to the homosexual fantasies, and enabled E.F. to understand them for the first time.

Summary

Ostow proposed that the last phase of this patient's treatment, as reported by the presenting analyst, illustrates the commonly found organic syndrome in response to electric shock treatment. The group agreed that the early occurrence of this syndrome promises poor results for the therapy, and that this organic syndrome might be facilitated by the simultaneous use of a drug which furthers the patient's confusion.

The case of E.F. also demonstrates the way one man, taking the same drug, recovered twice from depression in a similar time sequence, though the actual amount of time required was influenced by the dosage. On the first occasion the patient recovered in about five weeks, and the second time, exhibiting the same behavioral sequence, the recovery took about three weeks on double the dose.

Finally, on the subject of the relationship of drug therapy and psychoanalysis, in this treatment it became clear, as Klerman pointed out, that organic therapy always alters the transference, sometimes obscures it, and occasionally clarifies it.

___

EDITOR'S NOTE. This case demonstrates nicely the psychodynamic responses to drug therapy as the latter influences (or in some instances, failed to influence) one or another of the manic depressive states. What is especially well demonstrated is that anti-depression drugs helped this patient to resist the pathogenic effects of an external stress, but only relatively. The latter continued to influence his mood and every few years managed to overcome the protective effect of the medication and psychotherapy.

In retrospect, two issues were not considered seriously enough. First, there was the natural history of the manic-depressive illness. This had been a timid and fearful young man who by cleverness and an ingratiating manner had managed to get himself taken care of by others throughout his life. The episodes of illness occurred when this careful arrangement broke down from time to time, for example, when he was dismissed from employment, and when his wife turned away from him.

Second, as in the previous cases, the group did not understand that small doses of tranquilizing agents can reinforce the anti-depression effect of anti-depression drugs. For example, on October 18, 1968, when the dose of Taractan which was given along with the Niamid, was reduced from 50 mgs to 25 mgs per day, the patient promptly felt worse. However, it is doubtful that that effect alone could have been used to withstand the progressive withdrawal of his wife, and the progressive organic dementia which may have contributed to the downhill course. The dementia was probably attributable to arteriosclerosis, diabetes, and changes induced by chronic use of alcohol.

Following the period of treatment reported, the patient continued well on Niamid with varying but small doses of tranquilizers. In 1972 the family moved to another part of the country. After a few months, he became depressed once more and required further electric shock treatment. Thereafter he was maintained on Nardil and lithium, under the care of another psychiatrist in this other city. In January of 1973 he sustained a stroke, probably cerebral thrombosis, which left him with a left hemiparesis. He then developed a progressive dementia and died two years later. The fact that he ultimately showed this overt dementia may provide the explanation for his toxic response to tricyclic drugs and to electric shock treatment, that is, that at the time of this response, the dementia was incipient though invisible.

CASE 4

Introduction

In the early autumn of 1965 the reporting group member was contacted by a woman, the secretary of a colleague, who was concerned about her niece, Rhoda. She explained that the niece was working for a local pharmacist as a clerk and was being subjected to sexual advances by her employer. A week or so after hearing from Rhoda's aunt, the analyst received a telephone call from a friend of the same pharmacist who was also his internist. The internist felt that his patient should be seen by a psychiatrist because he was "acting funny," that is, he was involved in an affair with an employee. He had become irritable, he was sleeping poorly, and was losing weight. Within a few days the pharmacist, who will be called G.H., was brought to see the presenting group member by his internist and his wife.

Background

At the time of his first interview with the presenting analyst, G.H. was about thirty-six years old, though his crew cut, his generally youthful, athletic appearance, and his childish mannerisms gave the impression of a younger man. He was married to a woman several years his junior, and he was the father of seven children ranging from seven years to ten months in age. One of the children was reported to have congenital difficulties in walking.

G.H. grew up in New Jersey. When G.H. was fifteen years old, his father, then sixty-five, died of cirrhosis of the liver after a long period of excessive drinking.

The patient had done his undergraduate work at Rutgers University, where he majored in chemistry. After obtaining his B.A. in 1952, he served in the U.S. Merchant Marine for two years. When G.H. was discharged, he did not know what to do. During the following year he found employment as a chemist, he married his high school girl friend and, at the end of the year, he decided to study pharmacy. G.H. attended the pharmacy school in New York City and, after graduating in 1957, he set up his business in New Jersey. The patient had had no previous history of involvement with psychiatric agencies of any sort.

G.H. told the analyst that his current problem was his affair with Rhoda. This relation had been going on for about a year, during which time he had come to trust Rhoda and to confide in her. The patient explained that he was attracted by Rhoda's beauty, but, more than that, he found sexual satisfaction with her which was lacking in his marriage. After the affair had been going on for some time, Rhoda became hysterical and thereupon began episodes of histrionics and wrist-cutting. She told her lover that she did not want to break up his marriage; she could not live without him, but their relationship, as it was, had become intolerable to her.

Summer 1965   As Rhoda became increasingly hysterical, G.H. began to behave in a way which was out of character for him. He was arrested for driving under the influence of alcohol, and his license was taken away. Two weeks after this incident, he was again arrested, this time while driving without a license. He had run a police car off the road, and became embroiled in a fist fight with the patrolman driving it.

At this point, G.H.'s family sought counsel from the internist who, in an effort to control the patient's destructive behavior, hospitalized him as an internal medical patient with a fictitious illness. The internist's real concern centered on the patient's affair, which the latter flaunted openly, and which soon became public knowledge in the small town in which G.H. lived. The patient and Rhoda frequently went out to lunch together, and, after losing his driver's license, G.H. had his wife drive him to see Rhoda.

In August, Rhoda made another suicidal gesture, and was admitted to a local state hospital. G.H. then had himself admitted to the same hospital, claiming that he too was suicidal. This joint hospitalization lasted for about a week, after which time the psychiatrists at the hospital realized that they were being exploited, and discharged both Rhoda and her lover. One of the conditions of the patient's discharge from the state hospital was that he arrange for psychiatric treatment, and his internist brought him to see the reporting analyst with whom he began therapy twice a week.

First Week   G.H. told the reporting group member that Rhoda was very upset, and he wanted someone to help her. The analyst, who first heard of this case from Rhoda's aunt, was hard put to decide who, among the several people involved, was his patient. Since G.H. was the patient before him, the therapist observed him and noted that he seemed to be an immature, passive, narcissistic, phallic man with latent homosexual behavior relating to his father's alcoholism.

Second Week   G.H. and his wife came together to see the reporting analyst. It was the wife who spoke during most of the session. The group member described Mrs. H. as a quiet, very compliant, mousey woman. She told the physician that she came from a restrictive religious background; that she felt humiliated by this situation; and that she must have failed her husband if she could not hold him. She acknowledged that sexual intercourse was distasteful to her, and that she engaged in it out of a sense of duty and because she wanted to have a large family. Mrs. H., too, had been employed in her husband's drug store, but, as the size of her family grew, she had found herself increasingly housebound. For this reason, she considered her rivalry with Rhoda more than a sexual one. She also mentioned that the affair had begun when she was pregnant with her seventh child, who was, at this time, ten months old.

Mrs. H. recounted to the analyst that she had first heard of her husband's affair from rumors which had caused her to wonder why G.H. had begun to return to the drug store in the evening. G.H. would tell his wife he was going to play poker with the boys at times when she knew that there was no poker game. Mrs. H. understood that she was contributing to the problem, but, in this respect, she felt that she was caught in a dilemma. She really loved her husband, and she feared that if she did not acquiesce in the affair, she would lose him completely.

The patient's wife also described another side of her husband's personality. In the drug store, she said, G.H. was a hard-working, compulsive individual, who would become upset if he learned that he had made an error or had done an unsatisfactory piece of work.

Although G.H. was a very conscientious pharmacist, he was rather disorderly and depended entirely on his employees to keep the books properly and to control his inventory. Since Rhoda had slashed her wrists, the books were in disarray, bills were not being paid, and the family was in debt. Mrs. H. also pointed out that she was expected to help her husband keep his store in order, but no one ever helped her with her seven children and her husband would not play with them, even the oldest.

During this interview, G.H. sat quietly, and acknowledged that all that his wife said was true.

Group Discussion

Roose and Klerman commented that G.H.'s public display of his affair with his employee and his fight with the policeman indicate very poor judgment. Klerman emphasized that the relationship began when Mrs. H was pregnant, and wondered whether his wife's pregnancy was causing the patient to feel deprived. Ostow added that the affairs of husbands are frequently initiated during a wife's pregnancy. Linn, noting that the patient was himself one of seven children, speculated that it might be important that G.H. became involved with Rhoda when Mrs. H. was expecting her seventh child.

September 1965 G.H. began to see the presenting analyst regularly twice a week. At this time Rhoda was again working in the store and the affair continued, though the patient had told his wife it was over. During this month the analyst observed that, while the patient displayed various moods, he was basically discouraged, because he felt he was facing a dilemma. He explained: "I have no choice. This is ruining my life, but I can't stop thinking of Rhoda. I am obsessed by her. She builds up my ego. I used to think I was sexually unattractive. My wife wasn't responsive to me, and I began to feel that I was losing my masculinity. Now Rhoda has made me feel like a man again."

The patient complained that his wife was too pious, and behaved as though sex were a burden. He remembered that, in his childhood, his mother had singled him out as her favorite and spoiled him. When she could not care for him personally, his mother would assign his older sister to take him to school and to supervise him. G.H. used temper tantrums to force his mother to give him what he wanted, and he became accustomed to having his own way. The patient seemed to expect his wife to give in to him and to take care of his needs as his mother had done, and he said resentfully that his life was being destroyed, and that he was five thousand dollars in debt.

October 1965   G.H. moved out of his wife's house, and took a room in a nearby town, after an episode in which Mrs. H. followed him and Rhoda to the beach and confronted them, saying, "You are still playing the same game. You are never going to change." Living alone, the patient became angry and irritable. He complained that he was lonely and he missed the children, and he imagined that his wife was suffering now that he was out of the house. The analyst understood from this material that it was actually the patient himself who was distressed.

During this period the patient, for the first time, asked the doctor for a prescription for Dexedrine tablets, 15 mgs a day. He stated that he was feeling low and tied down by his marriage, and that, in the past, Dexedrine had given him a lift and had made him feel better at work. By the end of October, although G.H. assured the doctor that the Dexedrine was helping him and that he was feeling better, he began to report visual experiences. He would look up and would momentarily see a face across the room even though no one was there.

At this time, Rhoda was again feeling upset. She was telling people that she was suicidal, and she asked her lover for the name of a psychiatrist. The therapist told the patient of his concern about this rapid deterioration of the situation, and he suggestsd that G.H. be hospitalized. The presenting analyst explained to the group that he had recommended hospitalization because he suspected that G.H. was abusing the Dexedrine, and the situation seemed to be generally out of control. He discussed the issue of whether the hallucinations required a diagnosis of schizophrenia.

Group Discussion

Klerman wondered why G.H. asked his therapist for a prescription since, as a pharmacist, he didn't need any. Ostow was surprised that the request was for 15 mgs a day, since he claimed that he was taking the Dexedrine, not as an addict, but for an occasional lift.

End of November 1965 The patient began to display some paranoid characteristics. He claimed that his store had been broken into and would be broken into again. In an effort to thwart the expected intruder, G.H. had a burglar alarm system installed. He bought a pistol (without first obtaining a license), and he began spending evenings sitting in his car in the parking lot outside his pharmacy waiting for the burglar.

End of December 1965 One night the patient telephoned the police chief of the town where his store was located and said he was certain that his drug store would be burglarized that night. He requested the police chief to come and wait with him for the burglar and when he arrived, he found the patient sitting with his pistol in a store that was in complete disarray, with Dexedrine tablets scattered over the floor. Realizing that what G.H. needed was a psychiatrist, the police chief telephoned the reporting group member. The therapist understood that the Dexedrine was causing the patient to experience a paranoid episode, and he had G.H. admitted to the psychiatric ward of the local hospital.

Group Discussion

Ostow and Klerman suggested that the patient feared he was losing control of himself, and therefore called the police chief as a form of external control. Klerman noted that, though G.H. exhibited ideas of reference, belligerence, and paranoia, he suffered no confusion. Benzedrine (amphetamine) psychosis differs from other drug reactions in that confusion or stupor is absent. It is partly for this reason that the syndrome was recognized only recently as a drug-induced condition.

Ostow thought that, in maintaining that his store would be broken into, the patient was expressing the fear that his personal cache of pills would be discovered. Ostow wondered whether G.H. had an attachment to a male object other than the analyst. G.H.'s therapist elaborated on the patient's friendship with his internist, from whom he had also obtained prescriptions for Dexedrine. This internist was unmarried, had some homosexual friends, and had undergone psychiatric treatment during his training. He was, moreover, a kind person whose own therapy had sensitized him to the psychologic needs of his patients. Several of this doctor's patients confided in him, including G.H. and his wife, and he used to make many night calls which he recognized as unofficial occasions for psychological counseling.

The reporting group member summarized the incident with the police chief as a psychotic episode resulting from the toxicity of an increasing dose of amphetamine. He added that, after G.H. was discharged from the hospital, he admitted to the analyst that he had been taking Dexedrine intermittently since he was a student at pharmacy school. At that time, G.H. was married, had a child, and worked nights in a chemistry laboratory. The Dexedrine enabled him to stay up late. At the time of his encounter with the police chief, the patient was keeping a diary, which revealed that he was taking 90 mgs of Dexedrine a day.

G.H.'s Career in the Hospital: December 1965-February 1966

Once G.H. was admitted to the hospital, his psychosis resolved itself quickly. During the first week, the patient was given Librium to mitigate the effects of the discontinuation of the Dexedrine. No other drugs were administered. This particular hospital has an intensive milieu group program. G.H. and his wife attended couple group meetings which proved effective in opening up communication between them, and, when his psychosis cleared, G.H. became the favorite patient on the ward. He fitted in well with the adolescents, and his glibness, contrition, and cooperativeness endeared him to the nurses, though they suspected that some of the repentance shown was shallow. The reporting analyst saw the patient only twice during his hospitalization. The hospital, because of its focus on group therapy, discouraged private sessions with outside psychiatrists, and the analyst was angry with the patient for secretly abusing his prescription.

Group Discussion

Linn asked whether, in light of the therapist's admitted anger, the impulse to hospitalize this patient may have been punitive. The reporting group member replied that, in retrospect, he considered his behavior too permissive. The patient should have been hospitalized earlier. Ostow felt that the therapist's failure to notice the patient's amphetamine addiction earlier might be due in part to the fact that he was seeing the patient twice a week. Five-day-a-week contact with this patient would have been preferable.

End of February 1966   G.H. was released from the hospital and resumed therapy, twice a week, with the reporting analyst. He dismissed Rhoda, and his wife arranged for someone to look after the children so that she could work for him. G.H. also called in an accountant to set up his books and to check them monthly thereafter. In this way he began once again to bill his customers on a systematic basis and to repay his debts.

At this time G.H.'s psychotherapy became very productive, and the patient spoke at length of his early life with his parents. He referred to his mother as a strong woman, who held the family together despite the father's excessive drinking.

G.H. was also his father's favorite child, and he remembered his father as an intelligent man but a failure. The father had held many positions as a salesman, and ultimately opened a retail store, which the mother controlled. Although G.H. wanted to look up to his father, he felt ashamed of his father's weakness. The patient, like his father, was very eager to please people. He could say "No" to no one, and he was sensitive to rejection. G.H. compared his reliance on Dexedrine to his father's use of alcohol.

Despite this significant progress in the therapy, in the late winter of 1966, the patient began to show signs of depression. G.H. reported that he was feeling lethargic and was losing all sexual interest. In the morning, although he would awaken early, his wife would have to propel him into the shower to get him to go to work.

Group Discussion

Ostow commented that many patients become depressed after going through a period in which they seem to display a great deal of insight. It is actually the onset of depression which causes self-observation and self-criticism which in turn pass as insight. Linn added that this patient's self-criticism should also be seen as an effort to please the analyst.

Exacerbation of the Depressive Trend

Although Mrs. H. enjoyed working in the drug store and felt she should be there to supervise her husband, she began to engage in squabbles with his customers. Moreover, at this time, G.H.'s internist was drafted into the army, and the therapist became the exclusive male object in the patient's life.

As his depression deepened, the patient began to ask the analyst regularly for advice on how to handle his wife's quarrels with the customers, and on many other small problems dealing with getting through the day. The material he brought up during the analytic sessions focused on memories of his father's drinking binges. The patient frequently described sequences such as the following:

Father would come in at night, drunk and angry. Mother would pack us off to a neighbor's house so that we wouldn't see father, but we knew that there were fisticuffs, anger, and yelling. The next morning we would be brought home for breakfast, and father would be upstairs, sleeping it off.

Mother used to take me aside, and say: "Promise me that when you grow up, you won't be like your father."

The patient said he realized that he was being used by his mother in her struggle against the father, and that his mother provoked many of the fights by humiliating her husband in front of the children.

To combat G.H.'s depression, the therapist prescribed Elavil, and built the dose up to 150 mgs a day, but the drug seemed to have no effect on the patient's condition. To make matters worse, although G.H. maintained that he had had intercourse with his wife only once since he had left the hospital, Mrs. H. became pregnant again, and, fearing that the new child would impede their financial recovery, she became discouraged.

The new pregnancy provoked in the analytic sessions many references to the patient's mother, who was then complaining that G.H. was not sufficiently attentive to her. The patient felt that since, as a child, he had received special care and affection, he was obligated to his mother and she was calling in the debt. G.H. also spoke of his older brother, who was the hell-raiser, the "bad news" of the family.

Group Discussion

Linn and Roose emphasized the difference between Mrs. H.'s seventh pregnancy, which, they suspected, may have caused her husband to resort to amphetamines, and the current pregnancy, which seems only to have strengthened his pre-existing depressive trend. One might have expected the new pregnancy to provoke a more intense reaction in the patient.

May 1966   The patient told the therapist: "I'm a sucker to everybody. I can't say 'No' to anybody." This statement led to a long monologue about how important it is to be well-liked and how hurt G.H. felt when anyone appeared to reject or to criticize him.

The patient also remarked that playing with his older children gave him much pleasure, and he and the analyst had their first discussion about the handicapped child whose congenital cerebellar disorder made it impossible for him to walk. At this time, the therapist learned that the child, who was then five years old, was unable also to eat without assistance, or to control his bowels.

The reporting group member spoke with the pediatric neurologist who was following the child's development. The neurologist described the child's condition as a systemic problem involving hepatosplenomegaly, and he commented on how extraordinarily placid G.H. and his wife seemed despite having a child who was suffering what was significantly more than just brain damage. The couple showed no guilt or anxiety about the child's condition and they calmly went about following doctor's instructions. The child seemed content and passive; he was accepted by the other children in the family and treated like a doll.

Summer 1966   One of the major themes elaborated in the therapeutic sessions during this period was the patient's conflict with his wife about contraception, which Mrs. H., because of her devout upbringing, rejected. Another recurring topic was G.H.'s mother. The patient always felt that he was the secret paramour of his mother, who confided in him and turned to him out of her dissatisfaction with her husband. G.H. suspected that his wife maintained a similar relationship with their oldest child, Timothy. G.H. also spoke frequently of his older brother, the rebel of the family, who left home and enlisted in the navy.

Because the patient was not responding to the Elavil and was becoming more depressed, the analyst changed the prescription to 75 and then 90 mgs a day of Nardil.

Group Discussion

Furst and Ostow commented that the reporting analyst had not only changed the patient's medication, but had, in addition, increased the dose. Seventy five to 90 mgs of Nardil is considerably stronger than 150 mgs of Elavil. Roose suggested that the child's enlarged liver might have been attributed to the patient's father, and he wondered whether G.H. thought about it in those terms.

Autumn 1966   With the introduction of the Nardil, the patient's condition seemed to improve. G.H. appeared to accept and adjust to his wife's pregnancy, and he moved to a larger store. The early morning awakening, nausea, and food revulsion cleared up and, although G.H. claimed that beer suddenly seemed tasteless, he gained a significant amount of weight. During this time, the patient remarked to the therapist: "In retrospect, I must have been depressed since childhood. I can remember each time my mother would say 'Don't be like your father! Don't be a drunk!' "

As the patient recovered, he informed the doctor that he was increasingly able to talk back to his wife. Although he would explode at her when he became irritated, G.H. understood the extent of his dependence on her, and he seemed to enjoy his children greatly.

January 1967   The birth of his eighth child triggered in the patient a manic episode. As soon as the baby was born, G.H. went immediately to his mother's house. He kissed and embraced his mother, and, when she became visibly upset by his behavior, he began to speak to her in obscenities. The patient was very talkative, and did not sleep at all that night. He announced: "I've got a new crutch . . . I've got a new assistant . . . she is my new crutch . . . she is better than my mother . . . she is the one who really understands me." G.H.'s family became concerned about the intensity of his elation, and telephoned the analyst, who instructed G.H. temporarily to discontinue the medication, and advised the family to keep the patient at home for a few days.

During the first days after the birth of the baby, G.H. was extravagant in buying furniture for the nursery. When he visited his wife at the hospital, the patient told her he loved her and that he wanted her forgiveness for having had the affair. G.H. informed the therapist that he was very happy, and that his only worry was that the doctor had discovered a mass in Mrs. H.'s breast.

Group Discussion of G.H.'s Post-Partum Elation

G.H.'s analyst added to the comments about the new employee that, before her confinement, Mrs. H. had found someone to take her place in the store. Klerman remarked that G.H.'s post-partum behavior was an expression of his joy in his reconfirmed potency. Linn and Ostow understood the patient's elation as a confirmation of their suspicions that Mrs. H.'s eighth pregnancy was a far more serious ordeal for her husband. In going immediately to see his mother and speaking to her in expletives, G.H. may have been imitating his father's drunken behavior. Linn added that for G.H. the birth of the baby represented primarily an oedipal achievement, and, for this reason, he celebrated it with his mother.

Roose interpreted G.H.'s elation as an identification more with the infant than with the father. He reminded the group of G.H.'s bland acceptance of, and possible identification with his seriously crippled child. Ostow responded that identification with both the passive infant and the phallic father is neither inconsistent nor unlikely for this kind of patient. G.H.'s therapist mentioned that, during the latter portion of his wife's pregnancy, the patient had learned from the analyst's secretary that the analyst's daughter was also expecting a child, and, as a result, identification with the analyst as a prospective father-grandfather became an important element in the transference.

Ostow called attention to the apparent discrepancy between G.H.'s elation about having a child, and his lack of interest in the child itself. Linn noted that the baby would most likely become a rival to the patient by claiming Mrs. H.'s attention. Klerman pointed out that the patient seemed to deal with this problematic aspect of the birth by focusing on his new employee. The reporting group member confirmed Klerman's observation, and added that Mrs. H. quickly sensed this situation, and resumed her work within six weeks.

Roose understood this episode as a distorted living out of the four polarities of the oedipal situation, i.e., the positive and negative, as well as the active and passive relationships with each of the parents. Linn considered this explanation too complex. G.H.'s therapist saw the situation as both complicated and obscured by the fact that he had no information about the patient's relationship with his father in early childhood, though he suspected that the image of the father as an ineffective person and a drunk describes the father's behavior only during the last ten years of his life. In his early years, the patient may have looked up to his father as a strong man.

Ostow asked how much Nardil the patient was taking at the time of the birth. The presenting analyst replied that the patient reported that he had lost track of how many pills he was taking, but he seemed to be taking slightly more than the prescribed dose. In view of the uncertainty of the patient's dose of Nardil, Roose wondered to what extent the mania should be attributed to the drug, and to what extent it should be considered a transference phenomenon. Klerman felt that both the earlier paranoid episode and the mania represent a complicated interaction of drug effects with the dynamics of this patient's personality. The paranoid quality of the first incident must be related to the patient's consumption of amphetamines.

Linn, Ostow, and Loomis were impressed by the fact that, though previously the patient had occasionally taken amphetamines, he did not start to abuse them seriously, and suffer their toxic effects until his wife's pregnancy. With the birth of his eighth child, he exceeded his father's reproductive achievement. Linn elaborated that, in anticipation of this event, the patient must have found himself at an impasse. In his search for some kind of relief, he began to poison himself with amphetamines, and consequently suffered a psychosis. Ostow suggested that the mania which greeted the arrival of the eighth child was not driven by excessive drug dosage, but rather represented the beginning of the drug's loss of effect.

1967-1968   G.H. continued to see the presenting analyst twice a week, and to take Nardil. He was a compliant and dutiful patient, and he soon established a new personal equilibrium which permitted him to function well, though there was no evidence that he gained any true insight.

The store was beginning to flourish, and six weeks after the baby was born, Mrs. H. found a baby sitter and returned to work. At this time she started to take contraceptive pills, and became much freer sexually, to the point of obtaining some pleasure from sexual relations with her husband.

At one point, however, G.H. seemed to escape from the effects of the Nardil. He became depressed, gained a considerable amount of weight, and reported a craving for sweets, as well as retention of fluids.

Group Discussion

Roose remarked that the retention of water represents a substitute for manic flight. Ostow preferred to see G.H.'s weight gain and edema as an example of narcissistic tranquility, which, like mania, includes weight gain and fluid retention.

Late Spring 1969   Because G.H. was functioning well, and did not seem likely to gain much more insight from a protracted course of treatment, the reporting analyst stopped seeing him on a regular basis. Since that time, the patient has been coming to see the therapist two or three times a year to have the medication regulated.

Summary

Ostow proposed the following summary of the case. During his wife's seventh pregnancy, G.H. found himself in a "trap." Although he needed his wife because she was a good mother to him, she provided no sexual gratification, and his relationship with a woman who was sexually satisfying had become untenable. Feeling that he could neither leave his wife nor live with her as a husband, he had two options for resolving the situation: they were depression and schizophrenic detachment.

When G.H. took Dexedrine, the energizing effect of large doses of the drug combined with the ego-disturbances that they produced inhibited the incipient depression, and induced in the patient instead, a schizophrenic type of detachment syndrome.

With the withdrawal of the Dexedrine, however, the depression which the patient had been warding off became manifest. This depression was a mild to moderate one: the patient did not become sufficiently depressed to turn away from the therapist, but he was depressed enough to cling to him. The prescribed dose of Elavil proved inadequate to overcome the depression, but a larger dose of Nardil effected a clinical recovery without producing the ego-disturbing effects which had resulted from the amphetamine. The fact that the patient would occasionally escape from the Nardil signifies that the dose was just enough to support the patient under normal circumstances. Additional stress would precipitate depression.

In this context, G.H.'s manic episode after the birth of the eighth child should be seen as a defensive mania, and represents the incipience of an escape from the medication. In this respect it is interesting that, during the course of the mania, G.H. sought his wife's forgiveness for having an affair. Guilt is not characteristic of a pure mania or of an intense mania. G.H.'s worry about the mass in his wife's breast appears to be a hypochondria displaced to his wife, and based on his hostility toward her. Shortly after this episode G.H. suffered another period of depression. This sequence of events suggests that the second depression did not occur as a result of the increased dose of Nardil, but that the patient began to take more Nardil because he sensed that he was becoming depressed.

Group Discussion of Ostow's Summary

Klerman agreed with the summary, and he reopened the question of whether G.H.'s final mania represented an oedipal triumph or a fusion with his mother. Roose commented that behind every oedipal attachment to the paternal phallus one invariably finds a longing for the mother's breast. This phenomenon is especially evident in religious conversion experiences.

In relation to the discovery of the mass in Mrs. H.'s breast, Loomis wondered about the meaning of the breast to this patient. Loomis has treated several men who were preoccupied with the condition of their wife's breasts and the possibility of breast cancer. The patient's resort to amphetamines at the age of twenty-six and the buying spree that occurred during his mania might indicate a strong need to be fed and a feeling that he is not being fed enough. Linn suggested that, since G.H. has a severe character disorder, with strong infantile tendencies, and the reporting group member has no information about large blocks of the patient's life, an interview with Mrs. H. might serve to supplement the existing material.

Feder remarked that most chronic amphetamine users seek relief in amphetamines, not from a simple depression, but from a feeling of emptiness and isolation. Feder sensed such an emptiness in G.H. Klerman did not consider this patient to be a schizoid character type. The presenting analyst added that G.H. is a competent professional who is very sensitive to his customers' feelings. This man described the earlier years of his marriage as quite happy and fulfilling, and he always maintained a group of friends with whom he regularly played tennis and cards.

Linn emphasized that G.H. functioned well for the largest part of his young adult life. He broke down, in the sense of no longer being able to fulfill his expected role, during his wife's eighth pregnancy. Furst suspected that, perhaps, like the patients in Cases 1 and 2, G.H. is an individual who finds it difficult to assume adult responsibility. The reporting group member pointed out that G.H.'s happiest years were those spent in service and in pharmacy school. Once he returned to New Jersey, he settled within twenty miles of both his mother and mother-in-law, and his situation began to deteriorate.

Winkelman concluded that this case illustrates the, as yet unresolved, issue of distinguishing affect depression from a chronic state of inadequacy, dependency, and helplessness. This patient's difficulties at the birth of his last two children suggest that this dependent, indecisive man is approaching the outer limit to the amount of responsibility he can assume.

Postscript:

March 9, 1970   When G.H. came to see the presenting analyst, he announced that he had discontinued the Nardil in January, because it was causing him considerable discomfort. The patient maintained that because the Nardil bloated him, he had gained thirty pounds over the past year, and that the drug made him constipated, and caused him to sleep excessively. G.H. explained that he was now trying to lose weight and to get along without the drug. "I don't know what to do. There has been a gradual change over the past few years. There used to be a time when I would take any drug I could get my hands on—amphetamines, sleeping pills, etc. Now I would like to be able to get around without drugs." G.H. also expressed the feeling that life was beginning to seem like a chore.

Recently, the patient had seen some old school friends, and had discovered that many of his heroes have clay feet. "My generation has fucked up their life." Specifically G.H. heard rumors about his internist, who was, by this time, out of the army and back in private practice. The internist was reportedly drinking excessively.

G.H. mentioned that he thought about Rhoda from time to time. Of their past affair, he commented: "At that point I had a deflated ego, and needed someone like Rhoda. I was like a sponge, soaking it up. I am a lot like my father. I am always looking for an easy way out. Every so often I think about my father and my childhood. We were very poor. There were times when there was no food in the house." The patient then related a memory from his fourth year.

> Because our family was so poor, I was sent to live with my aunt in Philadelphia. I was convinced that I had been sent there forever, and I cried, had nightmares, and pleaded to be returned to my parents.

The therapist tried unsuccessfully to reconstruct with the patient the period when Mrs. H. was expecting her seventh child. G.H. could not speak of that time with much clarity, and he never related the beginning of the affair to his wife's pregnancy, or even spoke of them as occurring simultaneously. He did wonder, however, whether the Dexedrine he was taking, while in pharmacy school, might have caused the child's brain damage. The analyst replied that very little is known on that subject, but it is a possibility. G.H. ended the session by elaborating the following fantasy.

> You [i.e., the analyst] have a real magic pill, but you're not giving me the real stuff. You're giving me second-class stuff instead. When will you start giving me the real stuff?

Group Discussion

The group discussed first the origin of the child's brain damage. Ostow cited recent reports claiming that damage to male gonads from drugs could result in impairment to the fetus, and Feder added that many people who drink feel responsible for anything that goes wrong with a child who was conceived while they were inebriated.

Ostow's interpretation of this session was as follows. The patient's questioning the origins of his child's brain damage indicates guilt. Generally, when a patient who is on anti-depression medication begins to gain weight and to retain fluid, it means that the patient is experiencing additional stress. The weight gain and fluid retention represent an exacerbation of the narcissistic tranquility syndrome, i.e., the individual's effort to isolate himself from the stress. Frequently, at this point, the patient will incorrectly blame the medication for the weight gain and edema, will discontinue the drug, and, as a result, will slide immediately into depression.

The dynamics described above are evident in this session. G.H.'s reference to the time when there was no food indicates that, though he is on a diet, he feels hungry and wants to eat, and the story about the internist's drinking problem indirectly expresses G.H.'s disappointment with the analyst.

The patient's memory of moving to his aunt's house reminded Ostow of Karl Abraham's contention that every depressed patient has had an infantile "primal" depression which he is reliving in his adult illness.* Ostow believes that in every episode of depression, previous depressive episodes are reconstructed; it is for this reason that G.H. recounted this particular incident. Linn suspected that the presenting analyst might be the aunt in Philadelphia with whom the patient wanted to move in.

March 16, 1970   G.H. came to his session smoking a pipe, and wearing a sporty tweed jacket and a new crew-cut hairstyle. He informed the analyst that he had tried to play basketball, but had found that he was disappointingly slow: he had to face the fact that he was no longer in his twenties. The patient then mentioned that Monday was his day out of the store, but he was planning to change it to another day because his week-ends were becoming too long. Since he had no real hobbies, and he obtained only partial satisfaction from playing with his children, he did not know what to do with himself on week-ends and holidays. Moreover his wife was angry with him because she wanted to go out to parties and to "do things" on week-ends, and he had told her that those things didn't interest him.

*Karl Abraham, "A Short Study of the Development of the Libido Viewed in the Light of Mental Disorders" (1942) in *Selected Papers of Karl Abraham,* translated by Douglas Bryan and Alix Strachey. London: Hogarth, 1948.

"My legs feel hollow, and I have a feeling of lethargy. You know I think I married a mother figure. My mother was the strong person of the family, and carried my father, and I see the same things in my wife. I wasn't mature for anything at the time we married. I see myself now associated with people my own age, and I am really the youngest member of the group. I think my values have changed a little, but I still try to have everybody like me. It is tough to have to say 'No,' but I am slowly learning to do it. I have been off the Nardil for a month, and I feel I'm getting depressed. What are you going to do?"

Group Discussion

Ostow remarked that, at this point, he would reinstate the Nardil and add Navane, perhaps 6 mgs a day. Ostow has found that when a patient escapes from the influence of an anti-depression agent, very frequently the addition of Navane will restore the effectiveness of the original medication. Feder suggested prescribing Vivactil, a drug that would provide for this patient a "lift" similar to the relief he obtained earlier from Dexedrine. Linn feared that Vivactil might also possess the addictive qualities of an amphetamine. Feder replied that he had never observed a case of addiction to Vivactil.

EDITOR'S NOTE: This case again demonstrates the natural history of manic-depressive illness. The patient was an able but timid young man, whose illness began in early adult life and who broke down when external stress, in the form of sexual rejection and increasing family responsibility, challenged his defenses. He abused amphetamines in an attempt at a self-administered pharmacotherapy. With increasing stress, he built up the dose to the point of toxicity. Though he was not schizophrenic, the amphetamine-induced psychosis clearly resembled paranoid schizophrenia. Under treatment he responded to a high dose of MAOI anti-depression drug therapy. As in other cases, the relative importance of childhood trauma, constitutional predisposition, and adult stress could not be established. Unfortunately the patient was not seen often enough to be able to monitor the details of the ego fracture under the influence of the large amphetamine dose.

CASE 5

Introduction

In the fall of 1968 the reporting analyst was asked by another member of the group to see I.J., a twenty-three year old white female, who had reportedly made threats of violence against her parents. This young woman had, since latency, undergone several forms of psychiatric treatment with a number of competent therapists. The parents, both lawyers, described their daughter as progressively withdrawn and detached. They stated that she spent a considerable amount of time sleeping, and was frequently observed laughing to herself. When they questioned her about her behavior, I.J. would reply: "I've been hanging around people who professionally are interested in my mind alone." The presenting analyst recommended and arranged for the young woman to be hospitalized immediately.

First Visit   When the reporting analyst first saw her, the patient gave the impression of a very drab-looking, depressed young woman. Her face seemed almost expressionless, her hair was messy and unkempt, and her clothes were in keeping with the rest of her physical appearance. In response to the doctor's queries, she offered nothing spontaneous. Instead, she spent long periods of time looking around the room before answering, often in an entirely nonsensical fashion. She told the therapist: "I need to have people talk to me while I communicate with myself. l am depressed because I am Jewish."

I.J. denied entertaining any suicidal ideas, though she admitted having made the statement: "I'll either kill myself or knife someone." The young woman reported further that she was experiencing feelings of depersonalization and derealization, about

331

which she commented: "I think that is a good thing to practice." She also mentioned that she had come to the presenting analyst for drug therapy.

I.J. was admitted to the hospital on December 28, and was started on Navane, 1 mg, three times a day. At one point, the dose was doubled, and the patient, as a result, developed severe hypotension. When this happened, the dose was immediately reduced, and built up again, very gradually, over a month. Oral Neo-synephrine (phenylephrine) was also administered, 25 mgs, five times a day, to combat the hypotension, and the patient's blood pressure slowly returned to normal.

Her first night on the ward, I.J. woke up once and, betraying no affect, asked whether there was a man in the bed next to her. For the entire first month she suffered chronic insomnia. During this time the patient's melancholy affect and behavior did not change. Her response to all stimuli was very slow, and she spent her days idly fingering magazines or listening to music, interacting with no one. She avoided all staff members except those specifically assigned to her. She would frequently retreat to her bed, and she bathed only when someone directly asked her to. This young woman wore the same clothing every day, and she was not urged to change.

Group Discussion

Furst was surprised that the patient found comfort in derealization and depersonalization. Most of Furst's patients are tremendously fearful of this experience. In reference to I.J.'s initial hypotension, Ostow reported that one of his patients suffered hypotension caused by Navane, and the hypotension cleared up when the dose of Navane was halved.

Klerman felt that the account, so far, left it uncertain whether this patient's condition should be diagnosed as retarded depression or schizoid flattening of affect and withdrawal. "This woman seems at some times flat, and at other times severely depressed." The reporting group member replied that, at the beginning of the treatment, he too was unsure of the exact nature of the patient's illness.

The case report, so far, represents a composite of observations made by the therapist himself and by other staff members on the ward. It should be understood as a description of the patient and her behavior, not as a diagnosis. The presenting analyst added that, though the patient's facial expression and demeanor seemed melancholy, she never reported feeling sad.

December 28, 1968   The patient was taking Navane, 1 mg, three times a day, and Artane, 2 mgs, three times a day.

December 31, 1968   Although, for the first month, the analyst had avoided all pointed questions, I.J. continued to be extremely uncommunicative, and gave only 'yes' or 'no' answers. She did, however, make some spontaneous approaches to the therapist. Because her previous psychiatrists had always asked about her dreams, I.J. assumed that the presenting analyst too wanted to hear about them, and she volunteered that her dreams were confused and full of shapeless, grey objects. The therapist understood from these dreams only that the patient felt that her mother was a witch.

January 2, 1969   I.J.'s dose of Navane was increased to 2 mgs, three times a day.

January 6, 1969   The dose was again raised, this time to 2 mgs, five times a day.

January 8, 1969   At this time the reporting group member was seeing I.J. for a short period every day, and sometimes twice a day. On this day the patient remarked, for the first time, that she felt "left out of things," but that she had no desire to "get into anything," and that she comes from a family background which causes conflict within her.

She said that she was taught to see beauty in everything and everyone, but this attitude conflicted with "the technical basis of life." When asked what this statement meant, the young woman elaborated very clearly and extensively on how "everything is destructive." The content of this monologue was quite bizarre and consistently depressed. Although, for the previous week, I.J. had been eating fairly well, after this interview, it was noted that she refused to eat anything.

January 9, 1969   The patient began, for the first time, to verbalize fears. She described a number of fantasies, of which the theme was

The world is empty of people, and there is no one to take care of me.

January 14, 1969   The dose of Navane was increased to 5 mgs, three times a day.

January 20, 1969   I.J. began to spontaneously discuss with the analyst some material from her own life. She described, though without much feeling, several housekeepers who had taken care of her in her childhood. Although, before this analytic session, the patient had been up and about on the ward, after speaking of spending her childhood with housekeepers, she once more regressed to her bed. No attempt was made to rouse the patient from her bed, because it was felt that the young woman was becoming somewhat activated on her own, and it would be better not to deprive her of any feeling of initiative.

January 21, 1969   After telling the doctor more about her housekeepers, I.J. volunteered that she liked the theater, and, for the first time, she dressed and left her room for lunch. By this time the reporting analyst and the other staff members involved in the case agreed unanimously that I.J.'s behavior had become warmer and more outgoing. The patient was also experiencing renewed upsurges of hypotension, and the therapist did not know whether to attribute the hypotension to the drug or to the young woman's increased physical and social activity.

Group Discussion

Feder observed that the patient's initial report of her dreams illustrates Ostow's theory that there is a time lag between a change in an individual's dynamic state and a corresponding shift in the contents of that person's thoughts. Though the substance of these dreams seems to match I.J.'s earlier mood, the fact that she was willing to tell the dreams indicates a change in her approach to the analyst.

Group Discussion of I.J.'s Renewed Hypotension

Ostow proposed that during the time when a patient who responds to any of the anti-depression drugs with hypotension remains depressed, the depression, by virtue of the cortisone secretion which is associated with it, will combat the hypotension. When, as a result of the pharmacological effect of the drug, the depression is alleviated, the cortisone secretion subsides, and the patient experiences clinical postural hypotension. For this reason, hypotension frequently accompanies clinical recovery, or anticipates it by a few days. This observation, however, does not apply to hypertensive individuals. Linn cited cases, especially of patients suffering late-life depressions, where the patient responded to the medication with an immediate hypotensive reaction, though the clinical depression remained unchanged. Ostow responded that the phenomenon he described is not universal. Depression helps an individual to resist hypotension, but it may prove insufficient for a person who is extremely sensitive to the medication.

Klerman remarked that hypotension is found more frequently among depressed than among normal individuals. Feder wondered whether the incidence of orthostatic hypotension resulting from anti-depression medication is different for agitated and retarded depressions. Roose added that a difference might indicate whether the hypotension is an element of the depression or a result of the drug. Ostow reemphasized that, in most cases, the overt signs of hypotension do not appear until the patient begins to recover.

January 23, 1969   I.J. began to dress somewhat more neatly, to spend more time in the day room, and to speak with other people more spontaneously. She related to the analyst a series of fantasies which were variations on the following theme:

> As a child, I was out in space. Each person was allocated his place in space, away from the world. These were all isolated people who didn't understand anything about psychiatric theory.

The reporting group member understood these fantasies as the pa-

tient's description of her various therapeutic contacts and her inability to understand what the doctors were talking about.

I.J also volunteered some tentative comments about her
parents, but very soon she retreated and dropped this material.
She did, however, begin to read her mail, which had accumulated,
and, although she had been in the hospital for twenty-six days,
for the first time, she referred directly to her parents by expressing
the hope that they had returned home safely.

Although it was the general impression of the staff that the
young woman's spirits were rising, there were periods when she
would retreat to her bed. But, on these occasions, instead of lying
quietly on her bed, as she had done earlier, I.J would complain of
somatic symptoms, mostly stomach cramps. And, at this time,
there was an exacerbation of her hypotension. The therapist interpreted this new behavior as expressing the patient's conflict
between her desire to retreat and her refusal to be alone.

The presenting analyst gave the patient's parents permission
to visit her. I.J. received her parents; they asked whether she was
feeling better, and she replied that she did not know whether her
condition had improved. Everything appeared the same, except
that she was feeling less fatigued than she had felt previously.
After the visit, the patient remarked to the analyst that, in her
parents' presence, she felt swallowed up and deprived of individ-
uality. Because I.J. had handled her parents' visit so well, the
therapist decided to increase the pressure on her. He allowed her
to leave the ward, and he moved the location of her analytic
sessions from the ward to his office, which is on another floor of
the hospital.

For the first time I.J. spoke of her brother David, who is
three years her junior. At that time David was diagnosed as
psychotic, and was being treated at another hospital. The young
woman told the analyst that three years earlier, when she was
twenty years old and he was seventeen, David had destroyed a self-
portrait which she had painted, and her parents did not punish
him for it. This incident convinced her, beyond a doubt, that her
parents did not care about her at all. She also mentioned that the
people in her dreams were becoming more distinct.

January 24-27, 1969   On January 24, I.J.'s dose of Navane
was raised to 5 mgs, five times a day. During these four days, the

patient reported that she was waking up in the morning feeling confused, and she began to describe sadistic crimes perpetrated on her by her brother. Although, at the time, the analyst could not ascertain how realistic her accounts were, he later learned from the patient's mother that they were true, and that the parents had permitted them.

During these weeks I.J. would frequently become lost on the way to the analyst's office. Sometimes she failed to appear for her appointment, and just wandered around the hospital. The therapist never criticized her for failing to come to see him. He simply told the young woman that these were times when she was not ready to talk to him. On other occasions, the patient would come for only the last five minutes of her appointment, or she would arrive on time and announce: "I have ten minutes worth to talk with you." The doctor always allowed I.J. to leave after the time period she proposed had expired.

At this time the doctor also noticed a considerable expansion of the patient's general interest. She actively followed the unfolding of the Pueblo incident, as it was reported, and she spoke at length of the U.S. involvement in South Korea. The reporting group member was impressed, not only by the content of the analytic material, but by the fact that, for the first time, he and the patient were able to pursue a topic, and the young woman now had sufficient concentration at least to begin something similar to association.

I.J. returned to the theme of her brother's birth, stating: "I felt cheapened by his presence." When the analyst asked her what she meant, she responded: "The big difference was somehow in the body. He has a body and a mind, and perhaps I have neither. . . When I was young, I didn't see my brother as a person, he was just a thing." The patient described how, after David's birth, she lost her mother, and was "put into the clutches" of her grandmother, who, it turned out, was the real witch.

This latest advance in the therapy produced another period of regression. The reporting group member instructed the hospital staff not to accept this retreat, but to urge the patient to be active. I.J.'s response to this encouragement was: "You know, I really felt lonely in my room." She refused, however, to elaborate on this comment.

February, 12 1969   I.J.'s dose of Navane was changed to 5 mgs, three times a day, and 10 mgs h.s.

Mid-February 1969   The patient began to make new approaches to people, and, simultaneously, to express some paranoid trends. For the first time, I.J. spontaneously initiated a relationship with a new patient named Peter, though, after each conversation with him, she would retreat to her bed for awhile. The young woman explained that this behavior represented her way of "getting back from outer space" and it was not interfered with. The patient also asked the nurse whether the latter had heard anything about the date of her discharge. When the nurse questioned her interest in going home, I.J. replied: "Well I want to go, in a way, and, in a way, I don't." She thanked the nurse for talking with her about going home and making her realize she was not ready, though the nurse had said nothing to that effect.

February 25, 1969   The young woman was, at this time, entertaining the paranoid idea that a particular patient was staring at her. The analyst later learned that the patient in question was Peter. I.J. also expressed feelings of self-depreciation and an intense concern about being close to someone.

March 12, 1969   I.J. was beginning to interact more and more spontaneously with people on the ward, especially the young people. She compared her experience on the ward to that of living in a school dormitory, and she commented: "I don't feel so alone now." She said she knew that she was going to be in the hospital for longer than she had expected, and she was beginning to feel that a prolonged hospital stay would be beneficial. As she put it, "I'm glad I came here. I realize I was worn out physically and mentally, and I needed time out alone. I had not been myself for three years." The patient added that she was struggling with some kind of reality testing, and that never before, as far as she could remember, was life anything more than a jungle. "It is confusing when you are trying to mature and grow."

I.J. became attached to one of the nurses on the ward, and she soon began to ask this nurse questions that the analyst would normally expect an adolescent girl to ask her mother. For example, "What do you talk to boys about? Do you think this dress looks nice on me?" She told the therapist: "You know, sometimes I play up to people. Don't let it bother you if I play up to you." When she was asked to clarify that statement, the young woman explained: "Well, I pretend to like people when I really don't."

At this time the analyst observed a marked change in the patient's mood. Although at times her manner continued to be flat and bizarre, she would frequently smile and speak warmly. On one occasion the young woman stated that she realized what she had been for twenty-three years, and it had not been a very pleasant or nice thing. "I learned now that maybe in the past I have done things in a manner that I shouldn't have done." I.J. often made this kind of cryptic announcement, which she would elaborate on only two or three weeks later, and her therapist learned not to ask more than she was willing to discuss.

Immediately following the paranoid episode I.J.'s dreams had been violent in a very diffuse manner that she could not describe easily. In March the dreams continued to be violent, but the violence was more delimited and was associated with specific individuals in the patient's life.

Group Discussion

Ostow suggested that the earlier dreams represented world destruction fantasies, while the later ones express rejection of a specific object. The reporting group member agreed, and elaborated that the more recent dreams described the young woman's wishes to attack her mother, and they ended in the statement: "My mother would leave me for the child of another person." The other person turned out to be the patient's father, and this new material brought up, for the first time, I.J.'s homosexual feelings about her mother. The patient concluded this analytic session by commenting: "You know, I feel as if my mouth is a lot less tense."

Presentation Resumed   After this dramatic encounter, the patient withdrew, and became aloof. The therapist felt that, after verbalizing such intense anger at her mother, the young woman should be allowed time to pull herself together again. For this reason her off-the-ward privileges were not interfered with.

End of March 1969   As I.J. slowly emerged from her withdrawal, she began to speak of politics and competitiveness. She informed the doctor that she disliked competition, and considered it an indulgence. She also expressed appreciation of the analyst's having trusted her and having allowed her to leave the hospital during the time when "things weren't going so well."

The young woman's dreams were again changing. The violence and sadism which had characterized the dreams previously were now being identified as such, and were accompanied by guilt. In the patient's own words, "My analysis is going well . . . Now I know there is something wrong in my dreams. It is a sense of guilt. I have the feeling of being taught a new kind of reality." The analyst used this development as a basis for further efforts to clarify this guilt.

April 1969   I.J. told the doctor: "I feel that I am now old enough to move out from my parents." She said she did not know what her parents expected from her, but that, for the first time in her life, as far as she could remember, she was feeling like a whole person. Her body and head now belonged together, although, at times, she was not terribly fond of her body. The therapist understood from this statement that the patient was having difficulties with her sexual feelings, and the young woman soon brought up, mostly in dreams, some sexual fantasies about her father.

Mid-May 1969   By this time I.J. had been in the hospital for about six months, and had begun to go downtown regularly to make purchases for herself. The analyst felt that she was really functioning as an outpatient, and he discharged her from the hospital. Through the next year, she continued to take Navane, 25 mgs a day, and, as she began to function as a normal person, her therapy assumed more and more the form of regular psychoanalysis. In 1970, the young woman was living in a kind of halfway house arrangement, taking courses in sculpture and music, and seeing the reporting analyst five times a week.

Group Discussion

Bressler emphasized that I.J. was a person who needed time to progress at her own pace. Her need for leisure and concern was vital to her care, and was the key to mobilizing affect. Bressler and Feder described how this kind of therapy can be difficult to achieve in the setting of a hospital ward where many of the subordinate staff members often entertain a more interventionist philosophy.

The group member who had referred I.J to the presenting analyst commented that this woman had been treated by several of the most distinguished psychiatrists in Philadelphia, and had been subjected to many different psychiatric arrangements and manipulations. When the presenting analyst took over the case, I.J. was living alone in the university neighborhood of Philadelphia, with all her needs provided for. She was in treatment with a gifted analyst, but she would frequently fail to attend her analytic session for days at a time, and no one would contact her. What the reporting group member offered I.J. was freedom in a protected environment. Roose remarked that this kind of patient should not be left alone in an apartment. When an individual is incapable of reaching out to the analyst, the analyst must take the initiative and seek out the patient.

Bressler felt that the medication was responsible for the changes in the patient's dreams. Under the influence of the Navane, the violence and sadism in the dreams seemed to become more quickly organized and recognized as such by the patient, and were complemented by other affects. Navane is the only drug which has such a strong effect of this kind.

Linn maintained that so much happened to this patient above and beyond the administration of Navane, that it is not at all clear that the medication in any way facilitated her recovery. Feder suggested that the Navane enabled this woman to experiment in the relationships which were offered to her.

Klerman agreed with Linn that it is difficult to distinguish the effect of the drug from that of the therapeutic environment in which the patient was placed, and her doctor's skillful use of authority and limit setting. This exposition also leaves unclear the nature of the woman's pathology, that is, whether she was experiencing a schizoid withdrawal or a retarded depression. Klerman has had bad experiences administering Navane to two patients who suffered straightforward retarded depressions.

Bressler stated that he has never prescribed Navane for a directly depressed patient, but he has used it very successfully in cases where depression was a prominent element of a generally schizophrenic condition. Bressler once performed a double-blind experiment on fifty such patients, using Navane and Thorazine. The patients taking Navane very quickly became alert, smiling, and warmer; and their depressive aspect disappeared. These changes were less marked, and appeared more slowly in the patients who were given Thorazine.

Feder observed that the principal advantage of Navane is that it allows a person to emerge from a psychotic withdrawal and become active without becoming agitated and disorganized or depressed. He cited the case of a patient who had been withdrawn and apathetic for nine years. Shortly after beginning to take Navane his level of activity increased significantly, and he reported feeling much better. Klerman cited a similar case from his practice.

Large doses of Navane can induce depression in susceptible individuals. Ostow referred to a case in which he successfully substituted Navane for Elavil. On 6 mgs a day of Navane the patient became depressed, but, when the dose was cut to 2 mgs, the depression cleared up and the patient began to function well.

It should also be emphasized that the effects of Navane are cumulative. Therefore, to maintain the same effect, a patient's dose must be gradually reduced, at least for the first week or so. Lasting effects are frequently obtained at a dose of 1 or 2 mgs per day for patients who are not psychotic. And, as with other drugs, the effects of macro and micro doses are probably entirely different, and should be studied separately.

Feder and Ostow noted the anticholinergic effect of Navane, which may produce confusion and difficulty in attention. Ostow mentioned that two of his patients experienced difficulty driving on 1 mg a day of Navane, and Furst and Ostow reported that patients taking Navane frequently complain of memory impairment.

Summary of the Discussion of Navane

Bressler proposed that Navane has a better alerting facility than Stelazine, and produces a faster organization and recognition of hostility. In this way it protects the patient against his rage and destructive fantasies, and it counteracts suicidal tendencies. Furst added that Navane also relieves an agitated depression.

Bressler explained that he usually starts with a small dose, i.e., 1 mg, three times a day. Although he sometimes prescribes Navane in an ambulatory setting, most patients ill enough to require it are hospitalized. Feder warned against administering Navane to ambulatory patients in whom there is potential for excitement, and, as when starting any drug, he advises patients not to drive until the effects of the Navane are evident. Ostow suggested that Navane could be used to treat depression in doses of the order of magnitude of 1 and 2 mgs per day.

EDITOR'S NOTE: We have here an example of skillful blending of management, drug therapy and psychotherapy. It is difficult to imagine that the patient could have done as well had any element of the therapeutic program been omitted. Needless to say, every case requires a well thought out therapeutic program rather than a simple, routine intervention.

In retrospect it seems to me that the presenting analyst, by raising the dose of Navane gradually, actually ascertained the point on the dose-response curve at which the patient did best. I believe it is possible that had he started at a lower dose and increased it more slowly through the range from 0.5 to 10 mgs, he might have found a similar response at a lower dose. It is my impression that the dose-response curve is not merely U-shaped, but undulating, with respect to energizing and tranquilizing effects. If we assume that, when first seen, the patient exhibited a state of schizophrenic, melancholic depression, then what was required was a dose of tranquilizing medication that exerted an anti-depression effect, but one so mild that it did not propel the patient into a state of schizophrenic excitement. Perhaps an anti-depression drug, covered by a moderate dose of tranquilizer, would have done as well.

We do not yet have clinically determined dose-response

curves for the various medications that we use. It is my impression though that one can obtain with the tranquilizing phenothiazines an alternating energizing and depressing effect similar to that exhibited by the thioxanthines. Certainly this comparison should be studied on a controlled basis.

This case was presented only briefly. Had it been presented in greater detail, we should have had the opportunity to observe the influence of drug-determined ego changes on the dynamics of the recovery process.